BETRAYAL

ALSO BY JONATHAN KARL

The Right to Bear Arms
Front Row at the Trump Show

BETRAYAL

THE FINAL ACT
OF
THE TRUMP SHOW

JONATHAN KARL

DUTTON

DUTTON

An imprint of Penguin Random House LLC
penguinrandomhouse.com

Copyright © 2021 by Jonathan Karl

Penguin supports copyright. Copyright fuels creativity, encourages diverse voices, promotes free speech, and creates a vibrant culture. Thank you for buying an authorized edition of this book and for complying with copyright laws by not reproducing, scanning, or distributing any part of it in any form without permission. You are supporting writers and allowing Penguin to continue to publish books for every reader.

DUTTON and the D colophon are registered trademarks of Penguin Random House LLC.

LIBRARY OF CONGRESS CATALOGING-IN-PUBLICATION DATA

has been applied for.

ISBN 9780593186329 (hardcover)
ISBN 9780593186343 (ebook)

Printed in the United States of America
1   3   5   7   9   10   8   6   4   2

Book design by Nancy Resnick

While the author has made every effort to provide accurate telephone numbers, internet addresses, and other contact information at the time of publication, neither the publisher nor the author assumes any responsibility for errors or for changes that occur after publication. Further, the publisher does not have any control over and does not assume any responsibility for author or third-party websites or their content.

For my mom, the kindest person on the planet

CONTENTS

CONTENTS

KARL: Were you worried about him during that siege? Were you worried about his safety?

TRUMP: No. I thought he was well protected. I had heard he was in good shape. No. Because I had heard he was in very good shape.

KARL: Because you heard those chants. That was terrible. I mean, you know, those—

TRUMP: Well, the people were very angry.

KARL: They were saying, "Hang Mike Pence!"

TRUMP: Because it's common sense . . .

The interview, I was told, would happen right there in the middle of the lobby, a room with two enormous crystal chandeliers hanging from a towering gold ceiling, the ornate and glittering space that once served as the living room for Marjorie Merriweather Post, the heiress who built the place. Before long, Donald Trump arrived, wearing a suit and tie. He ordered a Diet Coke and got right down to business, not waiting for my questions.

"You know we are putting out releases," he said. "These releases are much more elegant than Twitter. We are really getting the word out."

The former leader of the free world—who had been banned by Twitter and every other major social media platform for spreading disinformation—had discovered a more effective way of communicating: the press release.

As the interview went on, members of Trump's Mar-a-Lago club began to arrive for drinks and dinner on the patio outside, each one of them passing right by us, each one of them seeing him being interviewed. He could have talked to me in a private area of the club, but why would he do that? He wanted everybody to see him being interviewed—out of office, but still the center of attention.

Over the next ninety minutes, I asked him about some of the darkest moments in the history of American democracy, when, for the first time, an American president refused to concede defeat, attempted to overturn an election, and inspired his most die-hard supporters to stop the peaceful transfer of power. As you will see later in this book, his words were chilling, but his demeanor cheerful. In his gilded exile, he feels abused and betrayed, convinced the darkest betrayals came from those closest to him.

But in our conversation, as Donald Trump lashes out at enemies real and perceived, he seems happy, joyful—joyfully aggrieved. He's plotting a new campaign, not necessarily a political comeback—that's far-fetched although not impossible—but a campaign to make his erstwhile friends and allies pay a price for their betrayal. All the talk of disloyalty and revenge made him so gleeful he asked me to stick around for dinner.

As I headed to the dining area outside, Trump went elsewhere. Another meeting, he told me.

The main patio of Mar-a-Lago overlooks the club's pool and,

beyond that, the lagoon that separates Palm Beach from the Florida mainland. It's a beautiful space, half enclosed by the curved colonnade that extends from the part of the club where Trump has his residence to the areas open to club members. As the sun went down, the tables began to fill with diners, a mostly older and enormously wealthy crowd. On this night, there were about a hundred people spread out over a few dozen tables.

Shortly after I began eating, I heard a few people begin clapping. The clapping, isolated at first, soon spread across the patio, turning into sustained applause. As everyone soon noticed, Donald Trump was making his way from his residence. The diners were then on their feet, giving a standing ovation for the former president as he slowly walked down the Mar-a-Lago colonnade—a structure reminiscent of the line of pillars outside the Oval Office and alongside the Rose Garden. The ovation continued until he got to the archway leading to the living room where I had interviewed him. He pointed to a few of the guests. He waved and pumped his fist and then made his way to a table just like the others, although this table had a small velvet rope around it.

The applause continued until Trump took his seat. As the guests returned to their dinners, I asked one of the members how often this happens. How often does the former president stroll along the colonnade on his way to dinner as the members of his club rise to their feet in rapturous applause?

Every night, he told me.

Every night.

INTRODUCTION

O ne of the first calls I made as I watched the rioters move toward the Capitol building on January 6, 2021, was to John Kelly, the retired four-star Marine general who previously had served as President Trump's first chief of staff. More than a year before the 2020 election, as I was finishing *Front Row at the Trump Show*, I had asked Kelly what would happen if Trump lost the election and refused to concede. Back then the question was a hypothetical one, but it was one I had been thinking about for a long time. What if Trump tried to stay in the White House? How would this all end?

"Oh, he'll leave," Kelly told me back then. "And if he refuses to leave, there are people who will escort him out."

As chief of staff, Kelly had seen firsthand how Trump operates and he knew how the White House really functions. Clearly he had thought about this before and had played out the scenario in his mind.

"If he tried to chain himself to the Resolute," Kelly told me, referring to the enormous desk in the Oval Office, "they would simply cut the chains and carry him out."

Kelly has a deep and commanding voice befitting a retired four-star Marine general. He said these words with authority, as if he was speaking an immutable truth that needed no further discussion. To Kelly it wasn't complicated. If Trump loses, he'll be gone at noon on January 20, 2021. That's what the Constitution dictates. It's as simple as that. I didn't ask any more questions, but I still had a few. Who would escort him out? Who would cut the chains? Who were "they"? Would it be the Secret Service? Would it be the Marine who stands sentry at the entrance to the West Wing? The image Kelly described was a crazy one: a defeated president getting dragged from the White House while he refuses to admit defeat. Since John Adams lost reelection to Thomas Jefferson in 1800, every defeated president has accepted the results and voluntarily left office. The scenario described by John Kelly seemed too disturbing—and too absurd—to consider any further. I tried not to think about it again.

By January 6, the question was no longer hypothetical. Trump wasn't due to leave the White House for two more weeks, but for nearly two months he had been denying the results of the election. And now his supporters were storming the Capitol and trying to stop the certification of Joe Biden's victory.

I broke off from ABC's live coverage of the terrifying scene unfolding on Capitol Hill, and I called Kelly.

"This isn't America," he told me.

Like any rational person in America, he was angry about what was happening. And he was clear that the man he had served as chief of staff was to blame.

"If he was a real man, he would go down to the Capitol and tell them to stop," he said, telling me that it was time for the Trump cabinet to step in and save the country by declaring Trump mentally unfit and removing him from office.

"If I was still there, I would call the cabinet and start talking about the Twenty-Fifth Amendment."

Invoking the Twenty-Fifth Amendment and getting a majority of the cabinet to agree the president is unfit for office is the equivalent of cutting the chains and forcibly escorting the president from the Oval Office. There would be more talk of the Twenty-Fifth Amendment that night and over the coming days, but the first mention of it I had heard on January 6 was from Donald Trump's former chief of staff, while the rioters were still inside the Capitol building.

Kelly's views were shared by many who had supported and served Trump, and by more than a few who were still serving in positions of authority in his administration. I spoke to people close to Trump during his final days and weeks in office who told me they thought Trump was mentally unstable—that he had literally gone mad.

Members of his cabinet began talking about invoking the Twenty-Fifth Amendment during the evening of January 6. They may not acknowledge this fact publicly while Trump is still a political force, but they were. Lawyers were asked to quietly look into whether the Twenty-Fifth Amendment made it possible for the cabinet to remove Trump from office under the current circumstances and whether such an action would survive legal challenge. When the Twenty-Fifth Amendment option was deemed unworkable—there were several unanswered questions, including whether all the acting secretaries in Trump's cabinet would have a vote—a couple of cabinet secretaries resigned. Others made a pact among themselves to keep the president they served from doing more damage to the country.

Even as I wrote this book, attempts to whitewash the history of Trump's final days in office had begun. There are those who say Trump didn't really want his supporters to storm the Capitol building or violently disrupt the certification of the election results. Although, as you will see later in this book, Trump himself made it clear to me that he looks back on January 6 fondly and believes that if events just had played out a little differently, he'd still be president. There are also those who say the violence that day has been exaggerated, that there was no real threat to our democracy, that it was just a protest that got a little out of hand. That's a lie. January 6 was an attempt to overturn a presidential election; it was an assault on democracy itself.

I knew that on January 6. We all did. But the more I learned about the events leading up to the day, the more disturbing the story became. Over the course of my research and reporting for this book, I spoke to many of Donald Trump's top advisors and closest confidants, and several members of his cabinet. Many of those conversations came in the days before and during January 6. Others spoke to me after it was all over.

The more I learned, the more I became convinced that as horrific as January 6 seemed as the events unfolded, our nation was far more imperiled than most of us realized at the time. It's something of a miracle that nothing worse happened between the time Donald Trump lost the election in November and when he left office in January. You will read in these pages that America was dangerously close to being led into a foreign war at least twice after the election by a president who was also flirting with a war at home.

The seeds of our potential peril were sown in early 2020. As a deadly new virus was spreading across Asia, Donald Trump embarked on two campaigns. The first was a reelection campaign designed to win by dividing the country, and, if that failed, to undermine the results. The second campaign, largely invisible to the public, was a campaign to root out disloyalists in the federal government, to seek out and remove anyone in the Trump administration deemed insufficiently loyal to Donald Trump. If there had been anyone around Trump who stopped him from acting on his most destructive tendencies during the first three years of his presidency, they were either purged or sidelined by the end. By January 2021, hardly anyone was left to challenge him, to tell him no.

One of the striking things about January 6 is how many of the most senior members of the Trump administration were missing in action as the Capitol was ransacked and the president failed to do anything to stop it. As things went so desperately wrong, most of the people left in the Trump administration who had the standing to confront Trump were running in the other direction. One cabinet secretary was in Qatar. Another was in Khartoum on his way to Israel. The national security advisor was in Florida. Trump son-in-law and senior advisor Jared Kushner was on a government charter flight returning from Riyadh, Saudi Arabia. There is no evidence any of those people even bothered to speak to the president by phone on January 6 or urged him to condemn the rioters. Most of them didn't even bring it up to him in the days after the attack. They were either afraid to confront the president they served or convinced it wouldn't do any good if they tried.

My first book on the Trump presidency, written before the disastrous events of 2020, explored the dilemma facing a journalist reporting on a president who had declared war on journalism, calling real news fake and a free press the enemy of the people. Donald Trump branded reporters and mainstream news organizations as the opposition party. He did that to undermine our credibility, to make it possible for him to dismiss negative stories as nothing more than attacks from his political opponents. I wrote in my first book that reporters sometimes played right into the trap set by Trump:

. . . all too often reporters and news organizations have aided and abetted the effort to undermine the free press by openly displaying how much they detest this president—his policies, his blatant disregard for the truth, or his vilification of the press—and behaving like anti-Trump partisans rather than journalists striving for fairness and objectivity. We are not the opposition party, but that is the way some of us have acted . . .

Even through the events of 2020—the reckless and dishonest handling of the pandemic, the relentless politicization of everything at the White House, the shameful and destructive lies that followed the election defeat—I tried to treat Trump fairly. I have never wavered from my belief that journalists are not the opposition party and should not act like we are. But the first obligation of a journalist is to pursue truth and accuracy. And the simple truth about the last year of the Trump presidency is that his lies turned deadly and shook the foundations of our democracy. That's the truth. And if that makes me sound like a member of the opposition party, so be it.

The darkness of this time is not diminished by acknowledging that, in 2020, we also saw the two most significant accomplishments of the Trump presidency: the development of a COVID vaccine on a timeline few thought possible, and the signing of an agreement that established diplomatic relations between Israel and some of its Arab neighbors. Trump didn't develop the vaccine himself, obviously, and the Abraham Accords didn't bring peace to the Middle East, but these were real accomplishments made all the more remarkable given the chaos swirling around and through the Trump White House during this time. Trump himself would have received more credit for these feats if he wasn't also torching everything else around him.

History, rightfully, will focus on how Donald Trump brought

American democracy to the brink of destruction. The riot on January 6 was the visual manifestation of this, but it was just one element of the disaster. And the threat did not end when the rioters were removed or even when Donald Trump walked out of the White House on January 20, 2021—with no need for an escort—for the last time.

BETRAYAL

CHAPTER ONE

THE PURGE

O n February 10, 2020, less than a year before the events of January 6, Chinese President Xi Jinping, wearing a white lab coat and surgical mask, visited a Beijing hospital where coronavirus patients were being treated. It was one of his first public appearances since the COVID-19 outbreak had shut down the city of Wuhan some two weeks earlier. The news was grim and signs were ominous. Deaths from the disease had now surpassed one thousand in China alone, with hundreds more dead outside of China. Hundreds of Americans who had been evacuated from Wuhan on State Department charter flights were in quarantine on military bases in Texas, California, Colorado, and Nebraska. The World Health Organization had just raised an alarm about an ominous new development—a small number of COVID-19 cases in people who had not traveled to China.

"The detection of a small number of cases may indicate more widespread transmission in other countries," the head of the WHO tweeted. "In short, we may only be seeing the tip of the iceberg."

At the White House, Donald Trump had a two p.m. meeting in the private dining room near the Oval Office with acting Chief of Staff Mick Mulvaney. The subject wasn't COVID-19. It was White House personnel. Trump, newly acquitted in his first Senate impeachment trial and enjoying the highest job approval of his presidency (49 percent in the Gallup poll), was looking to make some changes. He wanted to finally rid his administration of people who were disloyal to him.

"I want to put Johnny in charge of personnel," the president told Mulvaney.

He was talking about Johnny McEntee, Trump's twenty-nine-year-old "body guy," the person who carries the president's bags when he boards Marine One and just about everywhere else he goes. And he was talking about putting the body guy in charge of the Presidential Personnel Office, a little-known but powerful position in the White House. The director of presidential personnel is responsible for vetting and hiring presidential appointees throughout the federal government—everybody from ambassadors and cabinet secretaries and top officials in the US intelligence agencies to the boards that oversee the nation's military academies. The office has thirty employees and is responsible for the hiring and firing of more than four thousand political appointees across the federal government.

Mulvaney thought McEntee was an odd choice for the job. He had no experience whatsoever in personnel and had never in his life hired anybody for anything. Now he was going to be put in charge of perhaps the most important human resources department in the world?

Mulvaney called his top deputy, Emma Doyle, into the meeting. If Trump insisted on putting a twenty-nine-year-old with no experience in charge of all the hiring for the executive branch, it would be Doyle's responsibility to make sure he knew how to do the job. But Doyle, who had the responsibility of overseeing the current director of personnel, couldn't believe what she was hearing.

"Mr. President," she said, "I have never said no to anything you've asked me to do, but I am asking you to please reconsider this. I don't think it is a good idea."

As the principal deputy chief of staff in the White House, Emma Doyle had spent a lot of time around the president, but she had never told him so bluntly she disagreed with one of his decisions.

She had also never seen him as angry as he was about to become.

"You people never fucking listen to me!" Trump screamed at Mulvaney and Doyle. "You're going to fucking do what I tell you to do."

As the president continued to yell and pound the table, he was interrupted by a phone call. When Trump took the call, Mulvaney motioned to Doyle to leave the room. She had incurred enough of the president's wrath. The decision had been made. There would be no contesting it. It would be up to Doyle to break the news to the Presidential Personnel Office that their current director, Sean Doocey, had been replaced by a new boss whose only qualification for the job was blind loyalty to the president.

A few hours later, Doyle was on Air Force One, along with McEntee, en route to a Trump rally in New Hampshire.

"So, I hear you are interested in a new position," Doyle said to McEntee as they were getting on the plane. She was unsure whether Trump had actually talked to him about it yet.

"Yeah, people have been telling me I should do that for a long time," McEntee told her. "I didn't feel ready before, but I am twenty-nine now and I'm ready."

"Is there any reason?" Doyle asked. "You know it's a brutal job."

"I'm the only person around here that's just here for the president," McEntee answered.

McEntee hadn't yet taken the job, but he had already been telling the president he had too many people working for him who were not totally committed to serving and promoting the president. He needed more people like Johnny McEntee.

"Johnny understands people," Trump told me. "He understands loyalty."

In the months ahead, while the country battled a pandemic and fears of economic collapse, Trump's most loyal lieutenant would lead a witch hunt, browbeating cabinet secretaries, scouring voting records and social media accounts of officials high and low, conducting loyalty interviews, and installing inexperienced people with questionable backgrounds into some of the most sensitive and important positions in the US government. And as Trump became increasingly isolated in his final year in office, McEntee became his indispensable man. He wasn't just seeking out and firing disloyalists, he was also, as you will see later in this book, playing a role entirely invisible to the public at the time—aiding and abetting the president's efforts to overturn the 2020 election. As one senior Trump official who worked with McEntee told me, "He became the deputy president."

One of the many remarkable things about the outsized role McEntee came to play in the final year of the Trump presidency is that he had actually been fired from the Trump White House in March 2018. Then–Chief of Staff John Kelly abruptly removed McEntee after his long-awaited FBI background check revealed that he had deposited large sums of money in his bank account, amounts too large to have come from his relatively low-paying mid-level government job. The deposits looked suspicious—most of them just under the $10,000 amount that would have to be reported to the IRS. The deposits raised questions about whether the money came from illegal payoffs and whether McEntee could be a security risk.

It turned out the money was from gambling winnings that McEntee had not paid taxes on, but before he could straighten it all out, he was fired. It was reported at the time that McEntee was escorted out of the White House so quickly he wasn't even allowed to return to his desk to get his belongings or even his jacket. That's not exactly right. McEntee was escorted out of the building because once he was fired, his White House pass was immediately revoked. But he was offered a chance to retrieve his belongings—he was just too embarrassed to be seen clearing out his desk.

Trump didn't know about McEntee's firing until after he was gone. He wasn't pleased when he found out. He immediately called Trump campaign manager Brad Parscale.

"Take care of Johnny," the president told Parscale. And with that, McEntee was given a campaign job that included a paycheck but no real responsibility.*

I was shocked when I heard about McEntee's firing. He was one of just three people who were at the campaign at the beginning and who were still working at the White House. As I wrote in *Front Row at the Trump Show*, I had met McEntee at the Trump campaign headquarters on the fifth floor of Trump Tower not long after Trump announced he was running for president in the summer of 2015. He was polite, earnest, and eager to impress. In fact, he gave me a tour of the place, including the shuttered set of *The Apprentice*, which NBC had taped one flight up from the campaign headquarters.

He was a recent graduate from the University of Connecticut, where he had played quarterback on the football team and made a viral video (several million views on YouTube) throwing trick passes. After graduating from UConn, he worked briefly as an entry-level assistant at Fox News. When Trump announced he was running for

---

*McEntee did not stay at the campaign for long. He ended up landing a well-paying job with Anthony Scaramucci, who had served as White House communications director for a raucous eleven days. Ironically, McEntee, who would go on to lead a purge of anybody not loyal to Trump, had continued to work for Scaramucci even as Scaramucci turned viciously against Trump.

president, McEntee offered his services and became one of a handful of employees at the Trump campaign.

McEntee traveled with Trump throughout the campaign and was one of the few people who accompanied Trump to the White House two days after the election when he stepped into the Oval Office for the first time and met outgoing President Barack Obama. When Trump became president, McEntee naturally played the role he played in the campaign—going wherever Trump went and carrying his bags. He had a workspace outside the Oval Office—against the outside of the curved presidential wall. McEntee put his name on that wall right above his desk. He may not have had his own office, but in political terms, the real estate could not be any better. Nobody was closer to the president. As one White House staffer who worked closely with McEntee told me, "He loves the boss and he'll do whatever the boss wants him to do."

And the boss liked McEntee, in part because he looked the part. Not only had he been a college quarterback, he looked like a college quarterback. Trump liked having the good-looking athlete around him carrying his bags. He also liked that the guy was athletic and tall—but not too tall, about an inch shorter than Trump. When the president played golf on weekends, McEntee always volunteered to go along, even though it was a thankless assignment that meant blowing his weekend and spending hours around the club waiting for the president to finish playing eighteen holes. McEntee would volunteer for any assignment without complaint.

McEntee's exile from the White House lasted nearly twenty months. With John Kelly long gone, he came back to the White House in January 2020 and resumed his old job, sharing the same desk space outside the Oval Office with Nick Luna, Trump's other body guy. But McEntee was bound for bigger things. When he came back to work at the White House, the president was going through his first impeachment trial. McEntee told Trump just what he wanted to hear: He had too many people around him who weren't loyal and were leaking confidential information to reporters. McEntee wasn't just carrying the president's bags, he was telling him whom he thought should be fired.

On February 5, 2020, the first Senate impeachment trial of Donald Trump ended with a decisive vote against convicting Trump. Senator Mitt Romney joined all forty-seven Senate Democrats in voting guilty on one article of impeachment—never before had a senator voted guilty in the impeachment trial of a president belonging to their party—but the vote was still 48–52 against conviction, far from the two-thirds supermajority needed to convict and remove a president from power.

Within forty-eight hours, some of the people in the Trump administration who cooperated with the impeachment proceedings were gone. Among the first to go was US Ambassador to the European Union Gordon Sondland, who had testified candidly about Trump's efforts to pressure Ukraine to dig up dirt about Democrats. Lieutenant Colonel Alexander Vindman, who worked on the National Security Council staff at the White House and also answered questions under oath about Trump's pressure campaign against Ukraine, was also fired. They even fired his twin brother, Lieutenant Colonel Yevgeny Vindman, who also worked on the National Security Council but had no role in the impeachment proceedings. Both Vindman brothers were told to leave immediately and escorted off White House grounds.

The president made no secret of the fact that the firings were reprisals for cooperating with Congress during the impeachment hearings. Regarding Alexander Vindman, he told reporters, "I'm not happy with him. You think I am supposed to be happy with him? I'm not."

And the president's son Donald Trump Jr. mockingly offered a word of thanks on Twitter to the leader of the Democratic impeachment effort, Representative Adam Schiff (D-CA), for helping identify the people in the Trump administration who needed to be fired:

Donald Trump Jr.
@DonaldJTrumpJr

Allow me a moment to thank—and this may be a bit of a surprise—Adam Schiff. Were it not for his crack investigation skills, @realDonaldTrump might have had a tougher time unearthing who all needed to be fired. Thanks, Adam!
#FullOfSchiff

2/7/20

"There is no question in the mind of any American why this man's job is over, why this country now has one less soldier serving it at the White House," Alexander Vindman's lawyer said after his client was fired. "Lt. Col. Vindman was asked to leave for telling the truth. His honor, his commitment to right, frightened the powerful."

It was just a few days after the Vindman brothers were asked to turn over their badges and escorted out of the White House that President Trump ordered Mick Mulvaney to put Johnny McEntee in charge of the Presidential Personnel Office and screamed at Emma Doyle for suggesting the move was a mistake.

As Doyle flew back to Washington that night, a story came on the

Air Force One television screens, which were tuned to the Laura Ingraham show on Fox News: REPORT: TRUMP REMOVING 70 OBAMA HOLDOVERS FROM NSC. McEntee hadn't officially received his promotion yet, but the purges had begun—just as the White House, and the world, were facing a real crisis that had nothing to do with who was or was not loyal to Donald Trump.

CHAPTER TWO

INVISIBLE ENEMY

Exactly one week before COVID-19 shut down most of the United States, I had my strangest meeting ever with Donald Trump. The date was March 4, 2020—the day after Joe Biden's decisive comeback victories in the Super Tuesday primaries. Trump had called me and two of my colleagues on the board of the White House Correspondents' Association (WHCA) to talk about our plans for our annual dinner.

We were invited to the meeting by Press Secretary Stephanie Grisham, who sent me an email saying she thought it would be "nice for you to sit down with the President himself to discuss attending this year's WHCA dinner." She added that I could "make the case to him as to why it would be good (if it really would be)."

This struck me as odd because although I was busily planning a big dinner—Kenan Thompson of *Saturday Night Live* had just agreed to be our host and the brilliantly satirical comedian Hasan Minhaj had agreed to do a multimedia presentation on the First Amendment—I had not actually invited Trump. In fact, I had not decided yet whether I would invite him. On the one hand, for more than a century of White House Correspondents' Dinners, the president always had been invited. On the other hand, he had declared the free press an "enemy of the people" and had skipped the dinner for three years in a row. Twice he had gone so far as to prohibit anybody working in his administration from attending. I hadn't invited him yet because I wasn't sure I wanted to. But there's one thing I certainly was not going to do: I wasn't going to plead with him to attend.

Deputy Press Secretary Hogan Gidley brought me into the Oval Office along with my WHCA colleagues Zeke Miller of the Associated Press and Steve Portnoy of CBS News. As with previous meetings with Trump, we were told to take a seat and wait for the president to arrive. As the three of us sat there alone in the Oval Office, we noticed a sheet of paper on the president's desk with the words HASAN MINHAJ in big print on the top of the page.

A few minutes later, the president walked in. He was all smiles and began with a little joke about the health safety measures that had people everywhere obsessively buying up hand sanitizer and had all but eliminated the act of shaking hands.

"Should we shake hands?" he asked. "What do you think?"

I had just flown to Washington from New York. I wasn't worried about getting COVID-19, but I sure didn't want to be the guy responsible for infecting the president of the United States with a deadly virus.

"It's your call," I said, my hands firmly at my sides.

And with that the president reached out his hand.

"What am I going to catch from you," he said. "What the hell am I going to catch from you?"

That was the last hand I shook in 2020. But the meeting would soon get stranger.

The conversation began with a breezy discussion about the results of the Super Tuesday Democratic primaries, which left Joe Biden as the clear front-runner and Bernie Sanders as the only real rival with a chance to beat Biden. Trump said the Democrats were working to keep Sanders down just as he said they had in 2016. If Elizabeth Warren had dropped out before Super Tuesday, he said, Sanders would have won big. He also ridiculed Michael Bloomberg, who had spent some $500 million only to lose everywhere except for the territory of American Samoa. He called Bloomberg a loser and a schmuck.

A president's time is his most precious commodity. But Trump seemed like he had plenty of time to sit around and talk politics. He asked who I thought would be a tougher opponent in the general election—Biden or Sanders. I answered honestly: I thought either one of them would be tough to beat. But Trump was clearly feeling good about the campaign to come.

After several minutes, he finally turned to the subject of the meeting.

"So, what do we do about this guy Hasan Minhaj?" he asked me, holding the piece of paper that was placed on his desk. "He was very nasty about Trump," he said, referring to himself in the third person.

Before I could say anything, he asked another question: "What is the date?"

Trump sounded like he really wanted to come to the dinner, or at least wanted me to think he wanted to come. I still hadn't invited him, but I decided that if he wanted to show up, we would not say no. Every president since Warren Harding had been invited and attended the dinner at least once.

I told him the date and said Minhaj was a very smart and funny comedian who I believed would do a great job. I wanted to make it clear I would not be making any changes to the entertainment in order to please him. I wouldn't be begging him to come or negotiating with him about our program.

"How important is it to you for me to come?" he asked.

"We will respect your decision whether you decide to come or not."

"It would be a very big get for you, Jonathan."

When I didn't react, he turned to Zeke Miller, who was sitting next to me.

"Jonathan is very cool," he told Miller. "He is like my son."

Trump then proceeded to reenact a conversation with his son.

"'Do you love your dad?' 'Uh, I don't know.' But he does. But he's too cool. The kids."

Donald Trump, it seemed, was comparing me to his teenage son, Barron—and he was comparing my lack of excitement about his possible appearance at the White House Correspondents' Dinner with his son's reluctance to say out loud that he loved him.

As Trump's words hung in the air for a moment, I repeated my noncommittal response to his suggestion he might come to our dinner.

"Well, we'll fully respect whatever you do, obviously," I said. "It's going to be a produced evening. We are going to celebrate the First Amendment. We have our journalism awards—"

"What do you do with all the awards you gave—I could bring this up in my speech I guess—all the awards you gave to reporters for the great coverage of the Russia hoax and they turned out to be wrong," he said. "I think you should take them back."

"Well," I responded, "there was some great journalism on that subject."

He suggested that Sean Hannity should be given the Pulitzer Prizes given to the *Washington Post* and *New York Times* for coverage of Russia's interference in the 2016 presidential election. More potential material for his speech, he said.

He had more questions. How long would his speech be? Would we supply him with a speechwriter?

"What is the concept?" he asked. "Am I supposed to be funny up there?"

As I started to answer, the door opened and Vice President Mike Pence came in the room. He had just been on Capitol Hill meeting with congressional leaders about the first emergency spending bill to help confront the threat of COVID-19. It would be the first of many emergency COVID-19 relief bills. As Pence walked in, Trump made another joke about shaking hands.

"Mike has just been meeting with [coronavirus victims] at the hospital," Trump said, gesturing to Pence. "Would you like to shake his hand?"

Of course, Pence had not just been at the hospital and, regardless, we did not shake his hand. But before the vice president could speak, Trump again changed the subject. With Pence standing beside him and waiting to update him about the government-wide effort to confront the greatest crisis, by far, of his presidency, Trump turned to me and returned to our earlier discussion about Super Tuesday:

"Seriously, how do you see the election, whether it's either [Biden or Sanders]?"

I looked awkwardly at the vice president, who was still standing there patiently by the president's desk, waiting for his turn to talk. It didn't seem right to make him wait more, but the president had just asked me a question, so I answered.

"I think it is going to be a really close election," I said. "It's going to be a real fight. And it's going to be in those states that you won that people didn't think you were going to win—Michigan, Pennsylvania, and Wisconsin, and maybe Minnesota. And it's going to be down to the wire, no matter who the Democrats nominate."

"You would say it's sort of similar between the two of them," Trump responded, with Pence still looking on. "In terms of assets and liabilities?"

"I think so," I said, telling him while Biden may poll better, Sanders has some real strengths as a candidate and could generate more excitement. "There are some things Bernie has—he attracts big crowds, he has a real fervent following."

"You do know my crowds are much bigger than Bernie's."

"I've been to both," I said, and nothing more. I had learned a long time ago not to get into a debate with Trump about the size of his crowds.

And at this point Pence chimed in. He had things to do and couldn't stand around listening to us chat about politics. He quickly summed up his meetings with congressional leaders—the coronavirus emergency spending bill had just passed the House and Pence said it had strong bipartisan support in the Senate. Then he told the president he would be traveling to Washington State, where a coronavirus outbreak at a nursing home had already claimed the lives of eight people. Trump joked again—telling Pence to be careful in Seattle. He then told Pence he didn't trust Washington Governor Jay Inslee because he is "a real showboater."

Shortly after Pence left to go to his next meeting, somebody came in to tell Trump he had people waiting to see him in the Roosevelt Room.

As we got up to leave, Trump told me he would have an answer on attending the correspondents' dinner by the following week. We'll never know what his decision was because exactly one week later, life in the United States changed: The World Health Organization officially declared coronavirus a pandemic, Trump announced a ban on travel to Europe, and most of the country was on lockdown. Like every other major event in the world for the rest of 2020, the White House Correspondents' Dinner would be canceled.*

---

*In March 2021, after Trump left the White House, I had an on-the-record interview with the former president and talked to him about that conversation in March of 2020.

—

Looking back at that meeting on March 4, 2020, it is both remarkable and revealing just how detached Trump seemed from the threat of the virus that was about to change life in America. He was jovial, joking about shaking hands. He made Pence, who was not just vice president but also the head of the coronavirus task force, stand there and listen to me talk about the Democratic primaries before allowing him to speak about the pandemic. He simply didn't seem all that interested in the virus that would come to define his presidency.

On February 26, 2020—just a week before my Oval Office meeting—President Trump had returned to Washington after an eighteen-hour journey on Air Force One from India. It was a rough ride home. As Trump watched television in his cabin, he saw the stock markets tumbling down, the Dow Jones Industrial Average dropping by more than a thousand points—the second day in a row of brutal losses. The sell-off threatened to wipe away all the stock market gains since he took office and, with that, one of his strongest arguments for reelection.

The stock market slide was directly related to fears of a global pandemic, with much of Asia and Europe already shut down and the contagion already appearing in the United States. While he was on Air Force One, more bad news rolled in. CDC official Nancy Messonnier warned that COVID-19 spread in the United States was inevitable and if the virus wasn't contained, the United States would have to consider closing schools, canceling mass gatherings, and requiring people to work from home. "Disruption to everyday life might be severe."

_____

If the dinner hadn't been canceled because of the pandemic, would he have gone? Maybe, he told me. But he wasn't sure because, he said, the press had treated him "so unfairly."

Her comments sent the stock market into an even deeper fall. It also outraged Trump, especially because the comment came in a briefing held by his own Secretary of Health and Human Services Alex Azar, who was the first person to lead the coronavirus task force that had been created a month earlier following the outbreak in Wuhan. When Air Force One landed at six a.m., a furious Trump called Azar and demanded to know why Messonnier was scaring people.

When he got back to the White House, Trump called former New Jersey Governor Chris Christie. Trump had decided he had enough of Azar. He couldn't fire his HHS secretary in the middle of a health crisis, but he wanted to put somebody else in charge of the task force, somebody who wouldn't scare the stock markets. Trump asked Christie if he would come to Washington and take over leadership of the federal government's response to the crisis. After all, Christie had faced crises before as governor of New Jersey, most famously when Superstorm Sandy hit the state. Trump figured he could handle the coronavirus task force.

"I need to put somebody in there who is stronger," Trump told Christie. "Would you be willing to do it?"

Christie said he would have to talk to his wife about it, but, he said, "If you really want me to do it, I will do it."

A couple of hours later Trump called Christie back.

"I've thought about this," Trump told him, "and this thing is too small and too temporary for you."

Christie was put off by the president's sudden change of heart. He figured the job would be a nightmare, but he knew it was important and he had agreed to do it.

"This isn't too small or too temporary," Christie told him.

"It is," Trump responded. "I'm not going to drag you down here for this. After I get reelected, I'm going to bring you down here bigtime. But I'm just going to let Mike [Pence] do this."

A few hours later, Trump announced Vice President Pence would take over leadership of the White House Coronavirus Task Force—giving Pence the job on the very day he had offered it to somebody else.

There would be many times in the weeks ahead that Trump would suggest the threat was small and temporary. At the time he said those words to Chris Christie, there was not a single confirmed COVID death in the United States.

Trump held an early-evening press conference to announce he was appointing Pence to take over the task force. At this point—February 26, 2020—social distancing was a fact of life throughout Asia and Europe, but not yet in the United States. The briefing room was packed, every seat taken and every inch of space in the aisles and in the back occupied by reporters or photographers. The area around the podium was almost as crowded. Before Trump and Pence walked into the room, more than a half dozen senior officials walked in—including HHS Secretary Alex Azar, FDA Commissioner Stephen Hahn, the director and deputy directors of the CDC, economic advisor Larry Kudlow, and, in his first briefing room appearance of the Trump era, Dr. Anthony Fauci. When he took his turn at the podium and started speaking, a reporter interrupted, shouting out, "Can you identify yourself?" The man who would soon become one of the most well-known people on the planet responded, "My name is Dr. Tony Fauci."

Fauci, who had served every president since Ronald Reagan, was no stranger to the White House, but he had never seen any room there as crowded as the briefing room was at that moment. The lack of social distancing wasn't his first concern as he looked out at the jam-packed scene in the briefing; he thought the place was so crowded it was a firetrap, saying to himself that if a fire marshal had walked in, they would immediately throw everybody out.

Trump waited for the anticipation to build, making his entrance with Pence after everybody else had been standing there for several minutes. The subject was certainly not a pleasant one, but he loved the image he projected—a president taking command during a national crisis, surrounded by the government's top experts. Trump had made a few short appearances in the briefing room over the previous three years, but this would be the first time he answered questions and held a press conference there. It wouldn't be the last. The Trump Show had a new venue.

This first coronavirus press conference set the tone for those that followed. The president was joined by the experts, but he did most of the talking. And he spent most of the time boasting about what a great job he and his administration had done. He waved around a piece of paper that he said was a study showing the United States was "the number one most prepared country in the world" for a pandemic.*

The mere fact of the press conference and the appointment of the vice president to head the task force sent the message that the threat from the virus was deadly serious. But with his words, Trump sent an entirely different message. After the Deputy Director of the CDC, Anne Schuchat, told reporters it was inevitable that the disease would spread in the United States, Trump stepped to the podium to say, "I don't think it is inevitable." He made multiple statements about the virus that had absolutely no basis in fact, repeatedly comparing COVID-19 to the flu, offering what would be the first of many false statements about the virus: "In some ways it is easier, in some ways it is a little tougher." He offered a tragically wrong prediction, saying that

---

*Later, as it became clear the United States was woefully unprepared for the pandemic, Trump would say the opposite, frequently blaming any problems on the failure of his predecessors to leave him with adequate preparations. He repeatedly said, "The cupboard was bare."

while there were fifteen known cases of coronavirus in the United States, "in a couple of days it's gonna be down to close to zero."

In a measure of what was really on his mind, the next day Trump invited a "playwright" named Phelim McAleer to meet with him in the Oval Office. Mr. McAleer had written a play based on sexually explicit text messages between Peter Strzok and Lisa Page, former Justice Department officials whom Trump frequently attacked in speeches and on Twitter for the roles they played in the investigation of Russian interference in the 2016 election. How the president of the United States had heard about this obscure play is unclear, but it was to be performed at the upcoming Conservative Political Action Conference. Trump's meeting with Mr. McAleer was scheduled to last fifteen minutes but lasted nearly an hour. "He loves it," McAleer told the *Daily Beast* after the meeting. "He loves the play."

At this point, the coronavirus threat didn't seem all that immediate to me, either, but I got a wake-up call that morning when I dialed into the ABC News morning editorial meeting. This is a conference call held every day with bureau chiefs, show producers, and reporters across our news division to discuss the stories we will be reporting on that day. At one point during the call, our investigative unit invited Tom Bossert to say a few words about coronavirus. Bossert was an ABC News analyst who had worked as the homeland security advisor for President Trump's National Security Council during the first two years of Trump's presidency. He was speaking on a subject he knew well; part of his responsibility had been to prepare for a pandemic. Bossert predicted the virus was going to hit the United States soon—and hit hard.

"We could see a death toll in the US of 500,000," Bossert said.

His words stunned all of us on the call. I thought I must have misheard him. Somebody asked him to say the number again.

"Did you say 500,000?"

"Yes," he said. "This could kill 500,000 people in the US."

As Pence got to work on the task force, he was hearing similarly dire projections and the health experts were telling him exactly what Dr. Messonnier had said, which had so infuriated President Trump. There was no escaping the fact that there was a real potential for major disruptions to life in the United States. Pence added Deborah Birx to the White House staff as the coronavirus coordinator. The addition of Birx was seen as a sign of how seriously Pence was taking the problem; she was an Army colonel and had earned bipartisan respect for her work combating AIDS during the Obama administration. The task force had regular meetings in the White House situation room, often followed by a press conference in the briefing room. There would be four televised briefings over the course of the next ten days. They were serious and substantive and, with one exception, did not include Trump.

The news kept getting grimmer and grimmer. By March 5, the death toll in Seattle alone had already hit eleven. The city's restaurants and bars closed down and the biggest employers, including Amazon and Facebook, told employees to stay home, turning the city into a ghost town. As one resident told ABC News at the time, "Traffic doesn't exist." As bad as Washington State was, New York was starting to look worse. Adding to the fear and uncertainty, it was nearly impossible to get a coronavirus test. Even hospitals on the front lines of the emerging crisis found they couldn't get test kits, and if they could, it took some two weeks to get test results. Trump visited CDC headquarters in Atlanta on March 6 and tried the kind of bravado and exaggeration that had worked so well for him in the past.

"Anybody who wants a test can get a test," he said.

But it wasn't true. Not by a long shot. Just saying it didn't make it so. And all of Trump's talk about what a great job he was doing didn't make it so, either. Despite his February 26 prediction that the US would be down to "close to zero" cases in a matter of days, known coronavirus infections surpassed one thousand by the second week in March, and, with testing so scarce, the actual number of cases was undoubtedly much, much higher. On March 6, organizers canceled the big South by Southwest festival in Austin, the first major event in the United States to be canceled due to COVID-19.

Against that backdrop, there was intense debate inside the White House about shutting down travel from Europe and recommending a broader lockdown across the country. Treasury Secretary Steven Mnuchin warned the moves would cause the economy to tank. Others on the task force warned a shutdown was coming no matter what and that doing it sooner would ultimately mean less pain overall. As the internal debate played out, Donald Trump held an event with representatives of the banking industry at the White House. When the small group of White House reporters in the press pool came into the Cabinet Room for the start of the meeting, a reporter asked the president when he would be addressing the grim news on the coronavirus. The president and his senior staff had talked earlier in the day about the possibility of doing an address to the nation about the pandemic, but no decision had been made. The president surprised his senior advisors when he answered that he would be giving a prime-time address that night. It was almost four p.m. The White House communications team would have less than four hours to prepare for an Oval Office address on the greatest crisis Donald Trump had yet faced as president.

Trump's announcement of the Europe travel ban that night triggered chaos at airports overseas as Americans abroad scrambled to return before flights to the US were shut down. Almost no passengers were tested when they arrived—not surprising considering the scarcity of tests. The move itself was a decisive action that sent another signal that the White House—despite the president's repeated statements downplaying the threat—was taking the pandemic seriously and prepared to take drastic steps to defeat the virus. But the decision was made in such a haphazard way it may also have done more harm than good, bringing waves of people into the United States from coronavirus hot spots abroad with no plan to screen them or track them. In his speech, Trump said the ban would apply to cargo shipped from Europe as well as passengers. Shortly after the speech, the White House issued a clarification; cargo shipments were not banned.

Pence was still in charge of the coronavirus task force, but the task force would soon have a new spokesman: Donald Trump. With Americans increasingly panicked about the spread of the disease, the briefings by the task force started happening every evening. This was a seven-day-a-week operation. Every day at four p.m. the vice president would meet with the health and logistics experts in the White House situation room. Trump almost never actually attended those meetings, but Pence would bring the health experts up to the Oval Office to give the president a short synopsis of the latest developments before they all went in the briefing room to give an update to the country and take questions from reporters.

It's almost impossible to overstate the level of public interest in these briefings as they became a daily affair in mid-March. Every cable news network and all the major broadcast networks carried them live. With schools closed, professional sports shut down, and with no place to go, almost everybody was watching television, looking for the latest news on the virus and guidance on how to protect themselves and their families. But just as the White House briefing room became the venue for daily must-see presidential news conferences, the White House itself became a dangerous place to work. The briefing room itself is small, cramped, and poorly ventilated. The workspace for reporters behind the briefing room is even more cramped. As president of the White House Correspondents' Association, I worked with my colleagues to find a way to get some social distancing in the briefing room. On March 15, we announced that every other seat in the briefing room would be left empty and reporters could no longer stand in aisles. We also asked the television networks to agree to share a camera crew, further reducing the number of people in the room.

A week later, I got a call from Press Secretary Stephanie Grisham. She had terrible news: a White House reporter who had been attending the briefings was sick and she had all the usual symptoms of coronavirus. We had our first suspected case. I immediately convened a call with the WHCA and the television networks. We had to quarantine anybody who was in close contact with our sick colleague and we had to drastically reduce the number of reporters in the building. From now until the pandemic was under control, there could only be fourteen reporters in the briefing room at any one time, even during a presidential news conference. This was a brutally difficult process.* I had to limit the number of reporters in the room just as we were all covering the biggest story of our lifetimes. Nobody was happy about it, but I knew that if more reporters got sick, there was a real chance the whole briefing room would need to be shut down.

The newly sparse attendance at his press conferences didn't sit well with Trump. He loved looking out at a room packed with reporters and photographers almost as much as he liked being at a crowded arena for a rally. Now he couldn't have either. And as the news

---

*To bring the number down to fourteen, we created a complicated system to share the seats among news organizations that cover the White House. For the television networks, there were three seats to be shared among five networks. Some of the smaller news outlets had to wait more than a week for their turn to come up for the shared seats in the back.

continued to get worse—a virus doesn't respond to a president's bravado—he became angry, often taking his anger out on the small group of reporters there in the briefing room.

On March 20, NBC correspondent Peter Alexander asked Trump why he was downplaying the threat of the virus even as the death toll continued to rise.

"What do you say to Americans who are watching you right now and are scared?" Alexander asked.

It was a simple question, and it was a chance for the president to offer some empathy and to say something reassuring. Instead he lashed out at Alexander for asking the question.

"I say that you're a terrible reporter," Trump responded. "That's what I say. I think that's a very nasty question and I think it's a very bad signal that you're putting out to the American people."

The attack was especially jarring because of the strange intimacy of the setting. Tens of millions of people were watching it live on television, but Alexander was sitting just about five feet from the president, one of only fourteen reporters in the room.

A week later he lashed out at me when I asked if he could guarantee that every American who needed a ventilator could get one. "Don't be a cutie pie." Not long after that, he called me "a third-rate reporter," adding with a snarl, "You will never make it."

After Trump had been holding the briefings nearly every day for four weeks, *New York Times* media writer Michael Grynbaum wrote a story about the growing concern among public health experts that Trump's briefings were doing more harm than good because the president was regularly a source of disinformation about the pandemic.

The story began this way:

"President Trump is a ratings hit, and some journalists and public health experts say that could be a dangerous thing."

This was a harshly negative story but also entirely accurate, laying out how Trump was misleading the country with potentially dangerous consequences, downplaying the threat of the virus and touting quack treatments like hydroxychloroquine as miracle cures. It was negative and quite damning, but Trump loved the story, tweeting about it.

"Because the 'Ratings' of my News Conferences etc. are so high, 'Bachelor finale, Monday Night Football type numbers' according to the @nytimes, the Lamestream Media is going CRAZY," Trump tweeted. "'Trump is reaching too many people, we must stop him.' said one lunatic. See you at 5:00 P.M.!"

He followed that up with four more tweets quoting the story.

The point of the story wasn't the high ratings. The story was really about how briefings were spreading misinformation, but what really mattered to Trump was that people were watching. As they went on, Trump did more and more of the talking, the health experts taking a backseat. Sometimes, they seemed to be there as props, surrounding the president as he faced the cameras, battling the press, boasting about his performance, and attacking his political enemies.

On April 23, the Trump Show briefings reached the point of absurdity as Trump infamously suggested injecting disinfectant as a possible coronavirus treatment. This was the craziest and most surreal presidential press conference I had ever witnessed, and it was bizarre from the beginning. The president brought in acting Under Secretary of Homeland Security William Bryan, a career official who previously served in the Department of Energy during the Obama administration, to talk about a study DHS had conducted that showed coronavirus on surfaces could be effectively killed with disinfectant and with ultraviolet light. It wasn't really clear to anybody why this relatively obscure study should be the subject of a presidential press conference, but Trump apparently believed it qualified as good news at a time when there really wasn't much good news. After Bryan described the study, Trump had a follow-up question:

"Supposing you brought the light inside the body, which you can do either through the skin or in some other way?" Trump asked, adding, "And I think you said you're going to test that, too. It sounds interesting."

"We'll get to the right folks who could," said Bryan, who seemed as confused as the rest of us.

But Trump wasn't done yet. He later said he was joking, but there was no laughter in the room. This was not a joke.

"And then I see the disinfectant, where it knocks it out in a minute," Trump said. "And is there a way we can do something like that, by injection inside or almost a cleaning? Because you see it gets in the lungs and it does a tremendous number on the lungs. So it would be interesting to check that. So, that, you're going to have to use medical doctors with. But it sounds—it sounds interesting to me."

Dr. Fauci was not at this briefing. The White House had been routinely keeping him away by this point, in part because to many Trump supporters, Fauci had become a hated symbol of the COVID restrictions they detested and partly because Fauci had a tendency to speak the truth even when it contradicted the president, which it increasingly did. But Dr. Birx was there. I had never seen her contradict the president or suggest he was wrong about anything. Not even in this moment. She was sitting off to the side, a look of horror on her face. But she said nothing at all as the president spoke about "injection inside" of disinfectant. In fact, Dr. Birx sat mute for the next thirty minutes, only speaking near the end of the press conference when Trump again brought up the idea of using ultraviolet light and heat inside the body as a possible COVID cure.

"Deborah, have you ever heard of that?" Trump asked. "The heat and the light relative to certain viruses, yes, but relative to this virus?"

"Not as a treatment," she said. Then she tried to let the president down gently, as if she were a teacher talking to a young student who got the answer wrong, but was at least trying. "I mean, certainly fever is a good thing. When you have a fever, it helps your body respond. But, I've not seen heat or light as a treatment."

"I didn't know how to handle that episode," she later told ABC News. "I still think about it every day."

I was there for that briefing, sitting in the front row just about six or seven feet from Dr. Birx, and couldn't quite believe what I was hearing. I tried to catch her attention, but she just stared straight ahead. I was concerned that the president seemed to be directing his under secretary of Homeland Security to start experiments using injections of disinfectant.

I directed my question to acting Under Secretary Bryan.

"The president mentioned the idea of cleaners—like bleach and isopropyl alcohol you mentioned. There's no scenario that that could be injected into a person, is there? I mean—"

The poor guy had never been in the White House briefing room before, let alone shared the stage with a president at a news conference. He had played along, but now he knew he needed to set the record straight. What the president was suggesting was insane, and had nothing to do with his narrow study on cleaning hard surfaces.

"No," he said. "I'm here to talk about the findings that we had in the study. We won't do that within that lab and our lab."

And with that, the president partially backtracked.

"It wouldn't be through injection," he said, even though a few minutes earlier he had said "by injection inside." He now said: "We're talking about through almost a cleaning, sterilization of an area. Maybe it works, maybe it doesn't work. But it certainly has a big effect if it's on a stationary object."

The damage was done. In an indication that at least some people were taking the president's dangerous musings seriously, the state of Maryland's coronavirus hotline received hundreds of calls from people asking about injecting disinfectants, prompting state health authorities to put out a public noticing saying, "This is a reminder that under no circumstances should any disinfectant product be administered into the body through injection, ingestion or any other route."

By the following week, the press briefings were no longer daily as there was a growing feeling among some of the president's top advisors that the briefings were no longer serving any purpose other than to further erode public confidence in Trump's handling of the pandemic.

Bad news on the virus and negative news coverage put Trump in a surly mood. Making matters worse: he was cooped up in the White House. The shutdown had stopped his rallies just like it had stopped everything else. He was eager to get out again before his adoring supporters and he believed he needed to do that or risk losing the election. By April, polls consistently showed Americans disapproving of his handling of the pandemic and favoring Joe Biden in the general election matchup.

Against this backdrop, Trump met with his campaign team in the Oval Office in late spring. He had been hearing warnings from his advisors that the pandemic, and the economic downturn caused by lockdowns in much of the country, were hurting his election chances. Chris Christie had warned him that he needed to turn things around, and to make sure the message got through to him, he wrote a memo telling Trump he would lose if he didn't change course. Campaign manager Brad Parscale, citing the campaign's internal polls, told him essentially the same thing.

As the campaign team assembled around his desk in the Oval Office—including Vice President Pence, Chief of Staff Mark Meadows, campaign pollster Tony Fabrizio, and Parscale—Trump pushed back on the notion that the virus was making things worse. And the reason broke the boundaries of logic.

"You guys have to hear what Kayleigh has to say about this," he told them.

And with that he sent for Press Secretary Kayleigh McEnany.

"Kayleigh, tell them what you told me," Trump said when McEnany walked in the room.

"Mr. President, I think you are going to win this election because of coronavirus," she said.

That pronouncement was strange, but her reason for making it was even stranger.

"You are going to win because we won't have to talk as much about health care, which was the number one issue for Democrats in the midterms."

Yes, the White House press secretary was telling the president and his campaign team that the greatest public health crisis in more than a century meant that Trump wouldn't have to talk as much about . . . health care.

CHAPTER THREE

PHOTO OP

uring the final days of May 2020, it felt to me like the world was falling apart and, rather than holding things together, the president of the United States was accelerating the crack-up.

As America neared 100,000 deaths from coronavirus, people of all walks of life gathered across the country to protest the murder of George Floyd on May 25 by Minneapolis police officer Derek Chauvin, who cruelly pressed his knee against Floyd's neck for more than nine minutes as he struggled to breathe. The majority of those protests were entirely peaceful, but not all of them. By May 29, protests had grown especially violent and angry in Minneapolis as rioters fire-bombed local businesses, shattered storefronts, and even took over an entire police precinct headquarters. Blaming outside agitators and anarchists, Minnesota's governor, Democrat Tim Walz, described the scene downtown as "absolute chaos." He had already activated seven hundred members of the Minnesota National Guard to assist local law enforcement, but he acknowledged the situation was still out of control, telling reporters, "Quite candidly, right now we don't have the numbers."

The moment screamed out for forceful and compassionate leadership, but instead of attempting to unite the country, President Trump poured rhetorical gasoline on the growing fire. Regarding the protests, Trump used his biggest megaphone to threaten violence against those breaking the law, tweeting, "when the looting starts, the shooting starts." Whether Trump knew it or not, the words echoed those of Walter Headley, Miami's police chief, who used the phrase in 1967 to explain why he said Miami wouldn't have any race riots. Headley also said in 1967 about his campaign to combat crime in the city's Black neighborhoods: "We don't mind being accused of police brutality."

Shortly before seven p.m. on May 29, after I had finished my live report from the north lawn of the White House for ABC News, I walked toward the northwest gate to head home. As I approached the gate, I saw two clearly distressed Secret Service officers, one of whom appeared seriously injured, rushing into the guard shack just inside the White House fence. I was just a few steps away from the gate when another Secret Service officer emerged and ordered me to move away, motioning for me to head back toward the White House. The entire complex was going on lockdown; nobody could enter and nobody could leave.

I took a couple of steps back and looked around, trying to figure out what was going on. Through the black bars of the imposing iron fence that rings the White House, I could see protestors off in the distance coming through Lafayette Square. They were loud. Three Secret Service police cars sped across the plaza toward the area where protestors were gathering in front of the Treasury Department building next to the White House. Another Secret Service officer sprinted right past me and out the same gate where I had tried to exit. By now there were about a half dozen other reporters and photographers who, like me, had been walking out to go home and were now trying to figure out what was going on. The Secret Service officer who had ordered me to step back was now yelling at all of us:

"Get back into the building, now!"

Along with the other reporters and photographers, I rushed back down the White House driveway and into the press briefing room. Shortly after we got inside, the Secret Service bolted the door shut. We weren't going anywhere. This wasn't the first time I'd been locked inside the White House by the Secret Service—it can happen because a suspicious package is found or because somebody has jumped over the fence—but this was different. I looked at the Secret Service officers I see every day and sensed something I had never sensed from them before: fear.

I walked back to the ABC News booth located behind the briefing room and made a few calls to try to find out what was going on. A good source told me the Secret Service had just issued a "condition red" alert. *That sounds serious,* I thought, *but what is condition red?* I couldn't leave the building because the door leading outside was bolted shut, but I decided to see if I could walk out of the briefing room and into the West Wing, where I could try to get answers from the press secretary. I was a little surprised to find the blue sliding door behind the podium was still unlocked. I slid it open and walked through. Then I walked through the next door and turned up a ramp leading toward a short hallway that stretches from the press secretary's office to the Oval Office.

As I made the turn up the hallway leading into the West Wing, I saw an image I will never forget—a Secret Service officer standing with ramrod-straight posture, toting an SR-16 rifle. There is almost always an officer there, but they are usually sitting at a desk performing the mundane task of checking to make sure anyone walking down the hallway toward the Oval Office has a proper White House ID. This agent wasn't sitting and checking IDs. Her hands were on her rifle. She seemed ready for person-to-person combat in the West Wing. Making things even more surreal, she was wearing a mask. This officer was prepared for two threats: violent rioters and a deadly virus.

"Can I walk by?" I asked, too shocked to grasp the absurdity of the question.

Of course, I didn't take another step forward. She quietly and calmly told me to go back and I retreated to the briefing room.

Before long I learned what condition red meant. It's a threat level that almost never gets invoked, and on this occasion, it triggered a response that, to my knowledge, had never happened before. The president was taken from the Oval Office and escorted into a secure bunker beneath the White House. The reason for the extraordinary measures was that protestors had breached an annex of the Treasury building, which is technically part of the White House complex but is actually about a block away from the White House itself. About an hour later, the threat level was eased. The president left his bunker and I was allowed to leave the building. The condition red was probably an overreaction. No protestors actually got inside the gates of the White House, but it was getting intense outside. Secret Service officers sustained serious injuries as they worked with DC's Metropolitan Police Department to keep the crowds back. The frightening scene set the stage for even more disturbing events to come over the following days.

To understand Donald Trump's actions during this turbulent and unsettling time, it's worth looking at what he was doing on the day after Floyd's death.

While much of the country was recoiling in horror at the video of George Floyd's death, President Trump took to Twitter to promote a wacky and baseless conspiracy about MSNBC anchor Joe Scarborough, accusing Scarborough of murdering a woman some nineteen years ago. The woman died while working in Scarborough's office, but he was thousands of miles away at the time of her death. Trump's tweets on the subject started before Floyd's death and had prompted the woman's family to plead with Twitter to delete the president's tweets. But the day after Floyd's death, Trump was still at it, still calling Joe Scarborough a murderer.

Also on that day immediately following Floyd's death, Trump already was making unfounded allegations about voter fraud and declaring the results of the upcoming November election rigged. It was on that day that Trump launched what would be a sustained campaign to convince people, with no evidence, that voting by mail is prone to widespread fraud. "There is NO WAY (ZERO!) that Mail-In Ballots will be anything less than substantially fraudulent," he tweeted on May 26. "This will be a Rigged Election. No way!" Twitter added a fact-check warning to the tweet, prompting Trump to threaten action against the social media company for being unfair to conservatives. "We will strongly regulate, or close them down, before we can ever allow this to happen," he tweeted.

That's what was on the president's mind as millions of Americans started gathering around the country to protest the brutal murder of George Floyd.

Two days after Floyd's death, President Trump made his first comments about what had happened. The comments came while he was in Florida touring the Kennedy Space Center in anticipation of a SpaceX rocket launch.* As he paused to pose for photos with the first lady, Trump responded to a question from Kelly O'Donnell of NBC News, calling Floyd's death "very sad, tragic" and saying, "Justice will be served." In a tweet a few hours later, he said he had asked the FBI

---

*The SpaceX launch was aborted due to bad weather. Trump returned to the space center for the rescheduled launch a few days later and again spoke about Floyd. "I

and the Justice Department to investigate "the very sad and tragic death in Minnesota of George Floyd."

In the coming days he would speak out more about Floyd's death and eventually call Floyd's family. "It should never happen," he said of Floyd's killing, "should never be allowed to happen, a thing like that." But he did not speak to the larger question of racial justice. In fact, when he was asked why African Americans were dying at the hands of law enforcement, he snapped back, "What a terrible question to ask. So are white people. More white people, by the way." And as the protests grew, he became more forceful in condemning protest organizers, especially anything associated with the Black Lives Matter movement, and the rioters.

After the condition red was triggered on Friday, May 29, more barricades were erected around the White House, pushing protestors to H Street, right above Lafayette Square, an area that soon would be named Black Lives Matter Plaza. Over the weekend, protests in Minneapolis grew more violent. And in Portland, Oregon, protests that had started out peacefully turned ugly. After rioters set fire to buildings, smashed windows, and threw projectiles at police, Portland Mayor Ted Wheeler issued a plea to the rioters: "When you destroy our city, you are destroying our community. When you act in violence against each other, you are hurting all of us. How does this honor the legacy of George Floyd?"

In Washington, DC, the Apple Store in Georgetown was one of many places downtown that was smashed and looted. Rioters tossed flammable projectiles into Lafayette Square, setting fire to a small but historic building in the park, flames that were clearly visible from the White House residence. Across the street, St. John's Church, one of

---

understand the pain that people are feeling," he said. "But what we are now seeing on the streets of our cities has nothing to do with justice or peace. The memory of George Floyd is being dishonored by rioters, looters, and anarchists."

Washington's most treasured buildings, was vandalized—spray paint on its exterior walls and a fire set in the basement. Some bricks from the structure were pried loose, presumably used to throw at law enforcement officers on the scene. There are few buildings more historically significant in Washington than St. John's Church. Built in 1815, its iconic steeple was cast in a Boston foundry by Paul Revere's son. Every president since James Madison has attended a church service there. The damage to the church was not extensive, but it was heartbreaking. The windows of the church were boarded up to prevent further damage.

By the end of the weekend, fifteen states and the District of Columbia had activated the National Guard to assist state and local law enforcement. Donald Trump said little to calm the seething anger. He was angry about the scenes of violence and even angrier that news of his emergency trip to the White House bunker on Friday had leaked out.* Further enraging him, some commentators on cable television were saying the bunker trip was a sign he was running scared. As Democratic activist Adam Parkhomenko put it, "Big tough guy hid in the basement Friday then came out and told everyone how not scared he was. Sure thing, bunker bitch." Soon some protestors in DC made "Bunker Bitch" signs.

With the images of violence in Minneapolis, Portland, Dallas, and elsewhere dominating television news coverage and people accusing him of being a coward, Trump was determined to put on a show of force. Over the weekend, he tweeted about sending the military into cities to restore order. On Monday morning, Defense Secretary Mark

---

*President Trump insisted he only went to the bunker for an inspection, not for his safety, telling Fox News Radio host Brian Kilmeade on June 3, "I went down during the day, and I was there for a tiny little short period of time, and it was much more for an inspection, there was no problem during the day." Attorney General Bill Barr, however, directly contradicted that five days later, telling Fox News anchor Bret Baier, "Things were so bad that the Secret Service recommended that the president go down to the bunker."

Esper had to cut short a meeting with the senior Pentagon leadership. He and Joint Chiefs Chairman Mark Milley were being summoned to the White House to meet with the president. Separately, Attorney General Barr was called over as well. When they got to the Oval Office, the president told them he wanted an immediate deployment of ten thousand active-duty troops to deal with the protests, beginning with Washington, DC. Donald Trump was ready to be a wartime president. And the war he was ready to lead would be fought right here at home against American citizens.

Trump didn't like the responses he heard from Esper, Milley, and even Barr. All three of them told the president they thought it would be a mistake to deploy on the streets of American cities active-duty troops trained to fight foreign enemies. The National Guard, they tried to explain to Trump, is different because it is composed of citizen soldiers trained to deal with domestic emergencies; when the Guard troops are deployed, they serve as a show of force, but more important, as backup to local and state law enforcement.

Deploying active-duty troops would require the president to invoke the Insurrection Act of 1807, which allows the president to deploy the military to quell rebellion. The Insurrection Act had not been invoked since the 1992 Los Angeles riots, and even then, active-duty troops were authorized but not used on the streets of Los Angeles. It was the California National Guard that was deployed. Esper told the president there were many steps to be taken before resorting to deploying US troops on the streets of American cities. There was local law enforcement, state police, federal law enforcement agencies, and, of course, National Guard troops to support those law enforcement agencies. Barr told the president he could make available as many as five thousand law enforcement officers under various agencies of the Justice Department.

To Trump it all sounded like weakness. He kept repeating that the military needed to be brought in. It had to be more than just the National Guard. There needed to be a massive display of force, especially in Washington, DC.

Before the issue could be resolved, Trump had to break for a conference call with the nation's governors. Esper was relieved to see their meeting broken up because they had been talking around and around and were making no progress; the president kept insisting he needed active-duty units armed for combat in Washington, DC. Trump asked Milley, Esper, and Barr to join him on the conference call.

It was quite a call. The president lambasted the governors, calling them weak and telling them if they didn't get control over the cities, he would do it for them.

"If you don't dominate your city and your state, they're going to walk away with you," Trump told the governors. "You got to have total domination.

"You have to dominate, if you don't dominate you're wasting your time," the president said. "They're gonna run over you, you're gonna look like a bunch of jerks. You have to dominate. . . . You have to know what you're dealing with," Trump said. "And it's happened before, this happened numerous times and the only time it's successful is when you're weak, and most of you are weak."

For Barr's part, he said, "Law enforcement response is not gonna work unless we dominate the streets, as the president said, we have to control the streets. We have to control the crowds and not react to what's happening on the street and that requires a strong presence."

To emphasize the point, Trump told the governors Milley was on the line, introducing him as a fighter and a warrior who had won many battles and never lost one. "And he hates to see the way it's being handled in the various states," Trump said of Milley. "And I just put him in charge."

As a military officer trained to stay out of politics, Milley was put off by the president using him to criticize the governors. And it wasn't clear at all what Trump meant by saying he had put Milley "in charge." Milley wasn't in charge of anything; his role as chairman of the Joint Chiefs of Staff was to be an advisor to the president, not a commander of domestic law enforcement operations.

The call with the governors lasted fifty-five minutes. When it ended shortly after one p.m., Esper raced back to the Pentagon and embarked on a most unusual mission for a defense secretary: to keep the commander in chief from issuing an order he believed would do grave damage to the military and to the country. He figured the only way he could keep Trump from invoking the Insurrection Act was to get as many National Guard troops in Washington as soon as possible. He started calling governors, including Maryland Governor Larry Hogan and New Jersey Governor Phil Murphy, to ask them to commit troops from their state National Guard units to Washington. He also took steps to create the illusion of an active-duty deployment so that Trump wouldn't order it for real.

On Monday afternoon, Esper signed orders to begin moving some seven hundred members of the Army's 82nd Airborne Division, located in Fort Bragg, North Carolina, to the Washington, DC, area. He also issued orders for troops from Fort Riley in Kansas and Fort Drum in New York State. The moves generated alarming news headlines about the defense secretary bringing members of the 82nd Airborne Division, which had been among the first Army units to deploy to Afghanistan after September 11, to Washington. The headlines looked bad, but they were exactly what Esper wanted. In reality, the 82nd Airborne wasn't coming to Washington, DC. He had ordered them to Fort Belvoir in Virginia, about twenty miles away. He had no intention of bringing them into the city, but he hoped that Trump would be placated by the movement, buying him time to bring in more National Guard troops.

In other words, the defense secretary wasn't deploying troops to quell social unrest in American cities. He was deploying troops to quell the dangerous and dictatorial urgings of his commander in chief.

Like so many other people who worked at high levels in the Trump White House, he figured he had to manage the president the way you might manage the feelings of a self-destructive adolescent. The theory being, if Trump sees Army units "on the move," then the Army must be moving, and he won't sign the order to really deploy them.

At 6:04 p.m. on June 1, as protestors filled the streets above Lafayette Square and surrounding St. John's Church, the White House put out an alert to the press, announcing the president would be making a statement in the Rose Garden at 6:15. Even by the chaotic standards of the Trump White House, this is ridiculously short notice. While reporters and television crews were scrambling to get set up in the Rose Garden, Attorney General Barr was spotted out in Lafayette Square looking at the barricades and sizable presence of US Park Police and National Guard troops separating the protestors from the White House. Barr would later say projectiles, including frozen water bottles, had been thrown in his direction, but unlike the mayhem over the weekend, the protestors appeared peaceful.

As I went to get in place on the North Lawn for my report that night on ABC's *World News Tonight* program at 6:30, I started hearing signs of a major disturbance above Lafayette Square—including screaming protestors and loud booms that sounded like fireworks. I could see puffs of smoke rising above the trees in the park. I had no idea what was going on, but it seemed like a major battle had broken out on the other side of Lafayette Square—just about one block from where I was standing on the White House North Lawn. Meanwhile, the president was about to start speaking at the other side of the White House in the Rose Garden. The situation appeared even more ominous than the condition red lockdown two days earlier.

After finishing my report on *World News Tonight*, I tuned in to listen to what the president was saying in the Rose Garden. The remarks were short but explosive. As I was hearing flash-bang grenades and the screams of protestors getting beaten back by the Park Police, Trump was declaring himself the "president of law and order and an ally of all peaceful protestors." He issued an explicit threat: "If a city or state refuses to take the actions necessary to defend the life and property of their residents then I will deploy the United States military and solve the problem for them."

The whole thing was playing out on live television in split screen. The world could watch in real time as President Trump talked of "law and order" while protestors were being beaten with batons and forced back by officers on horseback.

Trump had not invoked the Insurrection Act, but as he spoke in the Rose Garden he made it sound as if he had: "As we speak, I am dispatching thousands and thousands of heavily armed soldiers, military personnel, and law enforcement personnel to stop rioting, vandalism, assaults, and wanton destruction of property."

After speaking for less than seven minutes, he concluded his remarks, saying, "And now I am going to pay my respects to a very, very special place." I knew instantly that he must have been talking about St. John's Church—and that if he was truly going to walk there, he would have to walk not far from me to get there. Sure enough, a few minutes later I saw him appear at the entrance to the south side of the White House and proceed right outside the same gate through which I had tried to exit three days earlier during the condition red.

I later learned that the White House had informed the Secret

Service at about 6:20 that after his Rose Garden comments, the president planned to take a walk out the front door of the White House and through Lafayette Square to review the damage to St. John's Church. A year later, an investigation by the inspector general for the Interior Department, which controls the Park Police who so forcefully and violently removed the protestors, concluded the officers did not clear the park to make room for Trump's walk across the park. Instead, the report concluded, the area was cleared so that a fence could be installed around the perimeter of Lafayette Square. Whatever the reason for the action, this much is clear: The Park Police frantically cleared the area just minutes before Trump's walk across the park, using flash-bang grenades and pepper spray—along with batons and riot shields and officers mounted on horseback—to beat back the protestors. It was an awful scene that looked more like what you would expect to see in a dictatorship than in America, let alone in front of the White House. It was also exactly how the president had been demanding that the protestors be treated. It was, in the words he had used hours earlier on his call with the governors, "total domination."

Flanked by Secret Service agents, Trump made his way out of the White House at 7:01 and through the park to the church. It would be a seventeen-minute round trip. He was accompanied by several of his senior advisors—including Chief of Staff Mark Meadows, National Security Advisor Robert O'Brien, Press Secretary Kayleigh McEnany, and Personnel Director Johnny McEntee. His daughter Ivanka and her husband, Jared Kushner, were there, too. And there, walking behind him, was Attorney General Barr and the military leadership: Secretary Esper and General Milley, who was wearing his combat fatigues. As they walked to the church, the smell of pepper spray and flash-bang grenades hung in the air.

When Trump arrived at the church, he didn't take time to survey the damage or attempt to go inside. He didn't give a speech. There was a singular purpose for the dreadful stroll. He wanted to be photographed standing—or as he saw it, dominating—the area that had been occupied for days by protestors. And so he stood next to the church and posed for the most absurd and outrageous photo op in the history of the American presidency. At first Trump stood alone by the church, holding a Bible as if it were some kind of foreign object. Initially, he held the Bible in his right hand with the cover facing the photographers. Then when he noticed there were no words on the cover of the Bible, he displayed the spine of the book so the cameras would see the words HOLY BIBLE. I've never seen anybody hold a Bible the way Donald Trump held the Bible there in front of St. John's.*

"Is that your Bible?" a reporter asked.

"It's a Bible," Trump answered.

He didn't read a passage from the Bible. He didn't even open the book. Responding to another question, he said a few words about making America great. But this wasn't about the words. This was about the photo. This was about showing the world that he could push back the protestors. This was about showing he was a strong man, not a bunker bitch.

After the first round of photos, he called over for his advisors to join him. For some, it was already clear that the whole thing was a disaster. General Milley stepped away, out of sight of the president. Ivanka and Jared, who over the four years of the Trump presidency had a knack for avoiding the most controversial moments, stayed away from the cameras. Those closest to Trump got roped in—Esper, Barr, McEnany, Meadows, and O'Brien. Meadows awkwardly turned away from the photographers while also standing next to Trump.

---

*During a CNN town hall meeting in September 2020, Joe Biden said Trump had held the Bible upside down during the St. John's photo op. That's not true. Trump held the Bible awkwardly, but he did not hold it upside down.

They all looked uncomfortable—all of them, that is, except McEnany. The press secretary stood there smiling, while the others looked as if they wanted to get away.

The entire episode was particularly damaging to Esper and Milley and to the idea of a military that stays out of politics and protects the American people. By being there, the defense secretary and the chairman of the Joint Chiefs of Staff seemed to be endorsing the idea of using the military to occupy American cities, even though the two of them had both argued with Trump earlier in the day, telling him it would be a mistake to invoke the Insurrection Act.

What most people didn't know at the time was that neither man knew anything about the planned photo op until minutes before they started walking across Lafayette Square. At almost precisely the time the Park Police started clearing the area of protestors, Milley and Esper got calls telling them to go immediately to the White House to brief the president on the National Guard deployments. Esper was in a car en route from the Pentagon to the FBI's Washington Field Office command center, where he had planned to meet General Milley before heading out to greet National Guard troops deployed around the city.

When they got to the White House, the president was already speaking in the Rose Garden. They were told to wait with a group of aides in the area outside the Oval Office. Neither man knew anything about the plan to walk across Lafayette Square until a presidential aide told them to line up along the side entrance to the Rose Garden colonnade because "the president may want to walk to see the damaged church and he wants you to go with him."

Esper looked at Milley and asked if he knew what was going on. Milley just shrugged his shoulders.

They had been summoned to the White House to brief the president, but as it turned out, there was no briefing. The real reason they had been summoned is so they would be seen walking with the president as he "totally dominated" the area above the White House.

As the impact of the day's events sunk in, Milley and Esper realized they had made a damaging mistake. They'd let themselves get used. The image of Milley walking along with the president was especially damaging because he was wearing his combat fatigues. If he had known he was going to the White House, he would not have dressed that way. He was in his fatigues because he had planned to spend the evening visiting with National Guard troops. The combat uniform looked ominous as he was walking behind the president through an area where peaceful protestors had just been beaten and forcefully removed. Compounding that unintentional mistake was something Esper had said earlier in the day on the conference call with governors, when he referred to National Guard troops being deployed to "battle space" in American cities. Esper later said he regretted using that phrase—and that he was simply using military lingo but didn't literally mean American cities were battle space.

Shaken by the experience, the two men attempted over the coming days and weeks to repair the damage they believed had been done to the military's image by their role in Trump's disturbing photo op. In a commencement address to the National Defense University ten days later, Milley didn't mince words.

"I should not have been there," he told the graduates in a prerecorded video message. "My presence in that moment and in that environment created a perception of the military involved in domestic politics."

Milley also used the speech to endorse the message of those who had been forcefully removed from Lafayette Square while peacefully protesting racial injustice in the wake of what Milley called "the senseless and brutal killing of George Floyd."

"The protests that have ensued not only speak to his killing, but also to the centuries of injustice toward African Americans," he said. "What we are seeing is the long shadow of our original sin in Jamestown 401 years ago, liberated by the Civil War, but not equal in the eyes of the law until one hundred years later in 1965." Citing the lack of African Americans in the senior ranks of the armed services he said, "We need to do better."

As for Esper, the day after the photo op, he issued a message to all employees, civilian and military, of the Department of Defense that was intended to make it clear he did not condone the forceful removal of peaceful protestors before the president walked over to St. John's Church. He reminded DoD employees that they all take an oath to defend the Constitution and, "As part of that oath, we commit to protecting the American people's right to freedom of speech and to peaceful assembly."

The next day Esper took an extraordinary step he thought would get him fired. He held a press conference at the Pentagon to announce he opposed invoking the Insurrection Act and sending active-duty troops to do battle in American cities, as his boss, the commander in chief, had been threatening to do for days.

"The option to use active-duty forces in a law enforcement role should only be used as a matter of last resort and only in the most urgent and dire of situations. We are not in one of those situations now," he said. "I do not support invoking the Insurrection Act."

He was going public with what he had already repeatedly told Trump privately.

Immediately after that press conference, Esper and Milley were both summoned, once again, to the White House. The president was livid, screaming that Esper had no authority to do what he just did. Invoking the Insurrection Act, Trump told him, was the president's decision and the president's decision alone.

Esper pushed back, saying that all he had done was say that he opposed it. He had not defied any order; he had just said what he had been telling Trump for days—that such an order would be a mistake. The clear but unstated message was that he would resign rather than carry out that order.

Months after the Trump presidency was over, I asked Esper what he thought would have happened if he and Milley had not fought back and told Trump they opposed deploying active-duty troops in American cities.

"I think we would have had active-duty troops on the streets, you know, with rifles and bayonets," he told me. "He wanted ten thousand active-duty troops in DC and then to prepare to use them across the country to deal with the violence and the protests. It was that simple."

After he survived his press conference opposing the Insurrection Act, Esper was determined to do everything he could to keep his job. His goal, he told me, was to prevent the use of the military against American citizens during "the days before, the day of, and the days after the election." Esper would keep his job through the election—but just barely.

CHAPTER FOUR

TO TULSA AND BACK

I n late April 2020, the day after the disastrous press conference where President Trump mused about using disinfectant to kill coronavirus—"by injection inside or almost a cleaning"—he invited the three top House Republican leaders to the White House for lunch. Before walking into the small dining room adjacent to the Oval Office, Republican leader Kevin McCarthy told the two others—Steve Scalise and Liz Cheney—that they had an important objective to achieve.

"We've got to get him off TV," McCarthy said.

McCarthy wanted to convince Trump to put an end to his daily live press conferences. More than two thousand people a day were dying from COVID-19 in the United States, and even as most of the country was on lockdown, the virus was spreading. Trump's daily ritual in front of the cameras wasn't helping. In fact, his press conferences had become political and public relations disasters. Every night at about six he was going into the briefing room and relishing his time before the cameras. Officially these were briefings about the federal response to the pandemic. In reality they had become a substitute for campaign rallies, which had been canceled since early March because of the national coronavirus lockdown. The briefings had become combative, unproductive, and filled with misinformation. Trump's gaffe about injecting disinfectant was the last straw. Trump's top political advisors agreed with McCarthy that the daily Trump Show in the White House briefing room needed to end.

In public, McCarthy rarely, if ever, said anything remotely critical of Trump, but in private, he occasionally told the president directly when he disagreed with him. This was one of those occasions. Over a lunch of grilled chicken and steamed broccoli, McCarthy told Trump the daily press conferences were backfiring. This wasn't an easy message to tell a president who loved being on television and who was constantly boasting about his ratings.

The message wasn't exactly a surprising one. In fact, the dining room was littered with piles of paper, including polls conducted by campaign pollster Tony Fabrizio. The polls were not looking good, reflecting increasing disapproval of the way Trump was handling the pandemic. But Trump pushed back, telling McCarthy the press conferences were the hottest show on television, drawing huge ratings.

As they finished lunch, White House Counsel Pat Cipollone stopped in, apparently to give the president a message. But before Cipollone could say anything, Trump started berating him in front of McCarthy and the others.

"Pat, I'm here with the top Republican leaders and they are furious," Trump said. "They are demanding to know why you haven't moved on the lawsuits against Pelosi and Schiff. They are really upset. It's all they want to talk about."

On one level, this was bizarre. Nobody at lunch had said anything at all about lawsuits or, for that matter, about Pat Cipollone. The idea of suing Speaker of the House Nancy Pelosi and Democratic Congressman Adam Schiff was something Trump had floated months earlier, but nobody took it seriously. Trump was lying through his teeth. McCarthy, Scalise, and Cheney knew it. Trump knew they knew it. But Trump also knew he could lie with impunity. Nobody in that room would dare to contradict him.

On another level, this was typical behavior in the Trump White House. Trump routinely humiliated senior aides in front of other people. He seemed to especially relish humiliating Cipollone, an earnest, straitlaced lawyer and a devout Catholic who often had to tell Trump things he didn't want to hear. As counsel, Cipollone had one of the most important jobs in the White House, but he was used to the president browbeating him in front of others. He was also one of a handful of aides willing to tell the president when he was wrong.

Trump did another press conference that evening. There was no way he was going to let Kevin McCarthy tell him he should stay off television. But Trump also knew McCarthy was right. His standing in the polls was cratering. The Trump Show in the briefing room was not working. After his lunch with McCarthy and the others on April 24, Trump heard a similar message on a conference call with his campaign advisors. Campaign manager Brad Parscale walked the president through the polls conducted by his pollster. The numbers were dreadful.

"In February, you were on track to win more than four hundred electoral votes," Parscale told him, saying he had been poised to win even bigger than he won in 2016. "But now you are losing ground everywhere."

Parscale later told me he didn't sugarcoat the bad news, telling the president the pandemic, and public disapproval of his response, had been devastating to his standing and that if he didn't turn things around, he would lose.

"If I lose, I'm going to sue you," Trump said.

"I love you, too," Parscale answered. He insists the president was joking about the lawsuit, but he was obviously angry about his tanking poll numbers.

The next week, Trump did in fact take a break from his daily press conferences. They would come back, but only sporadically. The daily Trump Show in the White House briefing room was over. Trump needed another outlet. The key to turning around his polls, he told his advisors, was to get out on the road again. He had not held a campaign rally since March 2, and he was convinced that was his real problem. He was desperate to get out of the White House and in front of his adoring supporters.

"He was just beside himself," former New Jersey Governor Chris Christie, a close advisor to Trump whom he called frequently throughout the campaign for advice, told me. "All he could think about was the campaign. He didn't talk much about anything else. COVID would come into it, but really his focus was on the campaign."

During another contentious campaign conference call in May, Trump demanded that Parscale put together a plan to get him back on the road as soon as possible. He made this demand as coronavirus infections and deaths continued to skyrocket and all large events—from concerts and baseball games to weddings and funerals—were on hold due to a nationwide shutdown.

Parscale presented Trump with a series of options for a first rally in June. He first proposed a drive-in rally in Tampa, Florida. Parscale told him a drive-in rally would be a great spectacle, with a line of cars stretching for miles. But Trump hated that idea. He didn't want cars; he wanted a crowd. Parscale next put together a presentation of eleven other possible locations, most of them in outdoor venues, including Michigan, Arizona, Wisconsin, and Oklahoma. Parscale even pitched Trump on a twelfth option: holding a boat rally outside his Mar-a-Lago resort in Palm Beach, Florida. According to Parscale, Florida Governor Ron DeSantis told the campaign to pick a location outside of Florida because the state wasn't ready to hold a big event due to the threat of the pandemic.

Trump wanted to relaunch his campaign with a bang, a real Trump rally—indoors and packed with people. Exactly the kind of thing that was happening nowhere in America—or anywhere else in the world, for that matter. He chose Tulsa, Oklahoma, which had a friendly Republican governor and mayor—a place where, given CO-VID, holding a rally might be dangerous, but, unlike in most other states, it wouldn't be against the law.

The campaign announced the rally for June 19 and then moved it back a day after facing intense criticism for holding it on Juneteenth, the long-celebrated date marking the freedom of the last slaves in America. The controversy and the date change didn't slow the campaign's hype machine, which was portraying the rally as the Super Bowl of campaign events. "Trump #MAGA Rally in Tulsa is hottest ticket ever!" Parscale tweeted a week before the scheduled date. Days later, he tweeted again: "Just passed 800,000 tickets. Biggest data haul and rally signup of all time by 10x. Saturday is going to be amazing!" The following day, Parscale again bragged about the reservation numbers, claiming they'd received more than 1 million ticket requests.

Trump was thrilled. Not only would he be back on the campaign trail, his massive rally would prove America was back and the pandemic had been defeated. Trump's campaign aides believed the rally would show that the news media was overhyping the threat of the pandemic. But concerns were being expressed by public health officials in Oklahoma. One week before the scheduled date, the executive director of the Tulsa Health Department pleaded with Trump to delay the rally.

"I think it's an honor for Tulsa to have a sitting president want to come and visit our community, but not during a pandemic," Dr. Bruce Dart told the local newspaper, the *Tulsa World*. "I'm concerned about our ability to protect anyone who attends a large, indoor event, and I'm also concerned about our ability to ensure the president stays safe as well."

During an event at the White House on June 15, Trump brushed off a question about those concerns, boasting about the size of the crowd he expected to show up.

"As you probably have heard, and we're getting exact numbers out, but we're either close to or over one million people wanting to go," Trump said. "Nobody has ever heard of numbers like this. I think we're going to have a great time."

Privately, Trump was even more elated about his return to the campaign trail.

"We're back, baby," Trump told Chris Christie over the phone a few days before the rally, repeating the claim that more than a million people had signed up for tickets. "This is gonna be great. We are getting back on the road and the campaign back on track."

In reality, the Tulsa rally would end up being a political disaster and, for Trump, the worst day of his entire campaign.

The night before the rally, Trump campaign staffers who had traveled to Oklahoma partied together at the restaurant bar of the Hyatt Regency in downtown Tulsa. The tight-knit team had not been all together for a rally in months. They were ready to celebrate, drinking together until well past midnight. After the bar closed, some in the group retreated to a staff room in the hotel and raided the minibar—drinking and celebrating well into the morning hours. Nobody bothered to keep their distance or wear masks. As it turned out, the virus wasn't just spreading across the country—it was also spreading among the Trump campaign staff.

The following morning, staffers woke up hungover from the festivities and skulked downstairs for breakfast in the hotel restaurant. As one of the senior campaign officials described it, they were eating "crappy bagels" when word came that members of the team had tested positive for COVID-19.

"Put your mask on," one campaign aide told another, hunched over breakfast food. "We have staff popping positive."

"How many?" they replied.

"We're already at eight."

After that, members of the campaign staff in Tulsa frantically tried to retrace their steps from the party the night before, worried they would be next to test positive. "We were all trying to figure out who's testing positive, because we were all thinking, 'Oh, shit. Was I near that person last night?'" a senior Trump campaign official told ABC News reporter Will Steakin, who was in Tulsa to cover the rally but fortunately had stayed clear of the hotel bar and the infected Trumpers.

Back at the White House and the Trump campaign headquarters, there was less concern about the health of the campaign staffers who had been infected than about the political fallout of the campaign rally turning into a pandemic super-spreader event. According to two senior campaign officials, after the eighth person tested positive, two of them with the Secret Service, word came down from the campaign leadership: STOP TESTING. This directive came after NBC News broke the story that six members of the campaign staff who had traveled to Tulsa to set up the rally had tested positive, a report that actually understated the number of infected staffers. The headlines were embarrassing. Trump was furious that news about infected campaign staffers was getting in the way of news about his triumphant return to the campaign trail.

But that wasn't the only bad news spreading among the team that day.

The rally that Parscale and the president had hyped for days as the biggest ever—a rally that was to be so huge that the campaign built a large outside stage for Trump to address the overflow crowd—was turning out to be the biggest flop of his political career.

Staffers started to notice early in the morning that the lines around the arena weren't nearly as long as they normally were. Perhaps it was the heat, aides thought, so they opened the doors to the arena earlier than planned. But as attendees entered the arena, it became clear that the turnout was so dismal that the overflow stage became completely unnecessary. In fact, they weren't going to be able to fill every seat inside. The crowd was so small, the campaign briefly discussed moving the entire rally outside to the side stage and abandoning the arena entirely. But the day's high temperatures made that not a viable option. There were going to be empty seats, something you almost never saw at a Trump rally.

Parscale believed a major factor behind the abysmal turnout was the massive security surrounding the arena. The rally was taking place smack in the middle of a summer of protests around the country sparked by the killing of George Floyd and a national reckoning on racial justice. As Trump further divided the country by attacking protest organizers, there was fear of a violent clash in Tulsa between Trump supporters and racial justice protestors. The security in Tulsa was beyond anything ever seen for a campaign rally. There was a fully secured perimeter, with military Humvees lining the sidewalks and armed guards walking the streets. About 250 Oklahoma Army National Guard soldiers were activated to help provide security. It looked like a war zone.

Will Steakin was on the ground early outside the Tulsa rally, arriving around ten a.m. for a rally not scheduled until that evening. As a veteran of roughly fifty Trump rallies, Steakin knew you had to arrive hours early to have any chance of finding parking. He also knew that no matter how early he arrived, there would be scores of Trump supporters already in line, many of whom would have camped out overnight. But something seemed off when he made his way to the Tulsa rally—he easily found a parking spot right by the arena. And as he talked to Trump supporters outside, many of them weren't sure they would go in for the rally. They were concerned about coronavirus at what would be the first large indoor event in America in months.

As Trump flew to Tulsa aboard Air Force One, he watched the news coverage on television. It was all bad—television reporters talking about the positive COVID tests, the massive security, and, worst of all, the lack of a crowd.

As Air Force One prepared to land in Tulsa, Trump called Parscale to check in on the thing he cared about the most: the size of the crowd.

"Is it going to be full?" Trump asked.

"No, sir. It looks like Beirut in the eighties," Parscale responded.

Parscale, who had been watching in disbelief as the disappointing crowd trickled inside the arena, was depressed. He offered a heartfelt apology to the president. "I'm sorry. I threw everything I could at it," he said. In response, Trump hung up on him. The president was so enraged, some senior aides feared he would refuse to get off Air Force One and instead fly back to Washington.

Parscale, knowing Trump was fuming, told senior staff: "None of you should go anywhere near the president today, including me."

But Trump did speak at the rally, addressing an embarrassingly empty arena. The top sections were nearly entirely vacant, and no advance team magic was able to hide the large number of empty seats for a man who often claimed he'd never had an empty seat at one of his rallies. According to the Tulsa fire department, only 6,200 supporters attended the rally. Trump's campaign count was much higher at twelve thousand, but even that was far short of the nineteen-thousand-seat capacity for the arena. There were dozens of news stories at the time that the low turnout happened because thousands of teenagers using the video and music app TikTok and other social media platforms had duped the campaign by requesting tickets, taking them away from real Trump supporters. The requests flooding in from TikTok, Snapchat, Twitter, and Instagram may have contributed to Parscale's excessively optimistic expectations about how many would attend, but that's not why the place was so empty. At Trump rallies there was never a limit on the number of tickets; an unlimited number of people could sign up to attend. Those requests from young tricksters didn't take tickets away from anybody.

Trump's speech at the rally was rambling and lackluster. He made no mention of George Floyd or Juneteenth, or the coming hundredth anniversary of the infamous race massacre that had occurred in Tulsa. Instead, he complained bitterly about the way he had been treated by the news media and his political opponents. He lashed out at protestors and condemned the growing movement to remove monuments to Confederate soldiers.

"The unhinged left-wing mob is trying to vandalize our history, desecrate our monuments, our beautiful monuments, tear down our statues and punish, cancel, and persecute anyone who does not conform to their demands for absolute and total control," he said, reading from the teleprompter.

He also boasted about doing "a phenomenal job" combating the pandemic and insisted that rising numbers of infections across the

United States were driven not by the spread of the disease but by the spread of testing.

"So, I said to my people, 'slow the testing down,'" he said.

As it turned out, that was almost exactly the order his campaign staff had been given earlier in the day when they started testing positive.

For Trump, Tulsa was a disaster because of the empty seats, but it was much more than that. The rally was a metaphor for how Trump had mishandled the pandemic. He dismissed the warnings of public health professionals, downplayed the danger, believed he could talk his way out of it all, and showed a total disregard for the consequences of his actions.

Incredibly, the Trump campaign staffers who tested positive were told to grab rental cars and to drive, while infected with COVID-19, back to Washington. Under public health guidelines, anybody infected with coronavirus was supposed to self-isolate for at least ten days to prevent further spread of the disease. Instead, these infected Trump campaign staffers were instructed to drive more than 1,200 miles back home. At least one of the cars was pretty crowded with infected staff members.

"There was a car of three staffers who had tested positive that drove all the way from Tulsa, Oklahoma, to Washington, DC," a senior advisor said. "We called it a COVID-mobile."

The event caused problems for the Secret Service, as dozens of agents needed to quarantine after two agents who worked at the Tulsa rally tested positive. The consequences were more dire for one prominent Trump supporter. Herman Cain, a former Republican presidential candidate who the president's team flew out to attend the rally, tested positive for COVID-19 days after the event. Cain, who was seventy-four, was photographed inside the arena without a mask, sitting jam-packed with a group of other well-known Trump supporters who were also not wearing masks. Days after testing positive, Cain was hospitalized. A month later, on July 30, Cain died from complications of the coronavirus. The news devastated Trump campaign staff. Many felt like they were to blame for his death. "We killed Herman Cain," one senior staffer told Steakin not long after Cain's death.

There's something else neither Trump nor his campaign ever disclosed. One of the campaign staffers who tested positive became severely ill. This employee of the Trump campaign, whose name I've been asked not to disclose, was unable to drive home like the others. Instead, this staffer was hospitalized in Tulsa for a week. This staffer had been worried about the dangers of working on the rally because of preexisting conditions that made the prospect of being infected especially dangerous, but the president had demanded an indoor rally despite the warnings of public health officials, and the staffer faithfully responded by helping to organize it. Now that the rally was over, the president was back in Washington complaining bitterly that more people had not shown up, while this campaign worker was stuck in Tulsa, lying in a hospital bed thinking his life was about to end.

"It was really scary," a senior campaign official revealed for the first time in an interview for this book. "He was actually worried he was going to die."

CHAPTER FIVE

SWEARING ALLEGIANCE

Donald Trump had promised that the summer of 2020 would bring a massive American comeback—a "V-shape" recovery where the economy would quickly bounce right back to where it was before the pandemic shut everything down. Even the health experts had hoped COVID-19 would fade, at least temporarily, with the warm weather. But those hopes were crushed as infections reached new highs after the Fourth of July holiday.

By mid-July there were nearly twice as many sick people in hospitals with coronavirus than there were during the grim days in early April, and the COVID crisis was compounded by a social justice crisis. Public outrage over the killing of George Floyd brought mass protests and unrest to cities throughout the United States. In late May, metal barricades were erected around the White House, making the place look like a besieged fortress, eerily reminiscent of the US embassy compound in Baghdad during the Iraq War.

The view from inside the White House was further darkened by the president's reelection prospects. The economic gains that Trump's political advisors had hoped would be the centerpiece of the reelection message had evaporated. In late June, a Fox News poll had Joe Biden with a twelve-point lead over Trump. Even the polls conducted by the Trump campaign's pollsters showed him trailing badly. Trump mocked Biden for hiding in his basement in Delaware, forgoing campaign events and only making appearances via video from his home. But Trump was essentially locked in the White House, and in the wake of the disastrous Tulsa rally, it was unclear when he would be able to get back to holding packed political rallies. Even the Republican convention was in doubt. Coronavirus restrictions and a dispute with North Carolina's Democratic governor forced the party to scrap plans to hold the convention in Charlotte, but the alternative venue in Jacksonville, Florida, looked increasingly in doubt as infections there were on the rise.

Facing these multiple crises, Donald Trump's most fiercely loyal lieutenant, Director of Presidential Personnel Johnny McEntee, focused on an entirely different set of challenges. He had helped convince Trump to rid the administration of people who were disloyal to him—and those who were insufficiently exuberant in their allegiance. In short, it was time to dig in and conduct a full, old-fashioned witch hunt. With Donald Trump's blessing, Johnny McEntee waged a war within the Trump administration, one waged mostly below the radar with little news coverage or public comment.

Some of the high-profile moves were obvious. Just days after McEntee took over as head of the Presidential Personnel Office in February 2020, Trump announced on Twitter he would be replacing the government's top intelligence official, acting Director of National Intelligence Joseph Maguire, with Ric Grenell, US Ambassador to Germany. Grenell had no experience in intelligence, but he was one of the most unflinchingly loyal Trump partisans in the administration. Maguire's sin was twofold: 1) He had testified in the House impeachment inquiry and 2) given a classified briefing to the House intelligence committee on election security. Maguire had simply been abiding by his constitutional obligations, but Trump didn't think a member of his cabinet should be dealing with the opposition in Congress.

Less than two weeks later, McEntee pulled the nomination of Elaine McCusker to be under secretary of defense and comptroller at the Pentagon. McCusker was highly qualified and had the full confidence of the defense secretary, but she was purged because as acting comptroller she had raised questions internally about the fact that military assistance to Ukraine, which had been approved by Congress, had not been sent to the Ukrainian government. Although she did not testify in the impeachment inquiry, her emails raising the issue of Ukraine's military assistance became a key piece of evidence in the case against the president.

Those moves were controversial and got a lot of attention, but McEntee was just getting started. From his post, he scoured federal agencies to find the people who didn't truly support all things Trump. Beginning in the early summer, virtually every senior official across the federal government was told they would need to sit down for an interview—essentially to interview again for the jobs they currently held—with officials in the personnel office, most of them in their twenties with little or no experience outside of Trump's administration or his campaigns. The demand for interviews went out to every agency in the Trump administration—from the intelligence agencies and the Pentagon to the Justice Department and the Department of Housing and Urban Development. The interviews usually lasted about an hour and were conducted by members of McEntee's staff. The questions they asked made it clear there was one primary reason for the interviews: to determine who was a staunch supporter of the president and who was not.

The team conducting this purge was, for the most part, comically inexperienced. McEntee had staffed up his office with a group of very young Trump activists. He had hired his friends. And he hired lots of young women. As one senior official in the West Wing put it to me, McEntee had hired "the most beautiful twenty-year-old girls you could find and guys who would be absolutely no threat to Johnny in going after those girls."

"It was the Rockettes and the Dungeons and Dragons group," the senior White House official said to me.

In fact, one of the people McEntee had hired was literally a Rockette. Her name was Katie Forss and she was a dancer who had performed in the 2019 Macy's Thanksgiving Day Parade with the Radio City Rockettes. The only work experience listed on her résumé other than her time with the Rockettes was a stint, while in college, as a dance instructor, and a White House internship. McEntee gave her the title of "Executive Assistant to the Director, Presidential Personnel Office" and a salary of $48,800. McEntee also hired young women who had developed sizable followings as Instagram influencers. Camryn Kinsey, for example, had not yet graduated college, but McEntee hired her as the "External Relations Director," a job title that had not previously existed in the Presidential Personnel Office. Kinsey was just twenty years old and boasted on social media of being the youngest full-time staffer at the White House. In an interview with the online publication *The Conservateur*, she described her path to the White House this way: "Only in Trump's America could I go from working in a gym to working in the White House, because that's the American dream." Kinsey would go on to work for One America News Network.

McEntee dispatched his deputies to the Department of Justice to interview officials low and high. One of the many senior officials interviewed was Makan Delrahim, the head of the DOJ's antitrust division. Among the questions they asked him: "Do you support the policies of the Trump administration and, if so, which ones?" As the person carrying out the president's antitrust policies over the past three years, he found the question strange.

DOJ spokesperson Kerri Kupec was asked, "What are your political inclinations?" A little amused by the question, she responded, "Are you asking if I am Republican?" An office assistant at DOJ was asked to explain why voting records in Virginia, where she lived, showed that she had voted in a local Democratic primary a few years earlier. She was spooked that McEntee's enforcers had been digging through her voting records.

A senior official at the Environmental Protection Agency was asked, "Do you support the president's plan to withdraw all US troops from Afghanistan?" The question made the official nervous because he just hadn't thought much about Afghanistan policy. After all, he worked on environmental policy.

A president has a right to expect that his political appointees support his policies and will work to carry them out. These are, after all, political appointees. But during the summer and fall of 2020, Johnny McEntee and his young enforcers set out to harass and intimidate the very people who had been appointed by Trump to work in his administration. McEntee had helped convince Trump that his political problems were caused in large part by people close to him who pretended to support him but were really "Never Trumpers"— Republicans who would never support him. This was the deep state. The resistance. And McEntee told Trump he needed to fire them all and hire people who were totally loyal. Ironically, most of the people they targeted were already devoted to Donald Trump and believed they were helping him accomplish good things for the country. After all, they were still working for him three and a half years into his administration. For many of them, their reputations would forever be defined by their service to Trump.

The interviews conducted by McEntee's team were meant to be intimidating. The Presidential Personnel Office had the power to deny promotions and pay raises and the power to fire political appointees. The Justice Department assistant who was asked about her past vote in a local Virginia Democratic primary (she explained she voted in the primary because her parents had told her that's where her vote would count most because the Democratic primary winner was all but certain to win the general election) was denied a promotion and pay raise that she was eligible to receive. Another DOJ official received a call from McEntee asking for information on the status of a DOJ antitrust investigation into Google. She told McEntee she wasn't able to give out information about ongoing investigations. Shortly after that, she lost her job.

This all reached a new level of absurdity in late October. McEntee had decided that Ben Carson's Department of Housing and Urban Development had become a den of Never Trumpers. This was bizarre because Carson was one of a handful of Trump cabinet secretaries who had been there since the beginning and, unlike most of them, he had a close relationship with the president. Carson had never criticized Trump about anything. He had even defended the president's response to the rally of white supremacists in Charlottesville in 2017, saying the controversy was "blown out of proportion." Now McEntee was trying to purge some of Carson's top aides. He even targeted Carson's chief of staff, Andrew Hughes. Carson called the president to tell McEntee to back off. Then things got really weird.

In mid-October, Hughes, who had managed to keep his job, got a call from White House Chief of Staff Mark Meadows. Hughes missed the call. When Hughes called him back, Meadows was in the confirmation hearing for Supreme Court nominee Amy Coney Barrett. Meadows left the hearing to take the call in the hallway outside the hearing room.

Hughes figured this must be important if the president's chief of staff was leaving a hearing for his Supreme Court nominee to talk to him. He wondered, what could be so important?

Well, not much. Meadows was calling to follow up on some of the personnel issues McEntee had raised. Hughes told him Secretary Carson had discussed those issues directly with the president.

Keep in mind, this is the middle of October—less than three weeks before the presidential election, in the middle of a contentious Supreme Court confirmation hearing and at a time when the pandemic was killing hundreds of Americans every day. The president himself had just recovered from a severe case of coronavirus. And here was the White House chief of staff making a call to follow up on Johnny McEntee's efforts to purge HUD of people deemed insufficiently loyal to Trump. That was already strange, but the call wasn't over yet.

Meadows told Hughes that he had heard that one of Secretary Carson's personal assistants, a young woman who worked in his office, had "liked" an Instagram post from pop star Taylor Swift—that is, she had tapped the little heart below the picture on Instagram. The post was a photo of Swift with a message encouraging people to go out and vote in the presidential election. But an eagle-eyed member of McEntee's staff had noticed that the second photo in the post was a picture of Swift posing with a plate full of cookies emblazoned with the logo of the Biden-Harris campaign. It doesn't look good, Meadows said, for people working in Trump's administration to be liking social media posts boosting the Biden campaign.

One would think the president's chief of staff would have something more important to worry about. But this goofy episode is about more than that. It's an indication of just how determined McEntee and his cohorts were in rooting out anybody remotely unsupportive of Donald Trump. Going into a hotly contested election, the message was that everybody needed to be completely and totally loyal to the president and that any hint of treachery would be noticed.

McEntee and his team had much bigger targets than the assistant working in Carson's office. For one, they wanted a further house-cleaning at the Pentagon. The first to go, on June 16, was Elaine Mc-Cusker, the acting comptroller for the Department of Defense who had already had her nomination withdrawn in March. Defense Secretary Esper liked McCusker and relied on her to deal with the department's sprawling budget. But she still was on McEntee's target list because of the cameo appearance her name made in the hearings for Trump's first impeachment. The hearings unearthed emails Mc-Cusker had sent raising concerns that military aid to Ukraine, which had been approved by Congress, had not been sent to the Ukrainian government. Not spending money that had been appropriated by Congress for that purpose, she had warned, was illegal. She was correct to raise the issue, of course. Nobody really disputed that, but as *Defense News* put it the day she was fired, "Those emails would appear to have cost her the full comptroller's role, despite support from inside the department for the work she had done."

McEntee then took aim at a lifelong Republican national security and intelligence expert named Katie Wheelbarger, an acting assistant secretary of defense who had been nominated for a top intelligence post at the Pentagon. Wheelbarger was a graduate of Harvard Law School who had worked for the House Intelligence Committee during the Benghazi hearings and later as the policy director and counsel for the Senate Armed Services Committee. She was smart, qualified, and conservative. But McEntee's team discovered something "damning" in her résumé: When she had been on the Senate Armed Services Committee, John McCain had been the committee chairman! McCain had been dead for nearly two years, but McEntee knew how much Trump disliked McCain. Wheelbarger had only worked on

McCain's committee for two years (less time than she had worked for the Trump administration) but to McEntee's team, the association with somebody like McCain was a sure sign of disloyalty. Wheelbarger's nomination for the intelligence job was pulled and she was forced to resign.

Once again, the Pentagon press corps dryly noted the unusual terms of her departure, the *Defense News* reporting, "She becomes the second Pentagon official to resign this week under similar circumstances—with both having had nominations for new jobs reportedly scuttled by White House staffers over loyalty concerns to President Donald Trump." What the article did not say was that in both cases, the firings were directed by Donald Trump's twenty-nine-year-old enforcer of loyalty, and against the wishes of the secretary of defense.

This kind of thing was happening throughout the federal agencies. At the Department of Homeland Security (DHS), McEntee dispatched a twenty-five-year-old Trump supporter from New Hampshire named Josh Whitehouse. McEntee sent him to DHS in May 2020 to take the job of White House liaison. Every cabinet agency has a White House liaison, which is usually a relatively low-level job with responsibility for coordinating messages between the agency and the White House. But Josh Whitehouse took the title to mean that he was the real authority at DHS—the person sent to enforce the will of the president.

Whitehouse's office was on the second floor near the office of Secretary of Homeland Security Chad Wolf. He immediately started to throw his weight around, often threatening to fire people at DHS, although he had no direct authority to fire anybody. His mood swings were so wild—from super friendly to hot-tempered in a flash—that some of the officials who worked on the second floor were worried he could get violent. As one DHS official told me, "I was legitimately worried he was going to come and kill us." When I asked Whitehouse about this comment from one of his former colleagues, he told me, "They need help." He added: "I can't imagine anybody should be afraid of another person working there if they are in it for the right reasons and aligned with the agenda."

Whitehouse took a particular dislike to a senior advisor to the secretary who had an office across the hallway from him. Whitehouse had been working there barely a week when this advisor heard him screaming into the phone, "If they don't do this, I will literally go to their house and burn it down."* This official, who eventually asked to be moved away from Whitehouse, asked me not to use a real name, having an ongoing concern for personal safety.

In mid-August, Whitehouse had a loud confrontation with Secretary Wolf in front of several witnesses. It happened after Miles Taylor, the former chief of staff at DHS who would later be revealed to be the author "Anonymous" who wrote about a secret "resistance" within the Trump administration, wrote an op-ed article in *The Washington Post* criticizing the president he had served for more than two years. Taylor wrote that "the country is less secure as a direct result of the president's actions" and that he would be crossing party lines to vote for Joe Biden. Taylor hadn't worked at DHS for nearly a year, but Whitehouse saw a way to get back at him for betraying President Trump.

On one side of the door leading into the secretary's suite of offices, there is a plaque that includes the names of all the past secretaries of Homeland Security, each engraved on a bronze-colored metal plate. On the other side of the door is a plaque with the names of all the people who have served as chief of staff. As soon as he found out

---

*I asked Josh Whitehouse about being overheard saying this. He said the quote sounded "exaggerated" and he didn't think he had said it.

Taylor had endorsed Joe Biden, he set out to deface the plaque, re-moving Taylor's name from the list of former DHS chiefs of staff.

Whitehouse was in the process of unscrewing the metal name plate with Taylor's name when Secretary Wolf walked into the office.

"What are you doing?" Wolf asked him.

"I am removing the name of this traitor," Whitehouse answered.

"Stop. That doesn't belong to you. It doesn't belong to me. And we don't erase history here at the Department of Homeland Security."

With that, the twenty-five-year-old Whitehouse erupted at the cabinet secretary.

"Miles Taylor is a traitor! This just shows you don't really support President Trump!"

Whitehouse later explained to me why he did this. He told me Miles Taylor was like the ancient Roman figure Brutus who betrayed and helped assassinate Julius Caesar, and that he didn't deserve a place in history.

By the fall, Whitehouse would be reassigned to a more important job: White House liaison at the Pentagon. When his new job was announced, he told people, "I'm going to the Pentagon to fire [Defense Secretary] Esper and those deep state bastards!"

But before he left the job, he had one piece of unfinished business. At a moment when he saw Secretary Wolf was out of the building, Whitehouse snuck over to the plaque with the names of the former chiefs of staff and, once again, he removed the name Miles Taylor—one last chance to erase the memory of one of the many who could be considered Trump's Brutus.

CHAPTER SIX

COUNTDOWN TO DISASTER

Donald Trump had just finished a campaign rally at the Duluth, Minnesota, airport when he heard about the death of Supreme Court Justice Ruth Bader Ginsberg. His first comments were appropriately deferential. After all, Ruth Bader Ginsberg was more than a Supreme Court justice: She was a cultural icon, a legal pioneer, and one of the most admired figures in America. "She led an amazing life," Trump told reporters when he got off the stage at his rally. "What else can you say? She was an amazing woman—whether you agreed or not—she was an amazing woman who led an amazing life."

He paused for a moment and added one more thought about hearing of her death: "I'm actually sad to hear that, I am sad to hear that."

Then he turned away from the reporters, who were gathered under the wing of Air Force One, and walked up the stairs to board the airplane. As soon as he was on board the airplane, he called Mitch McConnell.

It was late in the evening—9:15 Eastern Time on September 18, 2020. The Supreme Court had announced Ginsberg's death less than two hours earlier, but Mitch McConnell knew exactly how Trump should proceed.

According to multiple people who listened to the call, the Trump–McConnell conversation took place while Air Force One was still on the runway in Duluth. McConnell's advice was specific. He told Trump he should wait until after Ginsberg's memorial service to announce a nominee to replace her. And he said that nominee should be Amy Coney Barrett.

McConnell later gave me a detailed account of the conversation. He told me he was direct and unwavering. He told Trump that Barrett was the only real choice. And he said he could get her confirmed before the election, just forty-six days away.

"I said to him if it is going to be anybody other than her, please let me know, because I want to try to talk you out of it," McConnell told me.

Trump was already inclined to choose Barrett but thought he should interview at least a few other candidates. McConnell disagreed.

"I said I wouldn't do that," McConnell told me. "I think it's pretty obvious who the best choice is and going through an interview process just slows you down."

There would be no slowing down. McConnell wanted this on the fastest of fast tracks. To get it done before Election Day, this would have to be one of the fastest Supreme Court confirmations of the modern era. Even noncontroversial Supreme Court confirmations—including vetting of nominees, hearings, and debate—usually take more than two months. The last one that didn't take more than two months was actually Ruth Bader Ginsberg's, more than a quarter century earlier. She was confirmed just forty-two days after her nomination in 1993—but her nomination was neither controversial (she was confirmed by a vote of 96–3) nor during the middle of a presidential campaign.

When the Supreme Court announced Ginsberg's death, I thought there was no way her replacement could be confirmed before Election Day. After all, when Justice Antonin Scalia died in February 2016—nearly nine months before the presidential election—Republicans wouldn't even allow a hearing on President Obama's nominee, Merrick Garland. How could there be a nomination, hearings, and a vote on Ginsberg's replacement before an election less than seven weeks away?

Of course, I had underestimated how aggressively Senator Mitch McConnell would move to make his mark on the Supreme Court. In 2016, McConnell had insisted the Senate shouldn't move forward on the Garland nomination because it was an election year and it should be up to the winner of the election to nominate Scalia's replacement.* It was a weak argument, but it didn't matter because McConnell was the Senate majority leader and he had the power, and the support of fellow Republicans, to do what he wanted. Within hours of Ginsberg's death, McConnell would be making the opposite argument—saying the Senate had to act quickly to confirm Ginsberg's replacement before the election. It looked like brazen hypocrisy but, once again, it didn't matter, because McConnell had the power to push the nomination through.†

Eight days after Ginsberg's death, on September 26, President Trump did exactly what Mitch McConnell said he should do. He

---

*In 2020, McConnell insisted his rule of not confirming a Supreme Court nominee during an election year only applied when the president's party did not control the Senate. But that's not the way it was interpreted at the time. In 2016, fellow Republican Lindsey Graham put it this way when he was justifying the decision to block Garland: "If there's a Republican president in 2016 and a vacancy occurs in the last year of the first term, you can say Lindsey Graham said let's let the next president, whoever it might be, make that nomination."

†There were just two Republicans who had said they would not vote to confirm a Supreme Court justice so close to the election: Susan Collins (R-ME) and Lisa Murkowski (R-AK). As Murkowski put it, "Fair is fair." Ultimately, only Collins voted against the nomination of Amy Coney Barrett.

nominated Amy Coney Barrett to fill the vacant seat on the Supreme Court. Trump made the announcement in the Rose Garden on a beautiful Saturday afternoon in what would become known as the most high-profile COVID-19 super-spreader event of 2020. But long before any of the attendees tested positive, it seemed obvious this was a disaster in the making.

The White House press office had gone to extraordinary lengths to ensure maximum news coverage for the event. Since the beginning of the pandemic, attendance at Rose Garden events had been limited to accommodate some degree of social distancing, but as I arrived that morning, I was told correspondents for all networks would be permitted to attend the announcement—and we would all be able to do our live reports from right there where the president and his supporters were assembling. In fact, more than one hundred journalists had been issued credentials to cover the event in person. There was also expected to be a large contingent of Republican senators, conservative activists, and White House officials at the event.

Under the best of circumstances, the Trump White House seemed like a dangerous place to be through most of 2020. This White House had displayed an almost total disregard for COVID safety protocols, and now they were determined to pack as many people as possible into the Rose Garden. The only place in the entire complex where masks were routinely worn was the area where the press worked and set the rules. And over the course of the pandemic, 1600 Pennsylvania Avenue often seemed like a COVID hot zone. Several White House staffers, including the president's personal valet and the vice president's press secretary, had been infected. Earlier in September, Crede Bailey, the director of the White House security office, had become so sick with COVID-19 that he had been rushed to the hospital, where he would spend more than three months. Bailey's condition was dire. He would ultimately suffer permanent damage to his lungs and have part of his right leg amputated.

So, no, I did not jump at the opportunity to be right there in the middle of an overcrowded event during a pandemic with my camera crew. I had attended White House briefings—over the objections of my family—throughout the pandemic and had, somewhat miraculously, not been infected with coronavirus. But this event seemed to me to be the most reckless and densely packed event at the White House since the pandemic hit the United States. I politely and firmly declined the invitation to go anywhere near the Rose Garden. Instead, I did my live report from the other side of the White House—at the ABC News camera position on the North Lawn—with no large crowd of maskless Trump staffers and supporters nearby. As it turned out, Senator McConnell also declined an invitation to the Rose Garden. As he explained to me months later, he thought the White House had been "flippant" about COVID safety and he didn't want to expose himself to the risk of being infected. Imagine that. The architect of this election-eve Supreme Court nomination did not want to be there because he believed the Trump White House was so reckless, he might catch a deadly disease.

Skipping the Rose Garden ceremony proved to be a wise choice. Within a week, at least eleven people who were there to see Amy Coney Barrett nominated tested positive for coronavirus.

In a reminder of just how close all of this was to the election, the president spent most of the weekend preparing for his first presidential debate, which was just three days after the Rose Garden announcement. Trump had huddled with his top political advisors for a debate prep session shortly before walking into the Rose Garden with Barrett and her family. And he attended two more prep sessions the following day. Most of the people who helped the president get ready for that debate would also get infected with COVID-19.

The debate prep sessions took place in the White House basement in the Map Room, with a small group of political advisors, including Trump campaign manager Bill Stepien, Trump campaign strategist Jason Miller, Rudy Giuliani, and Chris Christie. Also there were White House aides Kellyanne Conway, Stephen Miller, Hope Hicks, Kayleigh McEnany, and Chief of Staff Mark Meadows.

Trump has never been one to spend much time preparing for debates, but this time his advisors were determined that he couldn't just wing it. He needed to get ready. Trump was trailing badly in the polls and needed a strong debate performance to have a chance of beating Biden. The sessions were designed to look a little like mock debates, with Trump sitting at a conference table next to Chris Christie, who played the role of Joe Biden, and across from Kellyanne Conway, who played the moderator. Conway would pose a question to Trump and after he responded, Christie would offer the kind of rebuttal he thought would come from Biden. The others sitting around the table would chime in with ideas on how to make the responses better.

The first session that weekend didn't get far, however. The problem was Rudy Giuliani. The former New York City mayor wanted to talk about one thing—Joe Biden's son Hunter. He came to the meeting armed with piles of paper and an iPad. He said he had all the evidence needed to bring down Biden once and for all. Giuliani believed that Hunter Biden's controversial business dealings in Ukraine—he made $50,000 a month serving on the board of Burisma, a Ukrainian energy company, while his father was vice president—would sink Joe Biden's campaign. He argued that all Trump needed to do to win the debate—and the election—was to hit Biden's son hard and do it over and over again. No matter what the topic, Rudy would chime in, saying that Trump should bring it back to Hunter Biden.

"Rudy was being a disruptive force," one of the other advisors who attended the meetings told me. "No matter what we were talking about, all he wanted to do was talk about Hunter Biden."

Giuliani was single-minded and he was manic. He rummaged through his papers and kept bringing up names of obscure Ukrainian businessmen and political figures. The corruption, he said, went far beyond Hunter Biden's work for the energy company.

"Watch this," Giuliani said, directing everybody to look at his iPad.

But as he tried to play a video showing more evidence of Biden's corruption, the iPad froze up. He fiddled with it and tried again.

"You've got to see this," Giuliani said. Again, he could not get the video to play. He tried several times but never could get it to work.

But if Giuliani was disruptive and disorganized, he was also saying exactly what Trump wanted to hear. And as they worked through questions, Trump kept talking about Hunter Biden, just as Giuliani had urged him to do.

Chris Christie thought this was a risky strategy that would invite Biden to attack the business dealings of the Trump family.

"You have real nerve talking about relatives taking advantage of political power," Christie said, playing the role of Biden. "You've invited your daughter and son-in-law into the White House and they made $36 million last year* while they were doing the people's business. Your family traded the influence they have in the White House to make tens of millions of dollars."

---

*The number Christie used was from a financial disclosure Ivanka Trump and Jared Kushner were required to make to the Office of Government Ethics. In July 2020, the couple disclosed making between $36.2 million and $157 million in 2019.

Christie was just playing the role of Biden here, but the words stung, especially because Trump knew Kushner and Christie had a tortured history dating back to 2005, when Christie, in his role as US attorney for the District of New Jersey, had prosecuted Kushner's father for tax evasion and witness tampering. Christie believed he had an obligation to prepare Trump for an obvious line of attack that would come from Biden. But all Trump heard was Christie attacking his family right there in front of his top advisors. He was livid.

"That's absolutely untrue!" Trump yelled at Christie. "We've lost money here. My children are losing money being here. Jared has sacrificed more than anyone being away from his business. He hasn't made any kind of money."

"No, no, Mr. President," Christie said, continuing to play the role of Biden. "They filed disclosure statements that say they made at least $36 million last year. Are you saying they lied? They lied about how much money they made?"

"I'm not saying that," Trump shot back. "I'm saying they could have made a lot more money."

"But they made that money, sir," Christie continued, making Trump even more angry. "They made that money while they were working for you full time."

"I'm not going to sit here and put up with this shit," Trump said, glaring at Christie.

"Well, look," Christie said, stepping back out of his role playing Biden. "I'm not saying we shouldn't talk about the Hunter Biden stuff. But if you go too deeply into the Hunter Biden stuff, this is the kind of stuff he will hit you back on. You've got to be ready for that. My job is to get you ready."

Trump was done with it all. This was exactly why he hated preparing for debates.

"I don't want to hear anymore," Trump declared. "I know what they're going to say. Enough. Let's move on."

The session finally ended when Trump had to leave to prepare for the Amy Coney Barrett Rose Garden event. As the group started to break up, Meadows walked over to Christie and Stepien.

"I'm not going to let Rudy in the building for any more of these," Meadows told them. "We're not going to get anywhere if he continues to be here." Christie and Stepien agreed. The only way to effectively prepare for the debate was to literally lock Giuliani out of the White House.

And that's exactly what happened. When Giuliani showed up to the debate prep session the following day at 2:30 p.m., he was turned away at the White House gate. Meadows had his name taken off the list. But before the next session—scheduled for six that evening—Rudy was back. He had called Trump directly and Trump told his secretary to get him cleared to come into the White House. The episode demonstrated a fundamental truth of the Trump White House: there were no gatekeepers. All four Trump chiefs of staff had, in varying degrees, tried to keep crazy or disruptive people from meeting with President Trump. But there was always a back channel. The quickest, and surest, way to get to President Trump was to call him directly.

Just as Giuliani got himself back into the White House, Trump was preparing to have a Sunday-evening press conference, which was to be followed by the second debate prep session of the day. Christie was waiting with the others in the West Wing basement cafeteria, when he got a call from the White House press office summoning him upstairs. Trump wanted Christie there with him for the press conference. Christie thought that was a bad idea, but the assistant on the other end of the line said he needed to come now. "He won't start without you."

As Christie greeted the president in the press office, Rudy Giuliani walked in. This was more than a little awkward; Giuliani believed Christie was part of the reason he had been locked out of the White House earlier in the day—and he was right.

"How are you?" Christie asked him.

"I'm fine," a clearly irritated Giuliani answered.

Trump announced that he wanted both of them to walk into the press conference with him. He wanted the world to see that he had two heavyweight political brawlers helping to prepare him for the debate, just two days away.

"I want them to see you're both here, my two tough guys," Trump told the two men.

But before the three of them could walk into the briefing room, White House Press Secretary Kayleigh McEnany rushed out of her office to tell the president about a blockbuster story that had just been posted in *The New York Times*. It was one of the biggest political scoops of the year, a story big enough to sink a presidential campaign. The newspaper had obtained several years of Trump's tax returns—the returns he had been refusing to release since he launched his campaign five years earlier. And the opening sentences of the story were devastating:

"Donald J. Trump paid $750 in federal income taxes the year he won the presidency. In his first year in the White House, he paid another $750.

"He had paid no income taxes at all in 10 of the previous 15 years—largely because he reported losing much more money than he made."

The self-described billionaire had paid virtually no federal income taxes. And it got worse. The *Times* reported Trump was so badly in debt he was facing financial peril.

"As the president wages a re-election campaign that polls say he is in danger of losing, his finances are under stress, beset by losses and hundreds of millions of dollars in debt coming due that he has personally guaranteed."

It was a story that seemed likely to dominate the upcoming debate and final stretch of the campaign. And here was Trump, about to walk into a press conference.

But as big as the story was, it only took a few minutes for Trump to decide how to handle it. He would do what he always did with bad news: deny the story and attack the news organization and journalists that reported it.* And that's exactly what he did.

Before Trump walked into the briefing room, McEnany handed him some prepared remarks to read at the top of the press conference. The statement, which the president read with only minimal ad-libbing, was a foreshadowing of Trump's later refusal to accept the results of the election. After boasting about his nomination of Amy Coney Barrett ("one of our nation's most brilliant legal minds") and slamming her critics ("nasty . . . mean . . . disgraceful"), Trump launched into a tirade about voter fraud. Reading from the remarks handed to him by his press secretary, he made a series of claims designed to give the impression Democrats were engaged in a massive nationwide effort to rig the election. Most of the claims were either distorted or flatly wrong. Even the claims that were accurate were entirely misleading.

"Thirty-five thousand mail-in ballots were rejected in Florida's primary," he declared.

That was true. But what he didn't say is that two-thirds of those ballots were discarded because they arrived after seven p.m. on Election Day. The rest were discarded because the signatures on the

---

*For his part, Giuliani was still obsessing about Joe Biden's son. He told Trump the tax story wouldn't matter much after people heard the truth about Hunter Biden.

ballots did not match the signatures of the voters on file. Signature match and strict deadlines were measures the Republicans had demanded. The rejected ballots weren't evidence of fraud. They were evidence that Florida election officials were vigorously enforcing safeguards Republicans had demanded.

"In Wisconsin, three trays of mail containing absentee ballots were found in a ditch," he said. "They were thrown in a ditch. Three trays—it's a lot."

This was partially correct. A week earlier, three trays of *mail* had been found in a ditch near Appleton, Wisconsin. How such a thing made it into a statement prepared for the president of the United States by his press secretary is something of a mystery. But it prompted an investigation by the Wisconsin Board of Elections. It turned out there were no Wisconsin absentee ballots included in the three trays. Not one.

And he went on. Reading one misleading claim after another. The only difference between the claims he was making about voter fraud at this press conference more than a month before the election and the claims he would make after the election was that buried within these lies was some thin factual basis. Yes, there was mail in a ditch. No, there weren't any absentee ballots. Yes, absentee ballots were rejected in Florida's primary. No, that wasn't a sign of fraud; it was a sign the rules were being enforced.

With the *New York Times* story on Trump's taxes now dominating the campaign, I headed out the next morning to Cleveland to be in position for the upcoming debate. Because of concerns about the pandemic, I drove from Washington; I hadn't been on an airplane since before the COVID lockdown in March. General election debates usually have a carnival-like atmosphere, packed with reporters, political advisors, political tourists, and lots of supporters for the candidates. Not this time. The number of reporters was strictly limited and so was the live audience inside the arena.

When it came time for the debate to start, here's how I described the state of the race on ABC from my perch inside the debate hall:

"Donald Trump goes into this debate with his back against the wall. By every publicly available measure, he is losing this race—trailing in the national polls, no consistent lead in any of the top dozen most competitive battleground states. He needs to change the dynamic of this race and tonight is the best chance for him to do it."

It sounded like a harsh assessment, but I wasn't saying anything Trump's own advisors weren't thinking.

And everybody knew the playbook. Trump would go ruthlessly and relentlessly on the attack, because that is what he has always done when he has his back against the wall. It's what he did when he faced Hillary Clinton four years earlier after the release of the *Access Hollywood* tape. Of course it was what he would do now.

But the savageness of Trump's attacks exceeded everyone's expectations. The debate was an embarrassment, something parents would be ashamed to show their children. Trump came across like a bully. Biden came across as unsteady and occasionally confused. They both showed total contempt for each other and contempt for the people watching the debate. Trump interrupted Biden so much that the Commission on Presidential Debates decided that night something had to be done. They ultimately decided to install a mute button that would enable a producer backstage to turn off the microphone if either candidate started interrupting the other candidate's answers. When the debate was over, there was really only one way I could think to sum up what we had seen.

"The debate was a total mess," I told George Stephanopoulos on ABC. "It was a mess of interruptions, petty insults." I said Trump had unleashed an avalanche of lies.

Some of the lies were a direct extension of the statement he had read two nights earlier at the press conference, but the president took the carefully crafted distortions about voter fraud that had been prepared by his press secretary and turned them into full-blown lies without any factual basis whatsoever.

The trays of mail found in the ditch in Wisconsin, for example, became ballots sold and tossed in a river in West Virginia.

"Take a look at West Virginia, mailman selling the ballots," he said. "They're being sold. They're being dumped in rivers. This is a horrible thing for our country."

A few days later, at the next White House press briefing, reporter Jon Decker of Fox News asked Press Secretary Kayleigh McEnany what the president was talking about. Her responses—and her defensiveness—made it obvious Trump had just been making things up.

"Who is 'they' that found those ballots," Decker asked, "and where is this river anywhere in this country?"

"The local authorities," McEnany answered. "It was a ditch in Wisconsin that they were found, and I can get the article to your inbox if you'd like."

Decker asked if the president misspoke when he said "ballots" had been found in "rivers."

"No," McEnany snapped back. "That's what the president was referring to."

"I cover the news and I like to accurately report the news," Decker said. "And when the president said, 'they found ballots in a river,' I simply want to know where that river is."

"No," McEnany said, cutting off the line of questioning, "you simply want to ignore the fact of the matter."

Even for the Trump White House this was head-turning double-speak. Nobody in the White House, and certainly not his press secretary, was willing to disagree with anything Trump said.

But this wasn't about the carefully crafted distortions prepared by the press secretary or the outright lies said by the president. The Trump White House was making a bigger statement. They were saying the facts didn't matter. Trailing badly in the polls, the president was already declaring the upcoming election illegitimate. And the only truth that mattered was this one: Donald Trump was not going to accept any result in the upcoming election except victory.

CHAPTER SEVEN

PATIENT ZERO

I t was just a couple of minutes before one a.m. when I was jolted out of a deep sleep by a cacophony of electronic noises—in simultaneous disharmony, my cell phone, my landline telephone, and my wife's cell phone went off. I reached for my cell phone first. On the other end of the line a computerized voice announced the reason for the commotion. The message went something like this:

"President Donald Trump has tweeted that he and First Lady Melania Trump have tested positive for coronavirus."

Before I could tell for sure if I was awake or dreaming, I heard more beeping—another call. I answered. This time the voice belonged to an actual human being. It was one of my ABC News colleagues telling me Trump had COVID ("Yes, I just heard") and telling me to call into the ABC News control room in New York. I had been awake for less than sixty seconds, and they wanted me to go on live television via telephone—immediately.

"Okay, yes, of course—but what else do we know?"

"There's a statement from the White House doctor in your email."

I had only been sleeping for about an hour and my alarm was

scheduled to go off at 4:45 a.m. Every day for nearly a week seemed to bring monumental breaking news—a controversial Supreme Court nomination, coronavirus deaths worldwide surpassing one million, a blockbuster story revealing Trump had paid virtually nothing in taxes for years, the worst presidential debate in the history of presidential debates—and then, just hours earlier, news that Hope Hicks, one of Trump's closest aides, had tested positive for COVID-19. Just before dozing off, I had written what I thought would be the lead story for *Good Morning America* in the morning. My story, which would have to be completely rewritten because of the breaking news about Trump, had started like this:

"This one hits home. Few advisors, if any, spend more time with the president than Hope Hicks."

The story went on to explain that Hicks had been at the president's side at the debate two days earlier in Cleveland and then at a Trump rally the following night in Minneapolis.

"The White House has taken precious few precautions to avoid the virus—the president and his top advisors are almost never seen wearing masks," I wrote in the script that would never air. "When he announced Amy Coney Barrett's nomination to the Supreme Court over the weekend, the crowd in the Rose Garden was neither socially distant, nor wearing masks."

With all that had gone down, it wasn't exactly shocking that Trump had finally gotten sick. But this was a monumentally important story, which is why it had triggered the automated ABC breaking news alert system that called all my numbers simultaneously. This is the same system that had been activated when Osama bin Laden was killed. It enables the news desk to call all ABC News reporters and producers at the same time and to call not just our main numbers but our backup numbers and, in my case, the backup to my backup number (hence the call to my wife's cell phone). The date was Thursday, October 1 (or, technically, October 2, since it was after midnight). A COVID infection for somebody like Donald Trump—in his mid-seventies and overweight—could be a death sentence. Even if he avoided the worst, he would almost certainly have to be isolated for at least ten of the thirty-two days left between now and the election. And if the president had been infected with this highly contagious disease, it would likely mean that many of the senior officials at the White House were also infected.

As I dialed into the ABC live line from my landline phone, I read the emailed statement from Dr. Sean Conley, the White House physician. The statement was short and to the point—and I was awake enough to believe almost none of it.

"The President and First Lady are both well at this time, and they plan to remain at home within the White House during their convalescence," Conley's statement said.

They are both well? Would Dr. Conley tell us if the president wasn't well? His predecessor, Dr. Ronny Jackson, had told me during a press conference in 2018 that Trump's genetics were so great that if he had a healthier diet "he might live to be two hundred years old." I wasn't ready to take the White House's word—not even the White House doctor's word—on the president's condition.

"Rest assured," Conley's statement continued, "I expect the President to continue carrying out his duties without disruption while recovering."

Yeah, right.

By dawn, the president's entire schedule for the coming week would be canceled. And within eighteen hours, he would be taken in the Marine One helicopter from the White House to Walter Reed National Military Medical Center, where he would be treated by an army of doctors with the kind of aggressive experimental drugs only given to COVID patients with serious connections who were fighting for their lives.

Another reason to be skeptical about what Dr. Conley was saying about the president's health was the constant stream of misinformation coming from the White House about the pandemic. Just a week earlier, Trump had declared at a rally in Ohio that coronavirus "affects virtually no one." That was one of hell of a statement. Already 200,000 Americans had died from COVID-19 and nearly seven million had been infected. Over the course of the next forty-eight hours, just about everybody in the president's orbit seemed to become infected with coronavirus, including his campaign manager, his personal assistant, two of his most important political advisors, the chairwoman of the Republican Party, and three Republican senators.

The Trump White House's lack of credibility on the pandemic was well established. Exactly three weeks before Trump tweeted he had tested positive, I had enraged him by asking the most forcefully confrontational question I had ever asked of a president—or any other political leader.

"Why did you lie to the American people and why should we trust anything you have to say now?" I asked him during a press conference on September 10, 2020.

I had challenged Trump many times for saying things that were not true, but before that moment I had avoided calling him a liar. In fact, I had cringed when I heard other reporters use the word "lie" because the word means more than something was factually inaccurate; it implies an intentional effort to deceive. I understood why others used that word given the constant barrage of untruths coming from the Trump White House, but I had generally avoided it. I figured that I should stick to the facts and let others make the judgment about whether something was a lie or simply untrue. But the flagrant disregard for truth even about public health during a pandemic that was killing thousands of people a week had changed my calculus. Bob Woodward had just released recordings of his conversations with Trump dating back to the early days of the pandemic that showed Trump wasn't just saying things that were untrue—he was saying things he knew were untrue. He was lying.

Infuriated by my question, Trump lashed out at me, calling it "a terrible question" and branding me "a disgrace to the ABC television network."

"I didn't lie," he said, scowling at me. "What I said is we have to be calm. We cannot be panicked."

Now with the pandemic hitting Trump himself, the second part of my question seemed more relevant than ever.

"Why should we trust anything you have to say now?"

Under the best of circumstances, it is hard to trust what any White House says about a president's health. The Wilson White House deceived the country about Woodrow Wilson's dire physical condition during World War I. And the world didn't learn the extent of John F. Kennedy's health problems until decades after his death. Could we really trust what the Trump White House was telling us about Trump's health during the final stretch of his reelection campaign? Of course not.

At 3:05 on Friday afternoon, about fourteen hours after Dr. Conley issued his statement saying the president would remain at the White House carrying out his duties "without interruption," the White House called the Washington bureau chiefs of the five major television networks with the confidential guidance that the president was likely going to be checking into Walter Reed later in the day for emergency medical attention. The information, which was strictly off the record and given with no further details, was provided so that network camera crews would be prepared to capture the president's movements leaving the White House and arriving at Walter Reed. Even the Trump White House recognized the gravity of the situation and the need for it to be documented by the very news organizations Trump had repeatedly vilified as enemies of the people. They also trusted that the television networks would not leak the information—and they didn't.

At 5:17, the White House made the announcement public and said the president would be traveling to Walter Reed via the Marine One helicopter, a highly unusual move. When visiting Walter Reed, a president almost always makes the short nine-mile trip in the presidential limousine. The use of the helicopter was another sign of the seriousness of the situation—he was being rushed to the hospital. The announcement came with another factually challenged statement from the White House, this time from Press Secretary Kayleigh McEnany, who said, "President Trump remains in good spirits, has mild symptoms, and has been working throughout the day." He may or may not have been in good spirits, but he had not been working throughout the day; he had been battling fever, chills, and a blood-oxygen level so low he was receiving supplemental oxygen.

With the news of the president's imminent Marine One journey, I gathered as much information on the president's condition as possible and put together one of the longest, if not the longest, stories I had ever written for World News Tonight. The story would end up taking nearly a third of the evening's newscast and, because of the lack of reliable official information, focused heavily on the unanswered questions. When and how was the president infected? Who else among the top leaders in the US government had also been exposed to the disease? What was his true condition?

Senior producer Claire Brinberg, who had helped me pull together all the material for my story, sent word that *World News Tonight* wanted me to go to Bethesda, Maryland, to be live for the show from outside Walter Reed.

I was tired, grumpy, and exhausted from all that had transpired since receiving my noisy wake-up call at one a.m. Go to Walter Reed? I thought it was insane, but after complaining loudly for a couple minutes, I jumped into my car and raced to Walter Reed, hoping to get there in time to watch the president's arrival. News of the president's planned admission to the hospital had broken just an hour earlier, but there was already a carnival atmosphere on the street across from the main gate into the medical center—television crews were setting up along with a growing band of Trump supporters decked out with "Make America Great Again" gear and large blue Trump flags. The presidential campaign was suddenly moving to one of the military's greatest medical facilities.

As I looked for a parking space, I got another urgent call from the ABC News control room in New York. President Trump had just walked, slowly and with obvious discomfort, out of the White House and boarded Marine One. He was on his way to Walter Reed. How quickly could I get in front of the ABC News camera that had just set up outside the medical center? I ditched my car in what was almost certainly an illegal parking space and rushed to find the ABC camera, which was directly across the main entrance into Walter Reed and, I would soon realize, directly across from the hospital's helipad. As I put on a microphone and an earpiece, I heard the voice of George Stephanopoulos anchoring the special report.

"There again we see the pool camera of the president walking to Marine One just a few moments ago," I heard him say. "He's just about to land now at Walter Reed. Jon Karl now in place at Walter Reed. Can you see the helicopters?"

Five minutes earlier I had been searching for a parking space.

Now I was on live television watching the iconic presidential helicopter heading my way carrying a seventy-four-year-old president infected with a deadly and highly contagious disease.

"I can see Marine One headed this way," I said. "I am right across the street from Walter Reed. Looks like he'll be landing momentarily." I told Stephanopoulos we had very little information from the White House beyond a statement from the press secretary saying the president would be at the hospital for a few days and "working out of what they call the presidential offices here at Walter Reed." The statement made it sound like Trump just wanted to spend the weekend working out of a different office.

Marine One looked like it was heading right at me.

"I can now see the, the helicopter coming into view quite, quite clearly."

The helipad was right there on the other side of the gate across from where I was standing on a stretch of sidewalk we were sharing with several other network camera crews. A nondescript stretch of road in Bethesda had quickly transformed into the center of the broadcast news universe.

Stephanopoulos asked me what more information we expected to be hearing from the president's doctors, but Marine One was so close it was becoming difficult to hear.

"George, the thing that we have asked for repeatedly is information directly from the doctors, a briefing directly from the doctors," I answered, looking back at Marine One. "The challenge here, George, is that, as we get statements from the president's press secretary—"

I turned around to take in the sight of the presidential helicopter landing less than two hundred feet behind me.

"—there's just a real question about the reliability of the information given that they have not been particularly transparent, especially on issues of the president's health but on other issues as well, which is why the request is being made by me and by so many other report-ers to get official information directly from the president's doctor. And here, as you can hear the sound of Marine One, it is just about to land."

With the sound of the helicopter getting louder, I was politely and diplomatically saying that we really couldn't trust anything the White House press secretary had to say about any of this.

Stephanopoulos then began recounting how little we knew about the president's condition beyond the fact that, right there before our eyes, he was being taken to the place where he could receive the world's best medical care. As he spoke, I could not quite believe the scene I was witnessing. I interrupted him, unsure if my microphone was still on and if he would be able to hear me.

"George, are you still here?"

"Go ahead, Jon."

"George, it's quite a scene here," I said. "As, as I mentioned to you, I'm right across the street from Walter Reed. [There's] a crowd of people across the way. As word got out that the president was heading here to Walter Reed, you've had people coming over to try to catch a glimpse."

The helicopter had just landed on the other side of the gate.

"What a sight," I said, "to see Marine One essentially medevack-ing the president of the United States here to the Walter Reed Medical Center."

The next day the White House agreed to hold a press conference at Walter Reed with the president's doctor. Trump was well enough to choreograph the scene. He had been impressed with the size of the team of military doctors working on him and how they all looked. These were some of the military's top doctors and they looked the part. He wanted all of them out in front of the cameras for the press conference and he wanted them wearing their lab coats. When they assembled in front of the hospital for the press conference, it was indeed quite a spectacle: ten doctors in white coats standing in formation outside the steps of one of the world's greatest medical centers. Even when battling a deadly virus, Donald Trump knew how to choreograph a scene for television.

The press conference looked impressive, but it was a disaster. Dr. Conley repeatedly declared the president was doing "great" and clumsily dodged specific questions about Trump's condition, such as whether he had received supplemental oxygen ("He has not received supplemental oxygen today"). As soon as it was over, Chief of Staff Mark Meadows called reporters over to correct the overly rosy picture painted by Dr. Conley. Meadows asked to be identified only as a "senior administration official," but he was seen by the television pool camera covering the press conference for the five television networks. Everybody could see Meadows was the "senior administration official" telling reporters that, despite what they had just heard from the doctors, Trump was in rough shape.

"The president's vitals over the last twenty-four hours were very concerning, and the next forty-eight hours will be critical in terms of his care," Meadows told reporters, directly contradicting the happy talk from the doctors. "We're still not on a path to recovery."

In reality, it was even worse than that.

"We were worried that if the downward trajectory he was on continued, he would, at best, have severe complications—at best," one of the few people directly involved in the decision to move Trump to the hospital told me. "At worst, I was concerned for him on a personal level, knowing that people had died from COVID."

With the president in the hospital receiving the most aggressive and advanced antiviral medication, steroids, and the undivided attention of about a dozen doctors, attention focused on who else might be sick.

One of the first calls I made the day Trump went to Walter Reed was to Chris Christie, who had spent hours and hours with Trump earlier in the week as he helped prepare him for the presidential debate. Christie also had spent hours with Hope Hicks at those debate prep sessions. After several unanswered calls, I finally reached him that afternoon.

"I've heard from nobody at the White House," Christie told me.

This was remarkable. Nobody had bothered to check in on him or to tell him that he had been exposed now to at least two people infected with the disease.

One of the key steps in controlling a contagious disease like COVID-19 is to do contact tracing—tracking down and informing everyone who has been in contact with somebody who has been infected so that person can quarantine and not infect anyone else. But Christie first learned that he had been exposed to the virus when he received a text message from CNN reporter Dana Bash after the news broke that Hope Hicks had tested positive.

"Let's be clear that I was never notified by the White House ever," Christie later told me. "My notification came from Dana Bash, who texted me and said, 'Are you okay?' And I said, 'Yeah, I'm fine. Why?' And she said, 'Hope Hicks tested positive for COVID.'"

It was the first he had heard that he was at risk.

Christie went to an urgent care center to get a COVID test in the morning, and by the time I talked to him in the afternoon, he had a bad headache. He hadn't gotten his test result back yet, but he feared the worst. Within twenty-four hours, Christie had tested positive and checked himself into a hospital in New Jersey at the urging of his doctor. Like Trump, Christie was in a high-risk category because he was overweight and also because he had a history of asthma.

Christie eventually got a call from the president. Trump called Christie on his second day at Walter Reed after he heard Christie was in the hospital.

"They picked on the wrong guys," Trump told him. "Me and you? There's no way this takes us down."

Christie thought the president sounded like he was having trouble breathing.

They spoke for about five minutes—from one hospital bed to the other, both men among the highest risk groups for death from infection with COVID-19. Trump wanted to know where Christie thought he got the infection. By this time, former White House counselor Kellyanne Conway, who was also at the debate prep sessions with Christie and Hicks, had also tested positive.

"I think it's pretty obvious, Mr. President," Christie told him. "Four out of the seven of us who were in the room have it."

Both men got very sick. We may never know why they recovered in the coming days from a disease that had taken the lives of so many people in their situations, but both Christie and Trump received experimental monoclonal antibody cocktails available to very few people at the time because they had not yet been approved by the Food and Drug Administration. Trump's treatment was developed by the company Regeneron Pharmaceuticals; Christie's treatment had been developed by Ely Lilly. In his time of maximum peril, Trump did not get treated with hydroxychloroquine, the treatment he had been falsely touting as a miracle cure for months.

Among the many questions the White House steadfastly refused to answer about the president's condition was when he had last tested negative for COVID-19. This was no trivial question. Trump had appeared on the debate stage with Joe Biden just two days before he told the world he had COVID-19. The debate had been hosted by the Cleveland Clinic, one of the world's premier medical facilities. The

Cleveland Clinic had gone to great pains to keep the debate site COVID-free. Everybody was required to wear a mask in the debate hall—and to get a negative COVID test before entering. For all the staff, guests, and reporters at the debate, the tests were administered right there by the Cleveland Clinic. But the candidates and the people they traveled with were responsible for their own testing—and it was the honor system.

Honor systems, however, only work when people are honorable.

It was clear from the moment the Trump team landed in Cleveland for the debate that they had no respect for the rules. They arrived at the hall several hours before the debate for what is known as a walkthrough. This is where the candidate, with no cameras rolling and usually no reporters around, gets to check out the podium and the hall to make sure everything looks right. The staff at the Cleveland Clinic were horrified when they saw Trump and his closest advisors (including Hope Hicks, who would be sick twenty-four hours later) walking on the stage—none of them wearing masks. They violated that rule. The question is: Did they also violate the rule requiring them to get a test? The Cleveland Clinic was never provided with proof the president had been tested and nobody at the White House would ever say anything about this on the record.

Even if the White House had said when Trump was last tested, there would be reason to be skeptical. Back in July, Press Secretary Kayleigh McEnany had said Trump is "tested more than anyone, multiple times a day." At a press conference later that day, I asked Trump about that. His answer made it clear McEnany had just been making it up.

"Your press secretary said today you sometimes take more than one test a day. Why is that?" I asked him.

"I take an average of one test every two, three days," Trump answered. "I don't know of any time I have taken two tests in one day."

That was on July 21. But multiple White House officials familiar with the president's routine told me that by midsummer, he had stopped getting tested regularly, which may explain why nobody would say when he was tested before the debate. In fact, several people close to Trump privately told me they believed he simply didn't bother to get a COVID-19 test before coming to Cleveland for the debate, violating that rule just as he and his aides had violated the rules about wearing masks inside the debate hall. As I was writing this book, I asked former Chief of Staff Mark Meadows the same questions I had asked several times while Trump was still in the hospital: When did Trump first test positive for COVID? When was the last time he had received a negative COVID test? Did he have a negative test before joining Joe Biden on the debate stage? Even months after Trump had left the White House, Meadows would not give me an on-the-record answer to any of these questions.

The complete disregard for the safety protocols continued during the debate itself as those seated in the section reserved for the Trump family and guests walked in—almost none of them wearing masks.

You might think the experience of the president and so many people around him getting sick with COVID would have been enough of a wake-up call to change that kind of behavior. For a fleeting moment on his third day in the hospital, it seemed like Trump maybe, sort of, had learned a lesson. That fleeting moment came on his third day in the hospital when Trump released a short, one-minute video on Twitter.

"It's been a very interesting journey," he said. "I learned a lot about COVID. I learned by really going to school. This is the real school. This isn't the let's-read-the-books school. And I get it. And I understand it."

What did he get? Did he get how serious it was? Did he get why it was important to take precautions to protect yourself and the people around you?

Not a chance.

Before he made that one-minute video, Trump told Chief of Staff Mark Meadows, who had gone with him to Walter Reed, that he wanted to take a drive to see the now sizable crowd of Trump supporters lining the street outside of the hospital. The night before, Trump had dispatched Meadows to greet his fans outside and to pass out cartons of M&M's emblazoned with Trump's signature. Now he got inside the armored Secret Service SUV and essentially took a ride around the block—waving through the tinted bulletproof window to his supporters and to the television crews. His supporters loved it, but Trump's critics called the move profoundly reckless. He was a man with a highly contagious disease and here he was in a tightly sealed vehicle with Secret Service agents. One of the attending physicians at Walter Reed, Dr. James Phillips, expressed the outrage felt by some public health experts, saying, "Every single person in the vehicle during that completely unnecessary presidential 'drive-by' just now has to be quarantined for fourteen days. They might get sick. They may die. For political theater." He added: "Commanded by Trump to put their lives at risk for theater. This is insanity." The car ride was certainly not risk-free, but the two agents in the car had volunteered to take the ride and both of them were wearing the same high-quality N-95 masks that doctors at Walter Reed wore when treating patients infected with COVID-19.*

By the next evening, Trump was well enough to return to the White House. His return may have been the most impressively choreographed event of his presidency. He timed his departure from

---

*Months later, I checked in with the Secret Service and asked if either agent became infected with COVID-19. They didn't. Both agents remained healthy and virus-free.

Walter Reed at precisely 6:30. This timing accomplished two things: It ensured Marine One would be departing the hospital and landing on the South Lawn of the White House when the three broadcast network newscasts—a combined viewership of nearly twenty-four million people—were on live. And the timing meant that the helicopter would be landing against the backdrop of a beautiful October sunset.

Trump, wearing a suit and a tie, exited the helicopter alone and walked toward the White House wearing a mask. When he got to the entrance at the South Portico beneath the Truman Balcony, he briefly hesitated and turned to the right. Instead of walking into the ground-level entrance he had used every other time he had walked from Marine One into the White House, he walked up the grand arching staircase to the right to the balcony above. This was remarkable because Trump rarely walks more than he absolutely needs to—he's a guy who often drives the golf cart up onto the putting green to avoid the extra steps—and here he was walking up a large staircase as he was recovering from a respiratory disease that was still making it hard for him to breathe. When he got to the balcony he looked out at the South Lawn and dramatically took off his mask. Trump had talked to his aides about wearing a Superman shirt beneath his suit and ripping off his dress shirt to reveal the giant "S" symbol. That idea was rejected, but Trump stood there looking at the empty South Lawn for a good two minutes, and gave a thumbs-up and a salute long enough to make sure the cameras captured it all. He seemed to be grimacing a bit as he struggled to breathe, but he was loving the moment. Even after he left office, Trump remained proud of the way he had staged his return from the hospital.

"It was like a Broadway production," he told me in March 2021.

When he got back to the White House, Trump was still sick but feeling better—and his body was filled with the powerful steroid dexamethasone. He had beaten the killer virus and he was determined there was now no way he'd lose the election—no matter what the polls said. Instead of learning a lesson about the seriousness of the disease and just how wildly contagious it was, he was eager to get out there before large, packed crowds just as soon as he could.

If anything, the behavior of the president and his senior staff became even more reckless in the coming days and weeks. Even while the president was in the hospital, Press Secretary Kayleigh McEnany had talked to reporters outside the West Wing without a mask, despite the fact that she had had close contact with both Trump and Hope Hicks. On the day Trump returned to the White House, McEnany and two others in the White House press office tested positive. The president was out of the hospital and recovering, but the White House was still a COVID danger zone, and the virus was en route to killing more than half a million Americans.

CHAPTER EIGHT

THE GREAT MIRAGE

wasn't making any bold predictions going into the 2020 presidential elections, but privately I thought there was virtually no chance Donald Trump would win reelection. Sure, he had defied the polls and almost everybody's expectations in 2016, but I figured that was a fluke, and flukes don't tend to happen twice in row.

Trump won in 2016 in part because many Democrats who figured Trump had no chance to win didn't bother to vote. Why bother going to the polls to wait in line to cast a ballot if you already know the outcome of the election? But in 2020, Democratic voters were extremely motived—not because they loved Joe Biden, but because they were terrified of a repeat of 2016. They had seen Trump defy the odds and win and feared he could do it again with catastrophic consequences. They may have stayed home last time, but there was no way they would make that mistake again.

There were many other reasons to believe Trump was going down—ranging from his disastrous handling of the pandemic to battleground-state polls that were actually worse for him in 2020 than they were in the previous election, when they were dreadful. I thought Trump was a long shot in 2016, but in 2020, I believed he had virtually no shot.

Not everybody saw it that way.

Shortly before polls would start closing on election night, I ran into Will Steakin, who had been covering the Trump reelection campaign for nearly two years. He was one of the best young reporters at ABC News and somebody who never let his personal views get in the way of doing his job. Steakin was tireless, relentless, and had somehow managed to cover crowded Trump campaign events all over the country without becoming infected with coronavirus. He also had a personal background unlike anybody else covering the campaign. He grew up dirt-poor in Florida, raised by a single mother while his father was in prison. A high-school dropout, he played guitar in an indie rock band for three years before getting a GED. After studying at two different community colleges, he managed to get into Columbia University, where he earned a degree in political science. He was smart, but Will's real-world experience impressed me more than his Ivy League degree.

Will had just arrived in New York City after covering a rally the night before in Grand Rapids, Michigan, Trump's last campaign rally of 2020.

"So," I asked him, "what do you think?"

I valued Will's opinion. He wasn't some random observer. He was one of the very best reporters on the beat.

"Oh, I think he is going to win," he told me.

I almost fell over. Earlier in the year, Will, like almost everyone else, thought Trump was going to lose, primarily because of how he had handled the pandemic. How could he now be saying Trump was going to win?

From the ill-fated Tulsa rally in June until the final rally in Grand

Rapids, Will had attended more Trump campaign events than almost anybody other than Trump himself and the aides who traveled with him. He had seen the fervent dedication of Trump's supporters up close. He talked to people in city after city, in all the key states, as they waited in line for hours to see Trump. These people had endured bitter cold temperatures in the upper Midwest and heat-stroke-inducing temperatures in the South.

They showed up despite the real risk of getting infected with the same disease that had already killed more than 200,000 Americans and sent Trump to the hospital in early October. A Stanford University study of eighteen Trump rallies estimated the events had resulted in a combined total of 300,000 coronavirus infections that would ultimately lead to nearly seven hundred deaths. Those numbers were likely exaggerated (the study, after all, was conducted by economists, not epidemiologists), but coronavirus wasn't the only danger facing rallygoers. At some rallies the risk of hypothermia or frostbite was more immediate. At a late-night rally at Omaha's Eppley Airfield in late October, more than 20,000 rallygoers spent six hours or more in sub-freezing temperatures. When the rally was all over, many of them had to walk three miles in the bitter cold in the dead of night—three miles!—back to their parked cars because there simply weren't enough shuttle buses to accommodate all the people who showed up. At least thirty people at that rally ended up needing medical attention; seven of them were hospitalized. Despite all this, they kept coming.

By the final week of the campaign, Trump was doing five of these rallies a day, each seeming to be more crowded with die-hard supporters than the previous one. Decked out in Trump merchandise, these people had taken to interrupting Trump's speeches with chants of "we love you."

Will had seen it all with his own eyes. He had felt the energy of the crowds. Sure, the polls again showed Trump losing. The polls, he thought, would be wrong—once again.

As it turned out, it was Will who was wrong. But he was onto something. He was experiencing something that would help explain the calamity that would unfold after the votes were counted. The closer you were to Trump and his frenzied supporters during those final weeks of the campaign, the more certain you would be that he was going to win and, if you were a die-hard supporter, the more unlikely you would be to accept the results when he lost.

On board Air Force One en route to that last rally of the campaign in Grand Rapids, the president's son Eric didn't simply think his father was going to win, he thought he would win in a landslide. The campaign, he thought, was on fire. At each of the four rallies already held that day—in North Carolina, Pennsylvania, Michigan, Wisconsin—the crowds had been incredible, just as they had been at the five jam-packed rallies the day before. As Eric saw it, this wasn't a losing presidential campaign. This was a mass movement. Biden, on the other hand, had at most one or two events per day. And the Biden events were objectively lower-energy affairs that avoided large crowds by design because of the danger posed by the pandemic. Biden's events usually featured the candidate speaking to supporters parked in their cars, lamely honking their horns at his applause lines.

As Air Force One prepared to land in Grand Rapids, Eric started asking people for their predictions—how many electoral votes would his father win? Just about everybody on board predicted a Trump win, of course. Some talked of a win bigger than 2016. But Derek Lyons, one of the lawyers in the Trump White House, predicted the narrowest of narrow victories. He told Eric he thought the race would end in a tie of 269 to 269 electoral votes, with the race being decided in the House of Representatives. In this scenario, Trump would prevail because each state congressional delegation would have a single vote and the Republicans had a majority in twenty-six of the fifty congressional delegations.

Eric then turned to Chris Liddell, a low-profile senior official who had served in the Trump White House since the beginning and was currently a deputy chief of staff.

"I think it's going to be close," Liddell said. "But I think we have a chance of winning."

"You guys are nuts," Eric Trump told them. "We are going to win, and this is going to be a landslide."

The people running the Trump campaign also thought he could win, but they knew it was going to be close. To win in 2020, Trump was going to need significantly more votes than he had in 2016. Nearly sixty-three million people voted for Trump in 2016. That was three million votes less than Hillary Clinton, but enough to translate into a win in the electoral college. Democrats were more motivated this time and would turn out in higher numbers, but Trump's campaign strategists told him that if he could increase the Trump vote nationally to more than sixty-five million voters, he'd pull off another win.

And if he didn't, there was plan B—accuse Democrats of cheating and refuse to accept the results. Trump had been talking about it for months.

"The only way we're going to lose this election," he said during a rally in Oshkosh, Wisconsin, on August 17, "is if the election is rigged."

A month later, as his standing in the polls looked increasingly grim, he was even more definitive.

"It's a rigged election. It's the only way we're going to lose," he told supporters in Minden, Nevada, on September 12, adding this about Biden: "I'll tell you what, he is the worst candidate in the history of presidential politics. He doesn't know he's alive. He doesn't know he's alive."

Trump made no secret about it. He would never concede. He

would fight. He had laid the groundwork for months. By November, there was an army of supporters out there ready to believe everything he was saying about the election.

At the final Trump rally of the campaign in Grand Rapids, rally-goers told Will Steakin they simply could not conceive of a scenario where Trump would lose. It wasn't just what Trump himself was saying. It was what they were seeing with their own eyes. One Trump supporter showed Steakin a handwritten tally he had been keeping with a black Sharpie of all street signs he had seen for Trump and Biden on the way to the rally. The numbers were overwhelming: sixty-nine Trump signs and just seven for Biden.

"It's pretty obvious if Trump does not win, it's rigged," Judy Torp, who'd been in line for hours to get into the Grand Rapids rally, told Steakin.

"I truly believe that," a Trump supporter named Rosemary O'Conner, who had overheard the conversation, told Steakin. "And not just because President Trump said it."

With the pandemic making it dangerous to vote in person, states across the country had dramatically increased voting by mail, enabling people to vote without going to a crowded polling station and risking exposure to a deadly disease. As vote by mail expanded, Trump loudly proclaimed mail-in voting would be riddled with fraud. He raised the specter of truckloads of ballots mailed in with the names of dead people, foreigners, and even people's pets. He said ballots of people voting for him would be thrown out. It was nonsense; mail-in voting has been commonplace in several states for decades without any significant problems. Every state that has mail-in voting has procedures in place to prevent people from voting more than once and to only count ballots cast by registered voters.

Trump's drumbeat of complaints about mail-in voting had created a problem for his campaign. In states where voters historically vote by mail in large numbers, such as Florida, the Trump campaign had been working hard to get Trump voters to mail in their ballots. Now the president was telling voters it was all a big scam. As a result, many Republicans who might otherwise have voted by mail were convinced by Trump not to do it.

So, while there were safeguards in place to prevent the kind of fraud Trump was claiming, this much was also undeniably true: far more Democrats were voting by mail than Republicans. And the flip side was true as well: with so many Democrats casting their ballots by mail, the in-person voting on Election Day would skew heavily Republican. So, if you counted only mail-in ballots, Biden would win big. If you counted only votes cast in person, Trump would win big.

There was another factor that became something of an obsession for Donald Trump. Like everybody else following the election closely, he knew it would take considerably longer to count mail-in ballots than in-person votes. The reason for this is easy to understand. When you vote in person, you check in at the polling precinct and fill out your ballot, which, in most precincts, is directly entered into the system, ready to be counted as soon as polls close. When you vote by mail, the envelope containing your ballot must be opened. There is usually a barcode that must be checked to confirm the person mailing in the ballot is a registered voter who has not already voted. And, in all fifty states, the signature on the ballot must be compared to the voter signature on file. Only then can the vote be processed. All of this takes time.

Some states—including Ohio, Georgia, Texas, and Florida—minimize the delay by preparing the ballots to be counted as they are received. In these states, as soon as the polls close, the mail-in ballots, many of which arrive days or even weeks before the election, can actually be counted before the votes that are cast in person on Election Day.

But there are other states that don't begin processing mail-in votes until after polls close. Under Pennsylvania law in 2020, for example, the envelopes containing ballots could not even be opened until after polls closed. State election officials had warned for weeks before the election that this would create a huge backlog of mail-in ballots to be processed and that verifying the signatures on the ballots and counting them would likely take several days.*

Trump knew all this. Which is why in the days before the election he put forth a preposterous new standard for counting votes. The counting, he absurdly told them, should stop on election night.

"I think it's terrible that we can't know the results of an election the night of the election," he told reporters two days before the election at an impromptu press conference on an airport runway in Charlotte, North Carolina, on November 1.

"We're going to go in the night of, as soon as that election's over," he told reporters, his voice straining to be heard over the sound of Air Force One's jet engines, "we're going in with our lawyers."

That morning on ABC's *This Week*, Trump campaign strategist Jason Miller told George Stephanopoulos that "many smart Democrats . . . believe that President Trump will be ahead on election night." Then, he said, Democrats are "going to try to steal it back after the election."

"We believe we'll be over 290 electoral votes on election night," Miller said, as if electoral votes are awarded before all the ballots cast by voters are counted. "So, no matter what they try to do, what kind of hijinks or lawsuits or whatever kind of nonsense they try to pull

---

*There had been a proposal to address this problem by doing what other states had done and allow the processing of Pennsylvania's mail-in votes as they were received, but Pennsylvania Republicans blocked the change.

off, we'll still have enough electoral votes to get President Trump re-elected."

The strategy was clear even before the first vote had been counted. Trump would declare victory before all those mail-in votes—votes almost certainly to be overwhelmingly cast for Joe Biden—could be counted. In fact, on the Sunday before the election, Jonathan Swan reported in *Axios* that Trump had been telling people close to him that was his plan.

Here's how Swan put it: "President Trump has told confidants he'll declare victory on Tuesday night if it looks like he's 'ahead,' according to three sources familiar with his private comments. That's even if the electoral college outcome still hinges on large numbers of uncounted votes in key states like Pennsylvania."

His report created quite a stir, prompting President Trump to flatly deny it. It would soon become clear the denial was a lie.

The idea of any presidential candidate prematurely declaring victory is disturbing, but it would be far more alarming coming from a candidate already in the White House. Back in 2016, Trump had predicted massive voter fraud and refused to say whether he would concede if he lost. It all became moot because he ended up winning. But even if he had lost and refused to concede, he would just be a sore loser sitting in his office at Trump Tower.

In this case, he would be a sore loser sitting in the Oval Office—a commander in chief with the full powers of the presidency at his disposal. If he refused to accept the results of the presidential election, what else would he try to do? If Biden won and Trump refused to accept the results, how far would he go to keep power? Could he order the military to get involved? This was, after all, the president who wanted to send active-duty troops into the streets of American cities over the summer. Defense Secretary Mark Esper had done everything in his power to prevent that from happening. But what if Trump fired Esper, as many expected he would do right after the election? Two years earlier, former Trump Chief of Staff John Kelly had told me, "If he refuses to leave, there are people who will escort him out." But back then it was a hypothetical question. It didn't seem hypothetical anymore.

There was tremendous unease about this at the Pentagon, where the military's top leaders were worried Trump would try to involve the US military in his effort to undermine the election, effectively turning the United States into some kind of military dictatorship. Trump was the commander in chief, but the top military leaders wanted to quietly make it clear they would never go along with an effort to interfere with the election. Military leaders have an obligation to carry out any lawful order from the commander in chief, but they also have an obligation to refuse any unlawful order.

On the day before the election, Joint Chiefs Chairman Mark Milley convened an off-the-record video conference call with top anchors of the five major television networks* to address the concern Trump might try to involve the military in an effort to contest the election results. It was an extraordinary call. To my knowledge nothing like this had ever happened.

Milley, accompanied by National Guard Chief Daniel Hokanson, the head of Cyber Command Paul Nakasone, and Vice Chairman of the Joint Chiefs of Staff John Hyten, told the anchors point-blank that the US military had no role in the election and would play no role. It was a simple message, but it was chilling to think they felt the need to deliver the message to news organizations before the election.

---

*The network anchors on the call were George Stephanopoulos of ABC News, Norah O'Donnell of CBS News, Lester Holt of NBC News, Jim Sciutto of CNN, and Martha MacCallum of Fox News.

The Joint Chiefs chairman felt a need to declare, essentially, that regardless of what President Trump might order him to do, he would not take part in a military coup.

Shortly before ABC's election-night coverage began at seven, I talked to chief anchor George Stephanopoulos about the need to begin our coverage by making it crystal clear to our viewers that election results would come in unevenly and, as a result, give a misleading impression about where the race was going. It's something we had been talking about for weeks. In states like Pennsylvania that wait until polls close to start processing mail-in ballots, Trump would jump out to an earlier lead that would likely diminish as mail-in votes were counted. This phenomenon was so widely anticipated it had a name: "red mirage." Conversely, in states where mail-in ballots were ready to be counted as soon as polls closed, you could see a "blue mirage" where Biden would jump out to an early lead that would likely diminish as ballots cast in person were counted.

Within the first few minutes of our election-night coverage we made the point.

"We should prepare everybody," Stephanopoulos said as he introduced me, "for something that has been called red mirages and blue mirages. Let's talk about the north first, those states, Michigan, Wisconsin, and Pennsylvania, where the early vote is not going to come in right away."

"Here's the big thing," I said in my first words aired during our election-night coverage, "Republicans tend to vote in person on Election Day. Democrats vote more heavily by mail. So, the in-person vote is going to favor the Republicans. Pennsylvania, Michigan, and Wisconsin are going to tend to count those in-person votes first."

"So you could see a big lead for Donald Trump," Stephanopoulos said.

"You could see a very big lead," I responded. "That's your so-called red mirage. A very big lead for Donald Trump that gets whittled away as they count the mail-in votes."

I then explained you could see the reverse—a blue mirage—in those states that started counting the mail-in votes first, including Florida, Texas, and Arizona.

So, the idea of wildly shifting vote totals as the ballots were tabulated—and the idea that Trump could have a big lead in Pennsylvania, Michigan, and Wisconsin that would evaporate—was not shocking. Virtually every reporter covering the election and every political operative, Democratic and Republican, who was working on the election had been talking about it.

And as the votes started to be tabulated, we did in fact see red mirages and blue mirages.

In Florida, Joe Biden had a fleeting lead before eight p.m. that faded away by nine. For a few hours, it even looked like Biden had a shot of winning Texas. He ended up losing by nearly 6 percentage points. And in Ohio, another state that processed its mail-in votes earlier, Biden had 60 percent of the vote at eight p.m. compared to just 39 for Trump—a lead of twenty-one points. Talk about a blue mirage! By the time all the votes were counted, Biden ended up losing Ohio by eight points. This wasn't because Republicans in Ohio cooked the books or went out and "found" votes later in the night. It's because of the way the state counted votes.

But the blue mirages in places like Texas and Ohio were much more fleeting than the red mirages we saw elsewhere. The reasons, again, were well known. It takes longer to process mail-in votes because of the meticulous process of ensuring every vote is legitimate. If you don't process mail-in votes until Election Day, you are going to have to wait longer for results.

So, in the first few hours of vote counting on election night, it looked like Trump had a massive lead in Michigan, Wisconsin, and

Pennsylvania—exactly the states that didn't begin processing mail-in votes until Election Day. And as the clock struck eleven p.m., there were some indications Trump might actually be on his way to pulling off another upset victory, that the red mirage might have been more red than mirage. As the first returns came in, we knew Trump would jump to a lead, but he seemed to be racking up even more votes than he did in 2016. Trump was building up a lead that started to look like it just might be big enough not to evaporate entirely when the mail-in ballots were counted.

During a commercial break in the eleven p.m. hour, Rahm Emanuel, the former mayor of Chicago and Obama chief of staff who was now a Democratic analyst for ABC, came over to me shaking his head. He looked glum. "It doesn't look good," he said, referring to Biden's chances.

He wasn't alone. I was hearing the same thing from other Democrats worried they were watching a replay of 2016.

Meanwhile, at the White House, the Trump team was ecstatic. The Trump vote totals were exceeding their expectations. They could already see that overall national turnout was likely to exceed the sixty-five million Trump voters they had figured they needed to win. In solidly Republican areas, including rural areas of North Carolina, Georgia, and in Western Pennsylvania, they could see turnout was significantly higher than it had been four years earlier.

Trump's election-night watch party was right there at the White House.* About 150 advisors and supporters—including several members of his cabinet and conservative media stars like Fox's Laura Ingraham—were assembled in the East Room of the White House,

---

*This was a massive breach in protocol. Although FDR gave his acceptance speech, via radio, from the White House to the 1940 Democratic Convention, presidents have avoided using the White House for explicitly political events such as an election-night party. But this tradition had already been shattered when Trump convened the final day of the 2020 Republican Convention on the South Lawn of the White House.

where a podium with the presidential seal was set up for Trump to eventually address the crowd. As the early returns came in, there was a clear sense in the room that the gathering was going to be a victory celebration.

Chief of Staff Mark Meadows, campaign manager Bill Stepien, and Trump's other top political advisors were tracking results in the basement of the White House in the Map Room, where Franklin Delano Roosevelt had tracked developments during World War II. FDR's old military maps are still on the walls. The Trump team had set up four big television screens to watch all the networks and about a dozen computers on a large conference table. Members of the Trump family—including Ivanka Trump, Jared Kushner, and Trump sons Eric and Donald Jr.—were there as well. Over the course of the evening, Rudy Giuliani and other guests at the party upstairs in the East Room also stopped by.

Trump himself was upstairs in the presidential living quarters, watching television coverage with First Lady Melania Trump. He, too, had multiple television screens set up so he could watch several networks at once.

The race was close—really close—in Georgia, North Carolina, and even Texas, but he didn't seem concerned. His political team was telling him Republican turnout was way up. He was winning Florida decisively. And he saw on television he was ahead in Pennsylvania, Wisconsin, and Michigan. Those were three states nobody expected him to win in 2016, and he thought it looked like he was going to win them again in 2020. If he did, he'd win reelection.

But it really was all a mirage.

After eleven p.m., the Trump leads in Michigan and Wisconsin started to fade away and most of the votes yet to be counted were mail-in ballots expected to heavily favor Biden. Trump still had a big lead in Pennsylvania, but it was starting to look like there would be enough mail-in votes yet to be counted to give Biden the win. Then at 11:21 came a big blow. Fox News projected Joe Biden as the winner in Arizona. Trump campaign strategist Jason Miller told me that Fox News anchor Bill Hemmer called him to give him a heads-up before he went on air to proclaim Biden the winner in Arizona. Through a Fox News spokesperson, Hemmer categorically denied he called Miller to tip him off. Regardless of whether the campaign got an advance heads-up, the Fox News projection for Arizona was a gut punch. Trump won Arizona in 2016 and now Fox News was proclaiming Biden the winner, making it the first state to flip from red to blue.

The Trump team couldn't believe it. Biden was up by seven points, but only 73 percent of the votes cast in Arizona had been counted. There were still more than one million votes cast in person on Election Day to be counted—more than enough, the Trump team believed, to overcome Biden's lead. Arizona's Republican governor was saying the same thing—that Trump still had a good chance of winning Arizona. And no other news organization had projected Biden the winner in Arizona. So why was Fox News, the one major Trump-friendly network, declaring Biden the winner?

Kushner called Trump upstairs in the residence to give him the bad news, and the core group went up to talk to a now infuriated president. Trump felt betrayed. What the hell was Fox doing? Trump didn't really see the network as a news organization; he expected it to support him because most of its viewers supported him.

"Jared, call Rupert," Trump told his son-in-law, referring to the eighty-nine-year-old Rupert Murdoch, who owned Fox News.

"And get Hope to call Lachlan," Trump told Kushner, referring to Hope Hicks, who had worked for Rupert Murdoch's son Lachlan and knew him well.

"They've got to change this!" Trump shouted.

After a few minutes talking in the hallway, Trump's deflated advisors went back downstairs to the Map Room and Trump went back to watch more television. After they got downstairs, Mark Meadows called Fox News headquarters in New York to demand the network issue a retraction, taking back its projection of Biden as the winner in Arizona. He was put on the phone with Bill Sammon, the Fox executive in charge of the Fox News Decision Desk, which was responsible for crunching the numbers and deciding when to project a winner for any of the states or for the entire election.

Meadows demanded to know how Fox News could project Biden the winner in Arizona when they had projected no winner yet in North Carolina. He had a point. Trump was ahead in North Carolina and it seemed unlikely Biden would overtake him. All the other networks deemed both states too close to project. Meadows believed Trump was in at least as strong a position in North Carolina as Biden was in Arizona. And, in fact, the other networks (including Fox) would soon project North Carolina for Trump. The AP called Arizona three hours after Fox, but it would be days before the other networks projected Biden the winner in Arizona, and when the votes were all counted, Biden only won the state by three-tenths of one percentage point. Trump's win in North Carolina ended up being significantly larger; he beat Biden by 1.3 percentage points.

The phone calls to the Murdochs and to the Fox News Decision Desk would not change anything. The Decision Desk had been empowered to make projections without political interference and there would be no unwinding of their decision to project Biden the winner in Arizona.

But Arizona was the least of Trump's problems. As the vote was tabulated in Michigan, Pennsylvania, and Wisconsin, his lead was shrinking. The decisive national victory he thought he had at ten p.m. was fading away . . . like a mirage.

———

By midnight, it was clear to everybody there would be no winner projected on election night. Despite what Fox News had said, Arizona was too close to project. So was Georgia. Wisconsin and Michigan were trending toward a Biden victory, but both were still too close to project. And election officials in Pennsylvania, which still had more than two million votes to be counted, were warning that it would likely take days to finish the count.

At about midnight a clearly inebriated Rudy Giuliani showed up in the Map Room. He had been at the party upstairs with his small entourage of assistants, clearly enjoying himself. As he walked into the Map Room, Trump's political advisors were reeling from the Fox News projection on Arizona and watching their lead slip away elsewhere. You could see the concern on their faces—and on the faces of Eric Trump and Jared Kushner, who were standing behind the campaign's data experts sitting at the conference table scouring the returns coming in on their computers for good news. Giuliani announced, to nobody in particular, it was time for President Trump to give a speech saying he had won the election.

"He should go out there and declare victory," Giuliani said to the group. "If he doesn't, they will steal it from us."

Nobody in the room took Giuliani's slurred words seriously, but he had been telling the president the same thing.

At 12:40 a.m., Joe Biden addressed supporters at his outdoor election-night party in Wilmington, Delaware. It wasn't a victory speech, but it was close to one.

"We knew this was going to go long, but who knew we were going to go into maybe tomorrow morning?" Biden said. "We feel good about where we are. We really do. We believe we're on track to win this election."

Biden's comments made Trump even angrier. He didn't wait for Biden to finish before he responded. While Biden was still speaking, he fired back on Twitter.

"We are up BIG, but they are trying to STEAL the Election," he tweeted. "We will never let them do it. Votes cannot be cast after the Poles [sic] are closed!"

And one minute later, another tweet.

"I will be making a statement tonight. A big WIN!"

I've spoken to several of Trump's political advisors about election night. None of them would speak on the record about what they told him before he came out to give his speech that night, but one of his closest advisors insisted to me that Trump was told the cold, hard truth: He was in danger of losing. He was told he still had a chance to win, but with the way the vote was coming in, there was a real chance he would lose.

"It was not a 'you've lost' conversation," said one Trump advisor who was with him on election night. "It was more like, 'It's not look-ing good. If the trends continue, you know, it's not looking good.'"

The advisor told me Trump reacted with total disbelief, saying, "There's no way this could be true. There's no way this could be happening."

It was a calm anger. Instead of yelling, he quietly looked at his political team and told them they were wrong. These were the very people who had told him he would win if more than sixty-five million people voted for him. Now they were telling him he might lose—even though it looked certain that he would get far more than sixty-five million votes.*

As we waited for Trump's speech in the ABC News studio, I made

---

*He ended up with more than seventy-four million votes, but the Trump campaign's turnout models were wrong, grossly underestimating how many people would turn out to vote for Biden, who ended up with more than eighty-one million votes.

my first on-air prediction of the day: "I assume he's essentially going to declare victory."

That was the understatement of the night.

As "Hail to the Chief" blasted from the speakers in the East Room, Trump walked in followed by the first lady, Vice President Pence, and the second lady. The packed, indoor gathering (a violation of Washington, DC's coronavirus safeguards, which had banned indoor events with more than fifty people) erupted in applause.

Trump proceeded to give the most dangerous speech of his presidency—perhaps the most dangerous speech ever given by an American president—a speech that set the stage for what he would tell his frenzied supporters on January 6, 2021. The January speech would be cited in his impeachment trial as evidence Trump incited the mob that attacked the Capitol building. But the real incitement began at 2:30 a.m. on election night.

With votes still being counted across the country and no winner yet projected, Trump declared the entire election a fraud.

"This is a fraud on the American public. This is an embarrassment to our country," he said, standing between the first lady and Vice President Pence in front of a row of American flags.

"We were getting ready to win this election. Frankly, we did win this election."

He declared victory. He made entirely unsubstantiated claims about the election being stolen. And then he made his most outrageous claim.

"We'll be going to the US Supreme Court," he said. "We want all voting to stop. We don't want them to find any ballots at four o'clock in the morning and add them to the list."

Of course, polls had closed. There was nobody still voting. He was referring to what he had been watching on television: the counting of votes. And because the overwhelming majority of the votes that were now being counted were ballots that had been mailed in, his lead was slipping away.

Before he stopped speaking, he declared victory one more time: "We will win this. And as far as I'm concerned, we already have won it."

He had made wild claims in the past about election fraud. But now he was telling a deeply divided country he was somehow going to get the Supreme Court to force the states to stop counting votes. And he was making this outrageous claim just days after Senate Republicans had rushed through the confirmation, on an entirely party-line vote, of the third Trump-nominated Supreme Court justice. His words were aimed right at the heart of American democracy, a system that can only work if people trust their votes will be counted.

Trump's message would have a toxic effect on both those who supported him and those who opposed him. He was telling millions of people who had voted for Biden he was going to use the power of his position to stop their votes from being counted. And he was telling tens of millions of people who had voted for him he had already won. Among those who applauded when he said the line declaring victory were Secretary of Health and Human Services Alex Azar and former Speaker of the House Newt Gingrich—people who had been put in positions of public trust and who should have known better.

When his speech was over, I feared the president's words were going to provoke violence and I felt a need to tell anybody who happened to be listening to ABC's election coverage that the president was wrong, that there was a process in place and it would be followed regardless of what he said. Nobody, not even the Justices Donald Trump had put on the Supreme Court, could stop it.

"The president can say whatever he wants to say at his party in the East Room," I said when anchor George Stephanopoulos turned to me after the speech. "But he has no power to stop the counting of the votes. And the Supreme Court is not going to stop the counting of the votes. There is no basis in law for doing this."

It didn't take a genius to see why he was calling for the vote counting to stop. By 2:30 a.m., the biggest battleground state still in play was also the state expected to be the slowest to count all its votes: Pennsylvania. In his speech, Trump claimed he had a 690,000-vote lead in Pennsylvania. He was right! He wasn't even exaggerating. But while Pennsylvania had already counted most of the votes that had been cast in person on Election Day (votes that we knew would favor Trump), there were still two million mail-in ballots yet to be counted.

And we had a good idea of how those votes were likely to turn out. Biden had won 78 percent of the 500,000 mail-in ballots that had already been counted. If that trend—or anything close to it—continued, Biden would easily overcome Trump's lead after every vote was counted.

"There is nothing the president can do to stop that counting," I said after describing the trend in Pennsylvania. "There is still counting that has to happen in Wisconsin and Michigan. The president may win those states or he may lose them, but the counting will happen and we will have results. And the Supreme Court is not going to stop that and the president doesn't have the power to stop that."

The counting did continue. Trump never went to the Supreme Court to try to stop the counting because he had absolutely no basis to do so. And when all the ballots were finally counted in Pennsylvania, Trump's 690,000-vote lead was gone. Joe Biden had won the state by 80,000 votes. That's not because any votes were "found" at four a.m. It's because more people in Pennsylvania voted legally for Joe Biden than voted for Donald Trump.

But Donald Trump had used the biggest public platform in the nation—the White House on election night—to put the country further on edge. You could feel the tension everywhere. He was setting up a clash between those who believed his lie that the election was being stolen and those who believed his threat to use the power of the presidency—and even, somehow, the power of the Supreme Court— to overturn the results of the election.

His claim of victory was not campaign bravado. The campaign was over. This was the time for the country to come together and accept the results of a hard-fought election. Instead, he was spreading lies and inciting fear. As bad as the events of January 6 were, Trump had lit the fire that led to them, on election night. It's not overly dramatic to say the survival of the republic had been put at risk. Or that our democracy may have ultimately been saved by a combination of Donald Trump's incompetence and the actions of a disparate group of people—some famous, some unknown—who stopped him.

CHAPTER NINE

THE BIGGEST LOSER

I n the days after the election, Donald Trump watched from the White House as the lead he had on election night faded away. Mail-in votes were being counted in Wisconsin, Michigan, and Pennsylvania and, as anticipated, the votes were coming in decisively in Biden's favor. In Arizona, the reverse was happening, with Trump gaining as the state continued its count of the votes cast on Election Day. The red mirage was fading in the Midwest. The blue mirage was fading in Arizona. No major news organization had projected a winner yet, but Trump was clearly heading toward defeat. On Thursday, November 5, Trump tweeted the one course of action that could guarantee him a win:

Donald J. Trump
@realDonaldTrump

STOP THE COUNT!

11/5/20, 9:12

Once all the votes were counted, he would be the clear loser. To make sure nobody missed his directive to stop counting while he was in the lead, ninety minutes later he retweeted himself: "STOP THE COUNT!"

At the television networks, election night was turning into election week. We were exhausted from being on the air for round-the-clock coverage of the tediously slow vote count—slow because of the time-consuming process of verifying and tabulating all the votes that had been cast by mail. At ABC, as with the other networks, the decision on when to project a winner lies solely with a group of experts who work on what is called, appropriately, the Decision Desk. They analyze all the information coming in from the states and make their projections without any input from the anchors, correspondents, or on-air analysts. They don't make a projection until they are absolutely sure a candidate has secured enough votes to win.

By Friday, November 6, Biden had a sizable lead in Wisconsin and Michigan and had pulled ahead in Pennsylvania. The race seemed to be over, but the ever-careful ABC News Decision Desk had not yet made the projection. Neither had any of the other networks. Among the experts on the air for ABC was Nate Silver, the data guru and founder of FiveThirtyEight who had looked at all incoming vote data as closely as anybody, but was not part of the Decision Desk. As we got into our fourth straight night of election coverage, George Stephanopoulos asked him point-blank if he thought the race was basically over.

"At this point, yeah," Silver answered with a shrug.

Silver's understated and matter-of-fact answer to the question the entire country had been on edge asking caused everybody on set to break out in laughter. The never-ending election was almost over, but still there was no official projection. There would be no projecting a winner until it was a sure thing.

While the world awaited a winner to be announced, Rudy Giuliani started showing up at the Trump campaign headquarters in Rosslyn, Virginia. The former New York mayor had long ago established himself as a political pit bull who would fight for Trump under any circumstance. During the last campaign, Giuliani was the only one willing to go on television to defend Trump after the release of the infamous *Access Hollywood* tape, where Trump was caught bragging about using his fame to sexually assault women. Giuliani hadn't spent much time around the campaign office before the election, but now he was there all the time, digging in for the long haul to challenge the results of an election where no winner had yet been declared. He set up his own operation in the campaign headquarters' largest room—a glass-enclosed conference room with sweeping views of the Potomac River, Washington Monument, and National Mall. Giuliani brought along his own mini-entourage, including two assistants and a handful of lawyers. Among them were Sidney Powell, who had represented former Trump National Security Advisor Michael Flynn, and Jenna Ellis, who had already been working with the campaign as a consultant. Giuliani also brought in a woman named Christina Bobb, an anchor for One America News (OAN), a far-right, pro-Trump cable network.

The people who had been running the campaign—including campaign manager Bill Stepien and deputy campaign manager Justin Clark—had not invited Giuliani and his entourage into the headquarters or sought their assistance. In fact, the campaign had announced that Dave Bossie, who had been the deputy campaign manager of the 2016 Trump campaign, was coordinating the legal efforts. But Giuliani and his makeshift team began convening their own meetings and showing up, uninvited, to meetings of the campaign staff.

During these first few days after the election, meetings at the campaign headquarters included two distinct groups. In the first were top officials of the campaign, including Stepien, Clark, and campaign strategist Jason Miller, along with Trump son-in-law Jared Kushner and White House advisor Eric Herschmann. The second group was Giuliani and his entourage.

People in the first group had a name for the second group: "The crazies."

The original campaign cohort wanted to pursue the usual methods for challenging a close election. They had taken steps to demand recounts in states where that was an option (including Georgia and Wisconsin), and they wanted to pursue legal challenges in states where they could argue voting rules had been changed or not followed. In Pennsylvania, for example, they were challenging a judge's ruling that mail-in votes would count even if they arrived up to three days after the election. In Wisconsin, they were pushing to challenge absentee votes cast in person at early voting precincts because the law required a written application to get an absentee ballot. These were technical arguments unlikely to prevail and, even if they did, would be unlikely to make enough of a difference to change the final outcome. None of the legal challenges spearheaded by the campaign alleged widespread fraud.

The second group, a.k.a. "the crazies," were making all kinds of outrageous and fact-free claims about election fraud, raising the specter of hundreds of thousands of dead people voting and declaring voting machines were magically switching votes for Trump into votes for Biden. Sidney Powell brought an international air of intrigue to all of this, suggesting a vast conspiracy that included elements of the CIA, the government of Venezuelan dictator Hugo Chávez (who had been dead since 2013), and a mysterious computer server "farm" in Germany.

The first group wasn't particularly well organized or effective and, for the most part, believed the Trump campaign's efforts to change the expected outcome of the election would probably fail. The second group was totally disorganized and ineffective but they spoke as if they were 100 percent certain Trump would win the election—if they could expose the conspiracy to steal it from him. The crazies, in other words, really were crazy.

On the Friday after the election, the two groups came together for a meeting in the campaign conference room. Giuliani dominated the meeting from the start. The election was being stolen right before their eyes, he said, and it needed to be stopped. Dead people had voted. Trump ballots had been destroyed. Sidney Powell chimed in about rigged voting machines. The fraud was massive and all over the place. As wild as the allegations were, it was clear Giuliani had neither evidence nor a coherent legal strategy. After a little while, Kushner excused himself to take a call. A few minutes later Stepien got up and left, along with Bossie, Herschmann, and the others who didn't come in with Giuliani. Before long there was nobody left in the conference room except Giuliani, Ellis, Powell, and the rest of the former mayor's entourage.

Down the hall, Bossie asked Kushner why Giuliani was there. Who invited him? Kushner said he had no idea. Eventually Giuliani emerged, asking where everybody had gone, pleading with them to come back. "We have work to do!"

Jared Kushner extricated himself from the effort to challenge the election results after that. He had heard enough to see the effort was more likely to result in massive embarrassment than victory. Rather than argue against a destructive effort to undermine a presidential election—and, in the process, faith in American democracy— Kushner decided to steer clear of Rudy Giuliani and, for the most part, his father-in-law as well. Kushner's disappearance was extraordinary. He had been effectively running the campaign, and now that things were about to get really bad, he simply checked out.

At 9:35 a.m. the next day, as the presidential motorcade waited at the White House to take the president to his golf club in Sterling, Virginia, Trump tweeted what seemed like an important announcement:

> **Donald J. Trump**
> @realDonaldTrump
>
> Lawyers Press Conference at Four Seasons, Philadelphia. 11:00 A.M.
>
> 11/7/20, 9:35 AM

Ten minutes later, as reporters covering the Trump campaign scrambled to get to the Four Seasons Hotel in Philadelphia on such short notice, Trump tweeted again.

> **Donald J. Trump**
> @realDonaldTrump
>
> Big press conference today in Philadelphia at Four Seasons Total Landscaping—11:30am!
>
> 11/7/20, 9:45 AM

The time was pushed back thirty minutes, and the words "Total Landscaping" were added after Four Seasons.

Rudy Giuliani did indeed plan to hold a press conference later that morning at a place called "Four Seasons," but it wasn't the Four Seasons Hotel in downtown Philadelphia. The press conference was to be held outside a small business called Four Seasons Total Landscaping, which was located not downtown, but on the outskirts of the city between a crematorium and a store called Fantasy Island, which had a sign out front touting its ADULT BOOKS and LIVE VIEWING BOOTHS.

You really can't make it up. The president assumed his esteemed legal team would be holding its press conference at the posh Four Seasons Hotel, but it was instead scheduled to be held on an industrial lot between a sex shop and a crematorium.

As the Giuliani team worked to quickly turn the lot behind Four Seasons Total Landscaping into a press conference venue—they taped lots of Trump campaign signs to an aluminum garage door at the landscaping company's office and brought in a lectern—there was a major intervening news event: Biden was projected the winner of the presidential election.

CNN made the call first at 11:24 a.m., followed a few minutes later by ABC, CBS, NBC, and the Associated Press. At 11:40, Fox News did the same, as anchor Chris Wallace proclaimed Joe Biden the president-elect of the United States.

Ten minutes after Fox News declared Biden the winner, Giuliani stepped to the podium at Four Seasons Total Landscaping and began what President Trump had billed as a "Big Press Conference." Among those with him was Bernie Kerik, who had served as Giuliani's driver and bodyguard when he was mayor of New York and later the commissioner of the New York City Police Department. Kerik had also served time in prison—more than three years for tax fraud and making false statements to investigators. He wasn't the only person with a criminal background at the press conference. Giuliani also presented a man claiming to be a Philadelphia resident and a poll watcher who turned out to be a New Jersey sex offender who had served three years in prison for exposing himself to underage girls.

Former Trump campaign manager Corey Lewandowski showed up at the Giuliani press conference about twenty minutes late, but he did offer the one and only piece of concrete evidence presented on what seemed to be voter fraud. He identified a ballot that had been counted in Allegheny County for a woman named Denise Ondick, who had died on October 22. The county received her absentee ballot application on October 23 and mailed a ballot to her home address. The completed ballot, Lewandowski said, was received back on November 2—more than a week after she died—and it had been counted.

"This is not empirical!" Lewandowski declared from the podium in front of the garage door entrance to Four Seasons Total Landscaping. "This is hard evidence!"

It turns out Lewandowski was right! Sort of. Denise Ondick's daughter said she had helped her mother fill out her application to vote absentee shortly before she died of cancer. Apparently her husband filled out the ballot when he received it several days after her death. Assuming Ms. Ondick's widower honored her dying political wish, the ballot would have been filled out for the candidate she supported in life—Donald Trump. A dead person had voted, and apparently she voted for Trump, not Biden.

Trump had been playing golf as news organizations projected Biden the winner of the election and his lawyer conducted his disastrous press conference on the outskirts of Philadelphia. When he arrived back at the White House, his political team was waiting to give him the hard truth about their efforts to challenge the results.

The president, still dressed in his golf clothes, met with his advisors in the Yellow Oval Room on the second floor of the White House residence. It's a large and beautifully ornate room with windows overlooking the South Lawn and a door that leads out to the iconic

Truman Balcony. It's a long way from Four Seasons Total Landscaping. Among those there to meet with the president were the core of his political team—Bill Stepien, Justin Clark, Jason Miller, and David Bossie. None of them had anything to do with Giuliani's press conference in Philadelphia. This, after all, was the group that had walked out of Giuliani's meeting at the campaign headquarters the previous day.

It fell to Justin Clark, the deputy campaign manager who also happened to be a lawyer, to give the president the true state of play.

"There's still a chance we could prevail," Clark told the president, "but I would put our odds of winning at no more than five or ten percent."

The path to victory, he said, would be a narrow one. Trump would need to win Arizona, where no winner had yet been projected and where the votes were still being counted and Biden's lead had narrowed to just half a percentage point. He'd also need to win Georgia, which also remained too close to project. And then they would have to win a long-shot lawsuit to throw out more than 200,000 absentee ballots in Wisconsin based on a technicality. If he won all three of those states, the electoral vote would be split evenly between Biden and Trump: 269 to 269. That would mean the race would be determined by a vote of the House of Representatives with each state delegation getting a single vote, which Trump would probably win because Republicans controlled a narrow majority of such state delegations.

As for Pennsylvania, Clark told Trump he had no chance. Biden had won and no legal challenge was going to change that.

I've talked to multiple people who were at that meeting. They all tell me Trump did not react angrily to what Clark told him, but he also did not accept it.

"No. You're wrong," Trump told Clark. "The chances are much higher."

He said he believed he was still going to win Pennsylvania and that his odds of winning the overall race were closer to 40 or 50 percent.

The president calmly told them to keep working.

"We'll see what happens."

Within days, the counting would be over in Arizona and Biden would be certified as the state's winner. Trump's odds, which were already far lower than the 5 to 10 percent suggested by Clark, would be zero. With the window slammed shut on his reelection hopes, Trump turned decisively in the direction of Rudy Giuliani and the group his top political advisors had derided as the crazies. They were no longer a fringe group showing up uninvited at the campaign headquarters. They were calling the shots.

The day after the meeting in the Yellow Oval Room, Dave Bossie got COVID-19 and the campaign announced he would no longer be able to direct the legal efforts. Bossie became quite sick, but he later told friends that getting infected with the deadly disease was one of the best things ever to happen to him because it forced him to drop out of the effort to challenge the election results just as Trump's legal team was going off the deep end.

"I'm one of the few people," Bossie would later say, "who can say getting COVID saved my life."

The Sunday Bossie got his COVID diagnosis, there was a sign of the impending insanity in the form of an interview on the Fox News show hosted by Maria Bartiromo. While Fox News was calling Biden the president-elect, Bartiromo used her Sunday show on the network to highlight the most outlandish allegations of election fraud—going beyond even anything yet alleged publicly by Donald Trump or Rudy Giuliani.

Bartiromo introduced her lead guest—Sidney Powell—as an attorney working with the Trump legal team, even though there had been no announcement yet that Powell had any role on the Trump team. Powell launched right into a wild conspiracy theory about the election.

"There has been a massive and coordinated effort to steal this election from we the people of the United States of America, to delegitimize and destroy votes for Donald Trump, to manufacture votes for Joe Biden," she told Bartiromo.

"They have done it in every way imaginable, from having dead people vote in massive numbers, to absolutely fraudulently creating ballots," she continued.

Instead of challenging her deranged allegations or asking her to produce evidence (Powell had none), Bartiromo suggested it was an outrage that Attorney General Bill Barr wasn't acting to stop this legal atrocity, saying, "If this is so obvious, why aren't we seeing massive government investigations?"

"When the votes are really audited, and the real votes are counted, Trump will win," Powell said. "He is the president, and he is in charge of this country."

Powell's fevered rant ended on this bizarre note: "They had this all planned, Maria. They had the algorithms."

They had the algorithms!

What the hell was she talking about? Bartiromo didn't express one ounce of skepticism about these wild allegations or ask what she meant; instead, she concluded the interview by thanking Powell and telling her, "Please come back soon."

It's not hard to see why Trump, who watched the interview from the White House, liked what he heard from Powell much more than what his campaign team had told him. His political advisors were telling him he had only a slim chance of prevailing. Powell might sound nuts, but she was telling Trump he would definitely win and that "he is in charge of this country."

It was all a lie, but Sidney Powell's deranged theories would have never taken hold if there weren't people in positions of power and influence who promoted them—people like Maria Bartiromo. Bartiromo had once been a widely respected and trailblazing financial journalist. As a correspondent for CNBC, she was the first television reporter to report live from the floor of the New York Stock Exchange. Now she had her own show on Fox News and she was using it to boost a series of unfounded allegations designed to overturn a presidential election. While writing the book, I reached out multiple times to Bartiromo to ask her to explain why she played such an active role promoting lies about the election and whether she had any regret for what she did. She did not respond to those questions.

Later in her show, Bartiromo interviewed Senator Lindsey Graham, who used his position of public trust to speak directly to Trump and to encourage his most destructive tendencies.

"Trump has not lost," Graham told Bartiromo. "Do not concede, Mr. President. Fight hard."

And that was a message the president heard loudly and clearly, with devastating consequences to come.

The next day—Monday, November 9—I went to the White House entirely unsure what to expect. How far Trump would go in refusing the results was not clear. On the one hand, there were the deranged musings of Sidney Powell and Lindsey Graham. But others close to the president had told me the president knew he had lost. "Give him time," one of the president's closest allies in Congress told me. "He'll come around."

Despite the networks declaring Biden the president-elect over the weekend and the embarrassing performance of Trump's legal team, Monday should have been a pretty good day to be president. The pharmaceutical company Pfizer had just announced its COVID vaccine was 90 percent effective. The end of the pandemic was in sight and financial markets were rallying. The Dow Jones Industrial Average shot up more than eight hundred points—its best day in six months. But there was no plan for the president to address the vaccine news—or the results of the election. Press Secretary Kayleigh McEnany was nowhere to be found. Newspapers and unopened mail were piled high on the desk outside her office. As I walked into the press office, I saw a junior assistant talking to another reporter about her plans for after January 20—when Trump's term would be over. There was nobody else around.

The lack of activity at the White House was unsettling. It was quiet, but we were witnessing something dangerous and entirely without precedent in American history: a defeated president refusing to admit defeat. I walked back to my small office in the area behind the White House briefing room and wrote this in my journal:

> There are signs the president is gearing up for a fight to undermine public faith in our democratic system and challenge the legitimacy of Biden's victory. The legal challenges are a joke, but he is convincing a lot of people that the election was fraudulent. Our long national nightmare may not be quite over yet.

Several people close to the president had told me he was, essentially, going through the stages of grief but would ultimately accept the results and ensure a smooth transition to Biden. I had asked Kellyanne

Conway if we would ever see a Trump concession speech. She said she was sure he would give a speech recognizing Biden as the next president and committing to a smooth transition, but that he would complain bitterly about being mistreated and he would not quite admit he had lost. In other words, she was saying Trump would concede that the election was stolen from him.

I called Corey Lewandowski, who was as fierce a Trump supporter as anybody, to ask him how this would all play out.

"He knows it is over," Lewandowski told me. "He just wants to create enough doubt about Biden's victory so that when he leaves he can say he didn't lose and that it was stolen from him."

Whether or not Trump really knew it was over, he was compounding his election loss in a multitude of ways. By refusing to concede, he went from being a loser to a sore loser. He was suffering embarrassing losses in courts throughout the country. And the desperate effort to find evidence to support the wild allegations of election fraud were turning his effort to challenge the election results into a joke.

In one of its more comically inept moves, the campaign had set up a toll-free number and a web portal for people across the country to report election fraud. They sought eyewitnesses by spreading the word about the election-fraud hotline on social media.

Trump War Room
@TrumpWarRoom

Help stop voter suppression, irregularities and fraud! Tell us what you are seeing. Report a case: http://djt45.co/stopfraud Call: (888) 630-1776

11/5/20

Campaign workers were assigned to answer some thirty phones set up in a large room at the headquarters and to review material sent in over the web portal. They fielded hundreds of calls a day, but the only thing the effort produced was traumatized young Trump campaign workers. Instead of voters calling in with evidence of fraud, pranksters flooded the lines with fake reports as well as vile, threatening, and pornographic messages. The material sent in through the web portal consisted almost entirely of pornographic images.

After working a shift in the call center, one young woman begged to never answer any more calls. Within a week, the toll-free number was disabled and the call center deactivated.

As the call center was shut down, most of the campaign staff was either not working anymore or working from home. But Rudy Giuliani and his team continued coming in just about every day, working out of the large conference room overlooking the Potomac River. The president was being advised by two factions that were virtually at war with each other.

On Thursday, November 12, Trump put Giuliani on speakerphone during a meeting with a large group of senior officials at the White House, including Vice President Pence, Jared Kushner, Senior Advisor Hope Hicks, White House Counsel Pat Cipollone, Director of Presidential Personnel Johnny McEntee, and several others. As Giuliani started outlining a legal onslaught that included going to federal court to get access to voting machines in Georgia, Deputy Chief of Staff Dan Scavino brought in Justin Clark, who had been nearby with the campaign team in the Cabinet Room.

"Rudy, let me see if we can get Justin Clark in here," Trump said, nodding at Clark, who was already in the room.

"Okay, here he is," Trump said. "Go ahead, tell him what you think we should do."

"We've got to go to federal court right now," Giuliani said. "We've got to get Georgia to open up the voting machines."

Before Clark could respond, Cipollone pointed out that Georgia had just started a recount—by hand—of all 4.9 million ballots cast.

"Rudy, they are doing a hand recount right now," Cipollone said. "We are going to know when they are done whether or not the machines were accurate."

"No, no, no," Giuliani said. "That audit is going to be crap. It's going to be garbage."

"Look," Clark said, "the bottom line here is that if you file a federal lawsuit, it's going to be immediately dismissed and we'll have another loss on our hands."

At this point, Giuliani could be heard yelling through the speakerphone.

"They are lying to you, sir," Giuliani said. "They are lying to you!"

"We're not lying to you," Clark said to the president. Then, turning to the speaker, he said, "You're a fucking asshole, Rudy."

"Okay, okay, okay," Trump said. "You guys work it out."

There would be no working it out. The next day, Trump tweeted that Rudy Giuliani was in charge of the legal team. The move caused even more tension out at the campaign headquarters.

My ABC News colleagues Will Steakin, Katherine Faulders, and John Santucci reported on a big argument between the two factions two days later at the campaign headquarters over what the campaign leadership saw as an attempted "coup" by Jenna Ellis and Rudy Giuliani.

"The attempted power grab hit a boiling point on Saturday when Jason Miller, who's been the campaign's chief strategist for months, and Ellis got into what sources said was a 'screaming match' in front of other staffers," my ABC News colleagues wrote. "They both threatened to call the president to settle who he wanted to be in charge, sources said. At one point, Miller berated Ellis and called her 'crazy.'"

The report was entirely correct and, if anything, understated the nastiness of the confrontation. Miller issued a statement denying the story. He later joked his denial was technically correct because "I didn't call her crazy, I called her fucking crazy."

Giuliani's leadership of the legal team reached the pinnacle of absurdity on November 19 with a press conference even stranger than the one held at Four Seasons Total Landscaping almost two weeks earlier. This time the venue was the lobby of the Republican National Committee's headquarters in Washington, DC. The location was more formal, but the content more ridiculous.

The request to use the RNC's lobby came from Christina Bobb, an OAN anchor who was working with Giuliani. RNC Chairwoman Ronna McDaniel signed off on the request—after all, it came from the president's legal team—but she told her staff she didn't want any RNC employees to be there. As for McDaniel, she watched it all unfold on television while she was in Michigan.

For at least a minute or two, the press conference looked entirely normal. Giuliani introduced the lawyers on the stage—including Jenna Ellis and Sidney Powell—and said there were many more working as part of the president's legal team. But then Sidney Powell came to the podium and unleashed a torrent of wacky conspiracy theories and misinformation. She vowed to expose not just cheating by Democrats, but a vast global conspiracy.

"What we are really dealing with here and uncovering more by the day is the massive influence of communist money through Venezuela, Cuba, and likely China in the interference with our elections here in the United States," Powell said.

Whoa! The election-counting software at the core of the conspiracy,

Powell said, was "created at the direction of Hugo Chávez." Chávez, the former dictator of Venezuela, was a bad guy. He had also been dead since 2013. The conspiracy Powell described was so vast, it included more than just Cuba and China and Venezuela—it also included financier George Soros.

Powell was spewing nonsense, but when Giuliani got back to the podium, he actually sounded crazier.

"Our votes are counted in Germany and in Spain, by a company owned by affiliates of George Soros and Maduro!" Giuliani declared, a bizarre and utterly ridiculous allegation. Votes are counted locally.

A few minutes later, when asked to respond to something the secretary of state of Michigan said, Giuliani was again talking about votes getting counted in Germany.

"The secretary of state of Michigan never bothered to find out that the votes in her state were being counted in Germany, by a Venezuelan company," Giuliani thundered. "And you want me to take her seriously or him seriously?"

Again, no votes were counted in Germany. Voting machines are not connected to the internet. Data is not sent off to Germany to be counted. It's fantasy. It's bizarre. And it was being said by the man leading the legal team representing the president of the United States.

As the presser unfolded in her conference room, RNC Chairwoman McDaniel started getting angry text messages from RNC members demanding to know why the spectacle was taking place at the Republican Party headquarters. "Does the RNC agree with this?" one RNC member texted McDaniel. "Of course not," she replied. McDaniel never saw the whole press conference. As soon as Powell started talking about Hugo Chávez, she turned off the television.

As strange as it all was, the press conference is primarily remembered because of what happened to Rudy Giuliani's hair. As he ranted in front of the hot lights, he started sweating. And as he started sweating, black liquid started oozing down the sides of his face— apparently the dye he used to make his gray hair look black. With his eyes bulging and his hair appearing to melt, he looked like a character in a bad horror movie.

Rudy Giuliani was an embarrassment. He was also not getting paid. A week before the press conference at the RNC, one of Giuliani's assistants had sent an email notifying the campaign leadership that Giuliani and his team would need to be paid a retainer of $20,000 a day for their legal work. A week later, Maggie Haberman of *The New York Times* broke the story about Giuliani's pricey demand. By then, Trump had already rejected Giuliani's request. In fact, he was so offended by what he saw as an effort by Giuliani to make a windfall off his campaign that he told his campaign manager he didn't want Giuliani to be paid anything at all. This would effectively be pro bono work. Trump said Giuliani would only be reimbursed for his expenses, and, furthermore, Trump demanded he would have to sign off on all of Giuliani's expenses himself.

The morning after the RNC press conference, Giuliani and his team assembled once again at the campaign headquarters conference room to plot their next steps. Giuliani was now seen as a pariah by most of the president's advisors and supporters, but Trump wasn't cutting him off. No way. Not only was he working for free, he was the one telling Trump he could still win. There was virtually nobody else in the building as Giuliani and his entourage sat around the table eating, drinking, and talking about the path ahead. Suddenly, at around ten a.m., Giuliani got a message from his son, Andrew, who had been with him at the RNC press conference. He had just tested positive for COVID-19. That meant everybody in the room had been exposed. They would have to quarantine.

The Rudy team got up immediately and rushed for the exits. Nobody went back into the conference room for weeks—no campaign staff, no janitorial staff, nobody.

Weeks later the conference room seemed frozen in time, exactly as Giuliani's team had left it—half-drunk soda cans, legal pads and pens, and a half-eaten burrito on the table; napkins, paper bags, and sandwich wrappers were strewn around the room. As one of the top people on the campaign described it to me, "It looked like a bunch of high school kids had been in there for days, and didn't clean up after themselves."

Giuliani would continue his lost-cause battle to overturn the election results, but he never returned to the campaign headquarters. And nobody on the Trump campaign ever again went into the conference room. The cleaning crew avoided the place as well, presumably because so many people who had been in that confined space had been exposed to coronavirus. For more than a month, the trash and the half burrito remained visible to anybody who walked by the glass-enclosed conference room with the majestic views of Washington, DC—a rancid and decaying monument to the most embarrassingly ineffective legal team ever to serve a president of the United States.

CHAPTER TEN

INFIDELS AT THE PENTAGON

The second time Christopher Miller was in the Oval Office, he was offered the job of secretary of defense.

Christopher Miller's first time in the Oval Office was Friday the thirteenth of December in 2019. A mid-level Defense Department official at the time, he had been at the White House for a midday holiday party when he was asked to attend a briefing for the president by members of his national security team. When he got to the Oval Office, Vice President Mike Pence, National Security Advisor Robert O'Brien, and Attorney General Bill Barr sat in chairs in front of the Resolute desk facing President Trump. Miller and several other aides took their seats a little farther away on one of the yellow couches he had seen so often on television. Trump kicked things off the way he often started meetings. He ordered a Diet Coke from his valet and asked if anybody else in the room wanted one. All of the dozen or so aides in the room demurred—except for Miller. *Hell, yes,* he thought, *of course I'll take one.* He was in the Oval Office and he was getting offered a Diet Coke by a president who famously drank them all day long. How do you turn that down? The valet emerged from the pantry just outside the Oval Office with two Diet Cokes: one for the president and one for Chris Miller. *Pretty cool*, Miller thought.

As the meeting got underway, Attorney General Barr said something that caught everybody in the room by surprise, about a fatal shooting a week earlier by a Saudi Arabian aviation student at a naval facility in Pensacola, Florida. Barr told the president there were another twenty Saudi nationals unaccounted for in Florida and suggested the shooting in Pensacola could possibly be part of a larger terror plot. The president wanted to know more, but nobody had answers because nobody knew what Barr was talking about. National Security Advisor O'Brien signaled to Miller, who was the deputy assistant secretary of defense for special operations and combating terrorism, that he should leave the meeting to see if he could get more information. Miller quietly got up and walked back the way he had walked into the Oval Office. But he immediately became disoriented. Where he thought the door had been, he now saw only a wall. What Miller did not know is that the Oval Office has two hidden doors that flank the fireplace opposite the presidential desk; they blend into the walls when they are closed. The door he had walked in was now closed. So, as Miller stood up to leave, he couldn't immediately see how to get out of the room.

He walked slowly around the edge of the room and thought, *The Diet Cokes!* He could see the door on the other side of the room where the valet had emerged with the drinks. As the president talked about the Saudis—and how he'd make them pay if there was a larger terror plot—Miller quietly worked his way over to the valet's door and slipped out of the Oval Office. But the door leads right into the presidential pantry—a small alcove that Trump often showed off to visitors as the place Bill Clinton had some of his encounters with Monica Lewinsky.

Uh-oh, Miller thought. *How do I get out of here?* He saw another door, turned the knob, and pushed. But the door only opened a couple of inches before it hit something, or, more accurately, some*one*: a Secret Service agent standing in the hallway outside.

"You can't come through here," the agent said quietly through the crack in the door. "This door is for the president."

Miller pleaded to let him out and the agent allowed him to make his escape.

The next time Christopher Miller was back in the Oval Office, less than a year later, he was asked to lead the Department of Defense.

Miller would serve for just seventy-two days as acting secretary of defense, but it was one hell of a seventy-two days. He was a Pentagon leader unlike any other—a career special operations soldier who had conducted missions in dangerous places around the globe but who had little experience in Washington and no real experience in the realm of politics. He served a volatile commander in chief who wanted to overturn an election and had supporters who believed the military should help him do it. And while the post-election drama played out at home, the United States moved perilously close—much closer than the public realized—to a dangerous military confrontation in the Middle East.

Miller got the call to come to the White House for his second visit to the Oval Office from the Presidential Personnel Office on November 9, 2020—the Monday after every major news organization, including Fox News, projected Joe Biden as the winner of the presidential election. By then Miller had become the director of the National Counterterrorism Center (NCTC), a federal agency headquartered in Tysons Corner, Virginia, about twelve miles from the White House. Miller had known for months that if Trump fired Defense Secretary Mark Esper, he'd likely get tapped to replace him.

But when Esper wasn't fired in the days immediately following the election, Miller assumed his moment had passed.

Out at the NCTC headquarters, Miller had urged his staff to dress more casually, or, as he told them, "We're not wearing fucking suits anymore!" Their job was to fight terrorism, he figured, and they shouldn't dress like bankers. So, when Miller got the call, six days after the election, to come immediately to the White House, he was dressed the way he wanted his staff to dress—a button-down shirt, khakis, casual shoes, and "no fucking suit."

But now he had to rush to the White House where he knew damn well he should be wearing a suit and he had no time to get one. He sped off to 1600 Pennsylvania Avenue. When he got there, he went straight to the office of Director of Presidential Personnel Johnny McEntee.

"We're going to the Oval," McEntee told him. "We're firing Esper and you're the next man up."

Miller borrowed a tie, which he hastily put on just before going into the Oval Office. This time he was invited to sit in one of the chairs right across from the president. The meeting was short and to the point.

"I'm firing Esper," Trump said. "It's time for him to go. You're going over there."

The meeting lasted only a few minutes. Miller agreed to go right over to the Pentagon but as he walked out of the room, he was a little shell-shocked. It all happened so quickly. He hadn't even talked to his wife about the massively high-profile and high-stress job he just agreed to take. And he was expected to head immediately over to the Pentagon with no time for a transition. McEntee looked at him and started laughing.

"I told you!" he said. "I told you this was going to happen!"

Yes, McEntee had been telling him for months that he was going to be the next secretary of defense, but who thought it would go down like this? It was haphazard and chaotic, but it was also a crowning achievement for McEntee. His mission was to purge the Trump administration of people who he believed were not sufficiently loyal to Trump, and Esper had long been right at the top of his list. A couple of months earlier, McEntee had deployed Josh Whitehouse—the twenty-five-year-old former Trump campaign volunteer who had made enemies browbeating senior staffers at the Department of Homeland Security—to the Pentagon to help root out people who didn't truly support Trump. As Whitehouse had boasted when he took the job, "I'm going to the Pentagon to fire Esper and all those deep-state bastards."

Now it was happening, and McEntee was laughing. After Miller left the White House, McEntee called retired Army Colonel Douglas Macgregor, a decorated combat veteran and regular guest on Tucker Carlson's Fox News show, and offered him the job of senior advisor to the brand-new acting secretary of defense. As *Axios*'s Jonathan Swan first reported, McEntee handed Macgregor a piece of paper with handwritten instructions for the new team at the Pentagon:

1. Get us out of Afghanistan.
2. Get us out of Iraq and Syria.
3. Complete the withdrawal from Germany.
4. Get us out of Africa.

"This is what the president wants you to do," McEntee told him.

Miller had served his country for nearly thirty years in the Army, most of the time in the Special Forces. He was among the first troops sent into Afghanistan after the September 11 terror attacks. Over the next decade and a half, he would be repeatedly deployed to war zones, living and fighting in Afghanistan and Iraq during some of the darkest days of the war on terror. He is a soldier who has served his country selflessly and with distinction. He was also widely seen as unprepared for the job that had just been thrust upon him. As one former official who likes Miller and worked with him at the Pentagon told me: "Never has there been anybody in the history of the United States government in over his head more than Chris Miller at the Pentagon." I'm not sure that's right—Miller may have had no political experience, but he had more real-world experience in the military than many of his predecessors—but, regardless, nothing could have prepared him for what was about to happen.

Miller described his surreal experience to me a couple months after Trump's presidency, and his tenure as secretary of defense, was over. He is a gregarious guy, instantly likable and a good storyteller. He's the kind of person you want to sit down and have a beer with, which is exactly what we did, talking about his time as Donald Trump's man at the Pentagon over Indian food and a pilsner in downtown Washington. He still seemed amazed by how strange it all was.

He told me that after Trump offered him the job and he walked out of the Oval Office, he thought about the man he was about to replace. Mark Esper hadn't even been told he had been fired yet, but Miller was already told to rush over to the Pentagon to take over. It just didn't seem right.

"My whole thing was, 'Give Esper some respect,'" Miller told me. "The president can be disrespectful, but I am not going to be."

Like so many others fired by Donald Trump, Esper didn't get much respect on the way out. Shortly after Miller left the White House, Esper got a call from Chief of Staff Mark Meadows that the president was about to announce his departure. Within a few minutes—less than five—the firing became official with a pair of tweets:

> **Donald J. Trump**
> @realDonaldTrump
>
> I am pleased to announce that Christopher C. Miller, the highly respected Director of the National Counterterrorism Center (unanimously confirmed by the Senate), will be Acting Secretary of Defense, effective immediately.
>
> 11/9/20, 12:54 PM

> **Donald J. Trump**
> @realDonaldTrump
>
> . . . Chris will do a GREAT job! Mark Esper has been terminated. I would like to thank him for his service.
>
> 11/9/20, 12:54 PM

About sixty seconds after those tweets were posted, Josh White-house walked into Esper's office with a terse two-sentence letter signed by Johnny McEntee. It read, "Pursuant to the direction of the President, your appointment as Secretary of Defense is hereby terminated, effective immediately. Thank you for your service."

Miller didn't want to immediately go over to the Pentagon. He wanted to give Esper at least a little time to move out and say farewell to the massive organization he had led for more than sixteen months. And there was something else on his mind.

"I just knew I needed to get a fucking suit," Miller told me. He wasn't going to walk into the Pentagon as the new secretary of defense without first putting on a suit.

So, as the president sent out his tweet shortly before one, Miller told McEntee he'd be at the Pentagon at two. He then drove as fast as he could to get a suit at his house in Burke, Virginia, about a thirty-minute drive from the Pentagon. Esper, meanwhile, began packing up his office and putting the final touches on a farewell letter to all employees of the Department of Defense. He'd had a draft of that letter ready to go for months because he knew he could be fired at any time.

When Miller got to his home, he had another issue to deal with. His wife and his twenty-seven-year-old daughter, no fans of Donald Trump, were horrified he had just accepted a job to be Trump's defense secretary. They tearfully tried to talk him out of taking the job he had already accepted. Miller's family had sacrificed a lot through the years with his repeated deployments to war zones, but they reacted as if this was even worse than all that. Miller figured he didn't have time for a big family discussion on this. He needed to get moving quickly or he'd be late for his arrival at the Pentagon as acting secretary of defense.

"This family is about public service," Miller told his wife and daughter. "That's what we do. It's our family brand. I've been asked to serve. I am going to serve."

While Miller was home trying to reassure his family about the job he had just accepted and getting dressed for his arrival at the Pentagon, McEntee called Ezra Cohen,* whom McEntee had placed at the Pentagon back in April as an assistant secretary of defense.

"Where are you?" McEntee asked him.

He was actually not at the Pentagon at the moment. He had taken a lunchtime break to walk his dog.

"Chris Miller has been named secretary of defense," McEntee told him. "I need you to be there to let him in—I can't get ahold of anybody over there."

---

*Cohen has often been referred to in news accounts as Ezra Cohen-Watnick, but his name is Ezra Cohen.

And with that, Cohen hustled back to the Pentagon and had a temporary pass issued for the incoming acting secretary of defense. Miller was about to take over what is arguably the most powerful position in the cabinet, but he had been appointed in such a haphazard way that there was no time to get him his proper Pentagon ID card. As he waited at the Pentagon's River Entrance for Miller's arrival, Cohen saw a mini-motorcade of two black SUVs driving away from the building. Mark Esper was heading home, taking one last ride in a government vehicle. Esper hadn't even finished packing his office yet, but had been told by his military aide he needed to clear out immediately because the new acting secretary of defense was about to arrive.

Esper had been fired because he was one of the few people left in the senior ranks of the Trump administration willing to disagree with the president he served. It wasn't always that way. Early in his tenure at the Pentagon, Esper had earned the derogatory nickname "Yesper" because of the way he seemed to go along with anything Trump wanted to do—from the abrupt withdrawal of troops in Syria and Germany to holding up military aid to Ukraine. But those days were gone. The White House now saw Esper as somebody who was constantly blocking Trump's agenda. To McEntee, Esper had committed a long list of transgressions. He had welcomed Lieutenant Colonel Alexander Vindman back to the Army, even approving his promotion to colonel, after Vindman had infuriated the president with his testimony in the 2019 House impeachment hearings and had been fired from his post at the National Security Council. He had publicly disagreed with the president on using the Insurrection Act to deploy active-duty troops to combat rioters on the streets of American cities, and Esper had enraged Trump by issuing a directive that effectively banned the flying of the Confederate flag on military bases after Trump, just three days earlier, had called flying the flag a matter of free speech.

In none of these instances had Esper defied a direct order from the president, but in each case he knew Trump would not be happy about what he had done. Before he had issued his order on the Confederate flag in July 2020, for example, Esper had given the White House a heads-up, and Mark Meadows, in several meetings and phone calls, tried to convince him to change course. Meadows told Esper that banning the Confederate flag would be giving in to "political correctness" and that if he did it, the "left" would demand other flags be banned, too. Esper thought that argument was ridiculous and told Meadows it was about military readiness, not political correctness. He explained the flag was a symbol of oppression and slavery and an affront to everyone who served in the US armed services, especially the 40 percent of the enlisted servicemembers who were minorities. Despite the resistance from the White House, Esper went ahead with the ban. Two days later, Trump criticized the move in an interview with Chris Wallace on *Fox News Sunday*, saying, "When people proudly hang their Confederate flags they're not talking about racism. They love their flag, it represents the South."

There were also less public issues where Esper had been at odds with the White House and had quietly worked to undermine what he thought were wildly contradictory and impetuous requests from President Trump. As the election approached, Esper worried that the president was looking for the Pentagon to do something dramatic to give his campaign a boost. At times Trump talked about big gestures to bring home American troops deployed around the world, saying he wanted to bring home all US forces in Somalia (which he eventually announced in December), Afghanistan, Germany (where he already had alarmed NATO allies by abruptly announcing a reduction of US forces), and South Korea. Esper didn't oppose reducing US troop levels around the world, but he believed withdrawals needed to be carefully planned and coordinated with America's allies. When Trump wasn't talking about quick withdrawals, he was demanding plans for military strikes on Iran and even Venezuela. An intelligence official in the Trump administration told me, "He would go from talking about turning Iran into a parking lot to saying he wanted to completely withdraw all US forces—sometimes in the same conversation."

Esper had a strategy for dealing with presidential musings he believed were erratic, ill-conceived, or dangerous. He and Joint Chiefs Chairman Mark Milley would express concerns, but not outright opposition to what the president was saying, and then delay action in the hope Trump would lose interest and move on to something else. After he left office, Esper explained the process to me this way:

"I would ask some questions and give some initial feedback—anything from 'I understand what you want to do' or 'I don't think that makes sense, but I owe you a formal recommendation once I've done my homework to make sure that I'm not wrong,'" Esper told me he would say to the president.

The delay tactic usually worked.

"The president had a short attention span," Esper told me. "So, if it was really not a good idea, chances were he'd forget about it for three or four months."

What Trump didn't forget was that he wanted to fire Esper. He came close several times before the election but held off out of fear that firing his defense secretary might hurt him politically.

On October 19, McEntee's Presidential Personnel Office wrote a one-page memorandum summarizing Esper's alleged transgressions against Trump. The document, which I obtained while writing this book and has never before been made public, provides remarkable insight into the minds of McEntee's enforcers of Trump loyalty and the degree to which they were calling the shots. The document includes ten bullet points outlining Esper's sins against the president. Esper is called out because he approved the promotion of "the star witness in the sham impeachment inquiry," Lieutenant Colonel Alexander Vindman, and because he banned the Confederate flag on military bases and "opposed the President's direction to utilize American forces to put down riots." He is also criticized because he "has focused the Department on Russia—directing in last September to 'sprint' at them—and to look at 'every facet of competition' with Moscow." Finally, he is slammed for "actively pushing for 'diversity and inclusion.'" Focusing on Russia and promoting diversity in the ranks of the military, it seems, were considered betrayals of Trump's mission.

The memo concludes with a recommended course of action—get rid of Esper the day after the election "and immediately remove [him] from the building" and "Designate Chris Miller, Director of NCTC, as the Acting Sec Def."

Trump waited until six days after the election, but he followed McEntee's plan. Esper was now gone, and Trump had tapped a new acting defense secretary he believed would do exactly what he wanted.

Less than five minutes after Esper left the Pentagon for the last ride in a government-owned black SUV, a red 2018 Ford Fusion pulled up to the Pentagon entrance facing the Potomac River. Out of the small car jumped the 6'4" Chris Miller. He had been driven to the Pentagon by a friend, no motorcade, no entourage, no government vehicle. Along with Ezra Cohen, a group of reporters and a network camera crew were there to witness the unusual changing of the guard. As Miller bounded toward the steps outside the Pentagon, he briefly looked down to make sure his fly was zipped and then he tripped, nearly falling as he made his way into the building. The image of him stumbling quickly went viral on social media—not exactly the image he wanted for his first minutes on the job.

Once inside, Miller was escorted up to the office of the secretary of defense, but he couldn't go into his new office just yet; Esper's now former chief of staff, Jen Stewart, was still packing up the belongings of the outgoing defense secretary.

With his new office not yet available, Miller set up to work in a conference room and was quickly joined by Generals Mark Milley and John Hyten, the chairman and vice chairman of the Joint Chiefs of Staff. Josh Whitehouse—who had already boasted to people about his role in getting Esper fired—tried to join Miller's first meeting with the military leadership as secretary of defense, but he was told he was not welcome. This was a deadly serious and highly classified meeting. Like every new Pentagon chief since September 11, 2001, Miller had to be briefed first on two critical matters: 1) the procedures for launching nuclear weapons, and 2) the procedures for shooting down a civilian airliner.

Miller has the affable demeanor of somebody who was a class clown in high school. He likes to joke around and doesn't take himself too seriously. But an official who was there with him for this first briefing told me Miller's demeanor quickly changed as he listened to the generals speak. His journey to this job may not have been remotely traditional—it all seemed like a lark—but the immensity of the responsibility he had just inherited seemed to hit him hard as he listened to the four-star generals explain what he would need to do to launch weapons capable of destroying the world.

The next day the White House conducted what you might call a Tuesday-morning massacre. Several senior officials who were close to Esper were purged and replaced by controversial Trump loyalists.

The chief of staff for the secretary of defense was fired and replaced by Kash Patel, a Trump devotee and former aide to Republican Congressman Devin Nunes; the under secretary of defense for intelligence was pushed out and replaced by Ezra Cohen, a former aide to Michael Flynn on the National Security Council; and the under secretary of defense for policy was fired and replaced by former Fox News commentator Anthony Tata, who was best known for calling former President Obama a Muslim and a terrorist leader and pushing the theory that Trump was being undermined by a "deep state cabal." *The New York Times* called the moves "a purge of the Pentagon's top civilian hierarchy without recent precedent."

To some national security experts—including more than a few veterans of the Trump administration—the moves were alarming. There was rampant speculation that the changes were designed to set in motion the kind of big military gambit Esper had feared Trump would attempt before the election. Was this a precursor to war with Iran—or to a devious plan to get the military involved in Trump's effort to overturn the election? In reality, there was no master plan. The driving factor in all of this seemed to be a desire to punish people who were seen as not loyal enough to Trump and to reward people who were. One former Pentagon official called it "the last gasp of vengefulness and cronyism" from the Trump administration.

As for Chris Miller, he told me his goals when he took the job were modest: "No military coup, no major war, and no troops in the streets."

On his third day on the job, he was summoned to the White House for a meeting with President Trump and the national security team. The date was November 12—the same day President Trump fatefully put Rudy Giuliani in charge of his effort to challenge the results of the election and angrily accused his campaign advisors of not working hard enough to overturn Biden's victory. But unlike the Giuliani meeting, which dealt with the fantasies about election fraud, this national security meeting dealt with cold hard facts about Iran's efforts to develop nuclear weapons and the very real possibility of war. The meeting was called because of an alarming new report from the International Atomic Energy Agency (IAEA) documenting Iran's flagrant violation of the nuclear agreement negotiated by the Obama administration. The IAEA report showed Iran dramatically increasing its stockpile of enriched uranium and projected Iran now had the capacity to produce enough weapons-grade uranium to fuel two bombs within six months.

The November 12 national security meeting has been described to me by multiple officials who were there, one of whom shared with me notes taken during the meeting. The president's tone was serious. Back in January 2020, Trump had vowed, "As long as I am President of the United States, Iran will never be allowed to have a nuclear weapon." The latest news from the IAEA showed the Iranians were not taking his threat seriously and Trump wanted to do something about it. Among those at the meeting were Vice President Mike Pence, Secretary of State Mike Pompeo, Joint Chiefs Chairman Mark Milley, National Security Advisor Robert O'Brien, Treasury Secretary Steven Mnuchin, and—in his third day on the job—acting Defense Secretary Chris Miller.

As the meeting got started, General Milley outlined the significance of the IAEA report. It was disturbing that Iran had dramatically increased its stockpile of low-enriched uranium, but they had not made the leap to turn it into the highly enriched uranium needed to fuel a nuclear weapon. In other words, the Iranian moves were concerning, but they had not crossed any red lines, at least not yet. Despite the IAEA's assessment that Iran could have enough fuel for two nuclear bombs within six months, the U.S. military's assessment was that Iran was still twelve to eighteen months away from having the capacity to make a nuclear weapon.

Trump showed little interest in discussing the nuances of various levels of uranium enrichment. Iran was defying his warnings and he wanted to know his options—military options. What would it take to completely destroy their nuclear program? He turned to Miller and asked if the Iranian program could be taken out with air strikes.

"Yes, Mr. President," Miller responded. "We can absolutely do that."

And with that, Miller outlined what a US attack on Iran's nuclear program would look like. He described an attack that would include sending more than one hundred manned Air Force and Marine aircraft over Iran. He warned him that Iran has sophisticated air-defense systems.

"We're probably going to lose some planes," Miller said. "It's just the nature of the business. You'll probably see some three, four, or six planes shot down. I just want to make sure you are comfortable with that."

Miller told him the attack would be launched from aircraft carriers in the region and also with bombers flying from Barksdale Air Force Base in Louisiana.

"That's a long way to fly," Trump said.

"Air-to-air refueling, Mr. President," Miller said.

And with that, the conversation veered into a discussion of the tanker aircraft made by Boeing that supply fuel for bombers and fighter jets while they are flying. Trump's meetings, even on matters of war, rarely stayed on topic.

"Boeing? Boeing handles the air-to-air refueling?" Trump asked. "They can't build shit anymore."

The conversation then took another detour into the travails of the

Boeing Corporation and its 737 MAX civilian aircraft, which had been grounded all over the world due to technical issues.

As the conversation veered back to Iran, Trump turned to Secretary of State Pompeo. Pompeo was one of the administration's real hard-liners on Iran. What did he think about going in with massive air strikes to take out their nuclear facilities?

This was too much even for Pompeo. He said a military strike like this would be a mistake that would risk a larger war in the Middle East. Trump went around the room and just about everybody said the same thing. This was not the time to launch a military strike against Iran. Well, everybody in the room except one person: Chris Miller. The new acting defense secretary didn't want war with Iran, but he also didn't think he should be the one telling Trump he couldn't do it. Miller believed it was technically possible to deliver a debilitating strike on Iran's Natanz nuclear facility. It could be done, but it would also be a high-risk operation. Miller believed if Trump could see exactly what it would take, there was no way he would order it.

"I would play the fucking madman," Miller told me. "And everybody else would be like, 'All right, he's the new guy. He's fucking insane. Don't listen to him.' I was like, 'Hey, if we are going to do this shit, let's do it.'"

Miller explained to me that he was intentionally playing the role of the "fucking madman" as a way to get Trump to back away from the idea. It was precisely the opposite of how Esper and others would deal with Trump. They were constantly telling him what he couldn't do. Miller was telling him what he could do. But, in fact, they were using wildly different tactics to achieve the same goal—preventing Trump from acting on his most destructive ideas.

"I have found oftentimes with provocative people, if you get more provocative than them, they then have to dial it down," Miller told me. "They're like, 'Yeah, I was fucking crazy, but that guy's batshit.'"

Four days later, *The New York Times* broke the story that the president had asked for military options to strike Iran's nuclear program. The story reported that Trump had asked for options to move against Iran "in the coming weeks" but that "senior advisors dissuaded the president from moving ahead with a military strike." The story portrayed Miller as one of those who warned against a strike. That wasn't literally correct. Miller never actually told Trump he opposed the strike. In fact, he told him, in detail, how it could be done—and that it would be effective. The whole thing alarmed Secretary of State Pompeo, who later placed a call to Attorney General Barr. Pompeo told him he was concerned about what was happening at the Pentagon and that the new leadership over there could push the country into war. But to Chris Miller, it was a high-risk, high-stakes case of reverse psychology.

One of the most mysterious figures in Chris Miller's Pentagon was Ezra Cohen, the official who escorted him into the building just minutes after Esper's departure. Cohen had worked under Michael Flynn at both the Defense Intelligence Agency (DIA) and the National Security Council.* He wasn't active on social media and almost never spoke to the press. Little was publicly known about him aside from the basics of his biography—he was a graduate of the University of Pennsylvania who had worked at the DIA as a member of the Defense Clandestine Services, serving for a while in Afghanistan. Flynn had brought him into the White House as the senior director for intelligence programs. In July 2017, *The Atlantic* did a lengthy but highly speculative profile of him, saying, "Thirty-one-year-old Ezra

---

*Although Cohen worked at the DIA while Flynn was the DIA director, he served in a junior role and did not actually meet Flynn until 2016—nearly two years after Flynn was forced out of the DIA and retired from the army.

Cohen-Watnick holds the intelligence portfolio on the National Security Council—but almost everything about him is a mystery."

"Ask around about Ezra Cohen-Watnick, and people get defensive," wrote the author, Rosie Gray. "Some profess not to know him, or ask why anyone would want to write about him. Others simply refuse to discuss him."

Cohen was the subject of intense speculation because of his ties to Flynn, who was pushing some of the most outlandish conspiracy theories about the election and suggesting the military should play a role in preventing Joe Biden from becoming president. To Trump's critics—and more than a few of his allies—Cohen was seen as a protégé of Flynn—somebody who shared the retired general's lunatic views and now had one of the most important jobs in the Pentagon. The retired general apparently also believed Cohen was his man at the Pentagon. Not long after Cohen was promoted to the top intelligence post at the Pentagon, Flynn called him.

It was shortly after Thanksgiving 2020. Cohen was traveling in the Middle East and was surprised to see the call come in. It had been nearly three years since they had last spoken and Flynn had been through a lot since they last talked. He had twice pled guilty to lying to the FBI, and, for a time, was a cooperating witness in Robert Mueller's special counsel investigation into Russia's interference in the 2016 election. Flynn's cooperation, however, came to an abrupt end when he retained Sidney Powell as his attorney and he attempted to withdraw his guilty pleas. On November 25, 2020, President Trump gave Flynn a broad and unconditional pardon. It was a few days after Flynn received his pardon that he called Cohen.

"Where are you?" Flynn asked him.

When Cohen told him he was in Middle East, Flynn told him to cut his trip short and get back to the United States immediately because there were big things about to happen.

Cohen thought the call was strange and told him he could not come home early but agreed to talk to him after he returned. When they spoke the following week, the conversation was even stranger.

"We need you," Flynn told him. He said there was going to be an epic showdown over the election results. He said he needed to get orders signed, that ballots needed to be seized, and that extraordinary measures needed to be taken to stop Democrats from stealing the election.

Cohen had enormous respect for Flynn, and the retired general had given him one of the most important jobs on the National Security Council when he was just thirty years old. But as Flynn ranted about the election fight, he felt his old boss sounded manic. He didn't sound like the same guy he had worked for.

"Sir, the election is over," Cohen told him. "It's time to move on."

"You're a quitter!" Flynn yelled over the phone. "This is not over! Don't be a quitter!"

After another couple minutes of yelling, Flynn hung up the phone. It was the last time the two men talked.

But it wasn't the last time Flynn and his conspiracy-crazed allies attempted to reach out to the new team at the Pentagon. They seemed to think the senior ranks of the Pentagon leadership were now stocked with real Trump loyalists who would help them fight to overturn the election.

Shortly after Flynn called him, Cohen received a call from Sidney Powell, Flynn's former lawyer who was now advising President Trump and, like Flynn, promoting some of the craziest theories about the election. Powell called Cohen with a bizarre request.

Her request was specific, urgent, and highly sensitive. It was also completely insane.

"[CIA Director] Gina Haspel has been hurt and taken into

"Why did you lie to the American people and why should we trust what you have to say now?" That was my question to President Trump on September 10, 2020.
(Getty Images/Drew Angerer)

President Trump walks into the White House briefing room on April 23, 2020, for a press conference during which he infamously suggests injecting disinfectant as a possible treatment for coronavirus: "And then I see the disinfectant, where it knocks it out in a minute. One minute. And is there a way we can do something like that, by injection inside or almost a cleaning? Because you see it gets in the lungs, and it does a tremendous number on the lungs. So it would be interesting to check that." *(White House photo by Andrea Hanks)*

The day after he talked about injecting disinfectant, President Trump welcomed congressional leaders to the White House for a bill signing. Afterward he had lunch with Kevin McCarthy, Steve Scalise, and Liz Cheney. Over lunch, McCarthy told him he should stop holding daily press conferences. *(White House photo by Shealah Craighead)*

The coronavirus press conferences became contentious and combative. But the pandemic dramatically limited the number of people in the room—to just fourteen reporters. (*Doug Mills*)

White House briefing on April 22, 2020. (*White House photo by D. Myles Cullen*)

The Trump reelection campaign officially kicked off with a rally in Orlando on June 18, 2019. I was there with my ABC News colleagues Ben Siegel, Rachel Scott, and Will Steakin. *(Courtesy of the author)*

During the COVID-dominated final stretch of the campaign, nobody attended more Trump rallies than Will Steakin. *(Photo by Will Steakin)*

On June 1, 2020, Trump and his entourage head out of the White House gates for the most infamous photo op of his presidency. *(White House photo by Shealah Craighead)*

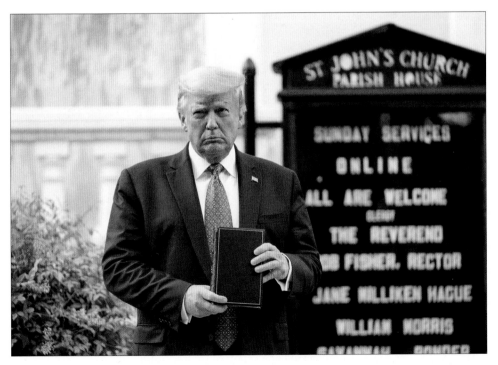

That evening, Trump held the Bible, but he did not open it. Asked if it was his Bible, he answered, "It's a Bible." *(White House photo by Shealah Craighead)*

On September 26, 2020, Trump nominated Amy Coney Barrett to the Supreme Court before a packed crowd in the Rose Garden. *(White House photo by Amy Rossetti)*

I declined to attend the event in person and reported from the other side of the White House. At least eight people who were in the Rose Garden became infected with the coronavirus. *(White House photo by Andrea Hanks)*

Trump poses with Johnny McEntee and the staff of the Office of Presidential Personnel. "It was the Rockettes and the Dungeons and Dragons group," a senior White House official said to me. In fact, one of the people McEntee hired had performed with the Radio City Rockettes. *(White House photo)*

Johnny McEntee was Trump's "body guy"—the person who carried the president's bags wherever he went. But in February 2020, the twenty-nine-year-old McEntee added a new title: Director of the Office of Presidential Personnel. He became Trump's enforcer, rewarding his friends and purging those considered insufficiently loyal. As one senior Trump official who worked with McEntee told me, "He became the deputy president." *(Getty Images/Saul Loeb)*

Cult of Personality. This photograph of Donald Trump, encased in a golden frame, hung outside the press secretary's office from late 2019 until early 2020. *(Courtesy of the author)*

Dr. Sean Conley and the team treating coronavirus patient Donald Trump at the Walter Reed National Military Medical Center. Trump was very sick—far sicker than Dr. Conley acknowledged—but even from his hospital room, he was thinking about the Trump Show. Trump instructed Conley to go before the cameras with his full team of doctors, all dressed in white lab coats. *(White House photo by Tia Dufo)*

Regarding his dramatic return to the White House after being treated at Walter Reed for the coronavirus, Trump told me, "It was like a Broadway production." *(White House photo by Andrea Hanks)*

Lawyer Lin Wood was brought in to help with the Trump legal effort by Donald Trump Jr. This photo was taken in the Oval Office in March 2020. On January 1, 2021, Wood predicted Vice President Pence would "face execution by firing squad." *(White House photo by Joyce Boghosian)*

Six days after the election, Trump fired Defense Secretary Mark Esper and installed Chris Miller as acting defense secretary. Here Miller is with Kash Patel, whom the White House made his chief of staff. *(Defense Department photo)*

Four days before the Capitol riot, I saw Kevin McCarthy walking on the National Mall. I asked him what kind of speech he was going to give when Congress convened on January 6, 2021, to certify the election. Would he denounce the lies about election fraud and finally acknowledge that Joe Biden had won the election? *(Courtesy of the author)*

Election night at the White House. At the beginning of the evening, the Trump inner circle was all smiles, thinking Trump was heading toward a big victory. From left to right: Lara Trump, Eric Trump, Bill Stepien, Jared Kushner, Ivanka Trump, Donald Trump Jr., Mark Meadows, and Stephen Miller. *(White House photo)*

The Trump campaign essentially moved into the White House on election night. This was the war room set up in the Map Room, where FDR tracked Allied progress during World War II. *(White House photo)*

As the night wore on and Trump's early lead started to evaporate, you could see the look of horror on the faces of the president's son Eric Trump and his son-in-law, Jared Kushner. *(White House photo)*

More worried faces in the White House Map Room on election night. *(White House photo)*

"I do regret the vote." When I interviewed Liz Cheney in May 2021, she told me she regretted voting for Donald Trump.
(Photo by Allison Pecorin)

Early in the evening of January 4, Trump summoned Vice President Pence to the Oval Office and made him listen to two lawyers who insisted he had the power to reject Biden's electoral votes when he presided over the certification of the election results. *(White House photo)*

On January 6, Vice President Pence was taken to an underground loading dock beneath the Capitol complex. That night, Pence put out this photo. I have seen many other photos of Pence during the siege, but he would not allow me to publish them. *(White House photo by Myles Cullen)*

Staffers planning Biden's inauguration barricaded themselves into S-407, a room on the fourth floor of the Capitol, during the January 6 riot. The only thing they had to defend themselves with were ceremonial hammers like this one. *(Courtesy of the author)*

During the riot, one Republican congressman retreated into a small private bathroom in Kevin McCarthy's office. He grabbed this Civil War sword that had been on display near McCarthy's desk to use in case the rioters broke in. *(Courtesy of the author)*

Representative Cedric Richmond (D-LA) barricaded himself in the Lincoln Room off Statuary Hall during the riot. He planned to go down this trap door if the rioters broke in. *(Photo by Ben Siegel)*

This is the handwritten tally of electoral votes during the certification of Thomas Jefferson's victory of John Adams in the election of 1800. As vice president, Jefferson presided over his victory. Trump became convinced Jefferson used his power as vice president to ensure his own victory. There is no historical evidence to back that up. *(National Archives)*

After January 6, 2021, Jennifer Krafchik of the Office of the Senate Curator showed me the three mahogany boxes used to hold the electoral votes. If these boxes had been seized by the rioters, it's not clear how the counting and certification could have proceeded. *(Photo by Allison Pecorin)*

Chris Liddell holds the record as the longest-serving member of the Trump White House staff. He asked me to take this picture shortly before noon on January 20. *(Courtesy of the author)*

After Senate Republicans rejected the formation of a special committee to investigate January 6, Liz Cheney sent Mitch McConnell a text message reading, "Historian David McCullough has described the statue of Clio, the Muse of History, standing over the North door and Statuary Hall. She takes notes in her book, reminding all of us that our words will be measured by history." *(Photo by Kevin Drennen)*

Police drew their guns on the House floor as rioters tried to break into the main entrance of the House Chamber. Representative Troy Nehls (R-TX), a retired sheriff and army veteran of the wars in Iraq and Afghanistan, comes face to face with the rioters looking through the shattered glass. *(Photo by J. Scott Applewhite [AP])*

Minutes before the Capitol riot started on January 6, a woman marching to the Capitol carried a sign proclaiming, "WE'RE NOT LIBERALS. WE DON'T RIOT." *(Photo by Frank Luntz)*

custody in Germany," she told Cohen. "You need to launch a special operations mission to get her."

Cohen had never before spoken to Powell and was shocked that she had called him at his direct phone line in his office. It's a phone that only rang with calls from within the Pentagon or from the White House—an unpublished number that somebody with access to the internal directory had to have given her.

Powell went on to explain that Haspel had been hurt while on a secret CIA operation to seize a computer server from a company named Scytl. The server, Powell claimed, contained evidence that hundreds of thousands, maybe millions, of votes had been switched using rigged voting machines. Powell believed Haspel had embarked on this secret mission to get the server and destroy the evidence—in other words, the CIA director was part of the conspiracy.

That's why Sidney Powell wanted Cohen to send a special operations team over to Germany immediately; they needed to get the server and force Haspel to confess.

Cohen thought Powell sounded out of her mind. He quickly got off the phone and reported the call to the acting defense secretary. But Powell didn't stop there. She then emailed Cohen with another bizarre request. She wanted help getting something called a "letter of marque."

This was a rather obscure demand. But a letter of marque from the US government would, essentially, allow Powell to act as a modern-day pirate, seizing property from US adversaries.

Seriously. It's actually a real thing.

In Article One of the US Constitution (Section 8, Clause 11), Congress is granted power to "grant Letters of Marque and Reprisal, and make Rules concerning Captures on Land and Water." At the time it was written, the idea was to give privately owned ships—privateers, a.k.a. government-authorized pirates—the authority to raid merchant ships aiding an enemy during time of war.

Why did Sidney Powell want a letter of marque? Did she want to conduct her own mission to seize some mysterious computer server in Germany? Who the hell knows.

The efforts of Michael Flynn and Sidney Powell to enlist Ezra Cohen in their efforts to overturn the election results, which are reported here for the first time, are among the strangest and most potentially dangerous actions taken by Trump's allies in the aftermath of the election. Just think about the request from Sidney Powell. She was asking the top intelligence official at the Pentagon to dispatch a special operations team on a mission to capture the CIA director. And the most disturbing thing about all of this is that Powell wasn't just a lone crackpot. She was working side by side with Rudy Giuliani as a member of the president's legal team and, by late December, she would be meeting repeatedly with President Trump in the Oval Office.

Although Cohen ignored Powell's emails, the fictional story about Haspel's alleged secret mission spread throughout social media on websites associated with the QAnon conspiracy, which claimed that a secret cabal of pedophiles inside the government was working to undermine Donald Trump. QAnon adherents would become a big part of the January 6 riot at the Capitol. There were several variations of the conspiracy theory about the CIA director's mission to Germany. In one version, Haspel had been captured and sent to the US prison in Guantanamo Bay, where she was confessing to all sorts of misdeeds. In another version, she had been killed during the mission. In yet another version, military special operations troops who had been helping her had been wounded or killed.

Of course, all if it was bunk. But the conspiracy theory spread so wide that the company, Scytl, had to put out a statement saying that no server had been seized and, by the way, they don't have offices in Germany and didn't have anything to do with tabulating votes in the 2020 US election.

The CIA also received inquiries from several news organizations, prompting the agency to release a response.

"Well . . . this is the most absurd inquiry I've ever addressed," CIA spokesperson Nicole de Haay emailed the Associated Press and Reuters in early December, "but I'm happy to tell you that Director Haspel is alive and well and at the office."

Crazy conspiracies about the election were also being pushed from within the walls of the Pentagon. In another incident in mid-December, Kash Patel, the acting defense secretary's chief of staff, attempted to use the resources of the Department of Defense to chase down a wacky report that military satellites in Italy had been used to rig voting machines in the United States. Patel apparently believed that two individuals who were imprisoned in Italy had information about this dastardly scheme. The two men had recently been charged with hacking into the computer systems of an Italy-based military contractor back in 2015, but Patel had heard that one of the men had confessed to Italian authorities that their hacking operation was really an elaborate effort to use satellites to rig the US presidential election for Joe Biden. It was nuts, but the theory had spread on fringe websites and social media accounts tied to QAnon. The theory even had a name: #ItalyGate.

In late December, Patel asked Ezra Cohen to send the US defense attaché at the US embassy in Rome to go talk to the two men in prison. As the under seecretary of defense for intelligence, Cohen had responsibility for overseeing defense officials in US embassies around the world. Cohen told Patel the whole thing was crazy and refused to do it.

But the wacky conspiracy would not go away. In fact, it soon captured the attention of the White House. Chief of Staff Mark Meadows called Chris Miller to ask him about it. And then on Saturday, January 2, Miller and Patel together called the director of the Defense Intelligence Agency, Lieutenant General Scott Berrier, and made the same request Patel had made to Cohen. They wanted DIA to dispatch the defense attaché at the embassy in Rome to go see the two Italian prisoners and find out what they had to say. Lieutenant General Berrier agreed to look into it and reported back to Miller a few days later that the strange story was entirely untrue. Neither prisoner had said anything at all about interfering with the election and their case was entirely unrelated to anything remotely involving the 2020 US presidential election. It's unclear whether the defense attaché at the US embassy in Rome was actually dispatched to talk to the men in prison. A spokesperson for Lieutenant General Berrier would not comment on the record.

It was a crazy QAnon conspiracy theory—something from the fringe of the fringe of the political extreme—and yet it had captured the attention of the White House chief of staff and the top leadership of the Pentagon, including the urgent phone call on a Saturday with the head of the Defense Intelligence Agency. And this went beyond the Pentagon. On December 30, Meadows emailed acting Attorney General Jeffrey Rosen asking him to look into the #ItalyGate conspiracy. Meadows's emails on this matter, which were made public in June 2021 by the House Oversight Committee, included a letter dated December 27, 2020, purportedly written by a man named Carlo Goria with a company identified as USAerospace Partners. The letter, which is addressed to "Illustrious Mr. President," spelled out the conspiracy and added a few wacky details tying the plot to the Italian defense company Leonardo S.p.A., which, the memo said, "changed the US election result from President Trump to Joe Biden" and had done so "using advanced military encryption capabilities." And the conspiracy, it alleged, was done "in coordination with senior US intelligence officials." When I tried to track down Carlo Goria, I found a Facebook page in Italian. I can't be sure if it is the same person, but the profile picture for "Carlo Goria" was a picture of the main character in the movie *Dr. Strangelove.*

Whoever the real Carlo Goria is, Chief of Staff Mark Meadows was asking the acting attorney general and the acting defense secretary to investigate this nonsense. In an attempt to get to the bottom of where all this stuff was coming from, I began to trace the conspiracy to its source.

Michele Ballarin, who also goes by the names Michele Roosevelt Edwards and Michele Lyn Golden, was known to senior officials at the Pentagon as "the heiress." Ballarin, who was sixty-five years old at the time, claimed to live in a twenty-two-bedroom Gatsby-like mansion in Warrenton, Virginia—but she didn't own it and never had. The place was actually for sale in 2020—with an asking price of $33 million—and she had used a real estate license to get access to the property, arranging meetings there as if it were her home. When I called the listing agent for the property, he said that Ballarin "is a great actor, but not an honest person" and that she had no connection whatsoever to the property.

Ballarin is listed in various websites and news stories as the chairman of USAerospace Partners—the same company as the purported author of the #ItalyGate memo Mark Meadows had sent to the acting attorney general.

This is where it gets weird. Or, I should say, weirder.

Ms. Ballarin's first contact with the Trump administration had come not long after the election. Through an intermediary, she arranged a secret meeting with Josh Steinman, senior director for cybersecurity on the National Security Council. Insisting on total secrecy, she convinced Steinman to meet her at a grocery store in Virginia.

Ballarin arrived at the grocery story dressed like a billionaire heiress, decked out with ostentatious jewelry. She had an entourage that included somebody she called "the sergeant major" and another person she called "my banker." The scene was so strange Steinman thought it was an elaborate prank and assumed he was being filmed by a hidden camera. Ballarin started spinning her story about Italian military satellites controlling voting machines. After I found out about this from another high-level official in the Trump administration, I reached out to Steinman. He would not talk to me about the meeting on the record. But Steinman did talk to at least one other senior official about what happened, describing Ballarin's information as "totally crazy" and saying the grocery-store rendezvous was one of the most bizarre experiences of his professional life.

Ballarin's attempted back channel to the National Security Council may not have worked, but she kept trying. Her goal was to get her "information" about the #ItalyGate conspiracy to President Trump. Two senior officials at the Pentagon—who both referred to Ballarin only as "the heiress"—told me that she had contact with others at the Pentagon. It wasn't the first time Ballarin had ingratiated herself to people at high levels of the government. In 2008, she had been featured in news stories as someone negotiating for the release of a Ukrainian ship that had been seized by Somali pirates. The pirates, it was reported, called her "Amira"—that's *princess* in Arabic—but her outreach interfered with the government of Ukraine's efforts to get the ship back and prompted the Ukrainian foreign minister to send a cable to then–Secretary of State Hillary Clinton pleading to keep Ballarin away from the negotiations. The cable, which was later posted by WikiLeaks, said Ballarin had "absolutely no authority from the owner of the vessel" but "her actions incite the pirates to the groundless increase of the ransom sum . . . thus creating an obstacle for the positive solution of this issue."*

When I attempted to reach out to Ms. Ballarin in June 2021, I received a call back from a woman named Maria Strollo Zack, who agreed to pass my questions about the grocery store rendezvous on to Ms. Ballarin. She got back to me a day later saying Ms. Ballarin was too busy to talk to me due to "international travel," but I found that Zack herself has had a central role in spreading the #ItalyGate conspiracy. In an interview on a far-right podcast called *The Right Side with Doug Billings*, Zack said she had spoken to Mark Meadows about #ItalyGate in December. "He listened and took my calls," she said of Meadows. And then she said she got her big breakthrough on Christmas Eve when she went to dinner at Mar-a-Lago and saw Trump himself. "I told him I had the best Christmas present ever," she said. "I know who stole the election."

Zack kept spreading the conspiracy theory after the New Year, posting a "news release" about it on the website of a group she founded called Nations in Action. The news release was headlined "Senior IT Expert at Global Defense Contractor Testifies in Italian Federal Court; He and Others Switched Votes throughout America in the U.S. Presidential Race." It included a quote from Zack, saying, "Make no mistake, this is a coup d'etat that we will stop in the name of justice and free and fair elections." The press release was posted on January 6, 2021—the day of the Capitol riot.

Zack says she also had been in touch with Michael Flynn about #Italy-Gate, but Flynn was doing more than spinning conspiracy theories

---

*Letter from Foreign Minister Volodymyr Ohryzko to Secretary of State Hillary Clinton, February 5, 2009.

during the final weeks of the Trump presidency. He was openly musing about declaring martial law and using the military to seize voting machines. In an interview with Newsmax on December 17, the retired three-star general outlined Trump's options.

"He could immediately on his order seize every single one of these machines around the country," Flynn told Newsmax anchor Greg Kelly. "He could also order, within the swing states, if he wanted to, he could take military capabilities and he could place them in those states and basically rerun an election in each of those states."

Again, it was all insane. Flynn was a highly decorated retired three-star general who had risen to the top ranks of military intelligence. I had learned he had called to try to get help for his manic plans from Cohen. It's hard to believe he wasn't making calls to others as well.

Acting Defense Secretary Miller wanted no part of any of that. After all, his goals for his brief tenure were "No military coup, no major war, and no troops in the streets." But while he felt totally confident there would be no military coup on his watch, by late December, Miller was less confident about there being no major war.

The problem again was Iran. This time the issue was not the nuclear program, but a steady stream of intelligence that Iran was planning to assassinate an American official as retaliation for the January 3, 2020, assassination of Iranian Major General Qasem Soleimani. And on December 20, Iranian-backed militias in Iraq unleashed a barrage of twenty-one rockets at the US embassy in Baghdad. It was the largest attack in more than a decade on the heavily defended Green Zone, where the US embassy and a US military base are located.

The next day, Trump convened his national security team at the White House. After the meeting, Trump publicly blamed Iran for the attack.

"Our embassy in Baghdad got hit Sunday by several rockets," Trump tweeted. "Guess where they were from: IRAN."

And then, in a second tweet, a warning.

"Some friendly healthy advice to Iran: If one American is killed, I will hold Iran responsible. Think it over."

In this case, Trump's tweets were more restrained and measured than what was actually happening. The intelligence on Iran's plans for the one-year anniversary of the Soleimani assassination was alarming and so was the rocket attack on the embassy compound. At Trump's direction, General Milley sent a message to the Iranians—a message that had to go through the Swiss government because the United States does not have diplomatic relations with Iran—that if an American were to be killed, the response from the United States would be overwhelming and disproportionate.

Here's how Miller summed up the message to me: "If you kill an American, we are going to fucking smoke you."

There was a real threat coming from Iran. There was less than a month to go of the Trump presidency. And Trump was desperately trying to stay in power. The whole thing was toxic and dangerous. The threat of a military confrontation was real and it wasn't just being driven by Trump. Miller no longer needed to be the provocative voice when Trump met with his national security team. The military leadership was advocating a major strike if Iran hit first and killed an American. General Kenneth F. McKenzie Jr., the commander of the military's Central Command, presented plans to hit Iranian targets in Yemen, Iraq, Syria—as well as inside Iran. Miller was on board, too, although he wanted to hit Iranian targets in the region and opposed plans for attacks inside Iran itself.

Here's how Miller summarized what he told the president. "We can fucking rip their guts out, but that risks an escalation cycle, and you got elected to get out of wars, not to get into wars."

What would have happened if Iran or a group tied to Iran had fired another rocket at the US embassy and, this time, succeeded in killing at least one American or more? What would have happened if Iran or one of its proxies followed through on threats to assassinate an American official? How would a president consumed in his effort to overturn an election have reacted? On this one, the military was fully ready to follow whatever order he gave.

For Miller, it was the most stressful time during his brief tenure as acting secretary of defense. Looking back, it was more than stressful. It was terrifying.

Visibly relieved it didn't happen, Miller told me, "I thought if we miscalculated, we could start a regional war."

CHAPTER ELEVEN

THE UNKINDEST CUT

One of the many strange things about 2020 was the way Donald Trump turned against Attorney General Bill Barr. For Democrats, Barr was the number one villain in the Trump cabinet. They saw him as a Trump lackey willing to politicize the Justice Department in the service of Donald Trump. It was Barr, along with Deputy Attorney General Rod Rosenstein, who made the decision not to prosecute Trump for obstruction of justice related to Robert Mueller's Russia investigation. Mueller had accused Barr of mischaracterizing his findings and Barr made it clear that he essentially agreed with Trump that the Russia investigation was a witch hunt. Barr also had tangled with career prosecutors, overriding their decisions in ways favorable to convicted Trump allies Michael Flynn and Roger Stone. As one liberal critic put it, "He transformed the Justice Department into a partisan cudgel for President Donald Trump, undercutting probes that might damage the White House and doling out special treatment for presidential allies who broke the law."*

---

*"Bill Barr Will Go Down in History as Trump's Worst Enabler," Matt Ford, *The New Republic*, December 15, 2020.

And yet Donald Trump spent much of 2020 bitterly complaining about Bill Barr, culminating in a break so severe that it resulted in what multiple witnesses have told me was the most frightening explosion of Trump anger they had ever seen in the White House.

The relationship took its first big hit in May 2020 after Donald Trump did an early-morning interview with Maria Bartiromo on the Fox Business Network. The interview, which was conducted in the Rose Garden, was bizarre even by the standards of Trump interviews with Bartiromo, which often went off the rails because she routinely cheered him on when he said crazy things. With the economy battered by the pandemic and the United States nearing its hundred thousandth death from coronavirus at the time, Trump still wanted to look back at the Russia investigation, which had ended more than a year earlier. Trump portrayed the investigation itself as a crime—a crime, he falsely claimed, that began when Barack Obama okayed spying on his campaign. Now he was telling Bartiromo that Obama—and Biden, too!—should be in prison for what they did to him.

"If I were a Democrat instead of a Republican," Trump told her, "I think everybody would've been in jail a long time ago, and I'm talking with fifty-year sentences. It is a disgrace what's happened. This is the greatest political scam, hoax, in the history of our country."

"Well, it is the biggest political scandal we've ever seen," Bartiromo preposterously agreed.

"People should be going to jail for this stuff," Trump continued. "This was all Obama. This was all Biden."

The interview irritated Barr. A year earlier, he had appointed US Attorney John Durham to investigate the origins of the Russia investigation. Trump applauded that move and Barr had taken heat for it from Democrats. There were legitimate questions about the way the Russia investigation began, including whether the FBI acted appropriately when it obtained a surveillance warrant for Trump campaign advisor Carter Page, but the idea that the Justice Department would prosecute Obama or Biden over any of it was nuts.

Barr felt he needed to respond publicly. So a few days after the Bartiromo interview, he scheduled a press conference on another matter, but came armed with a statement he planned to read when asked about the president's comments.

And, sure enough, the first question came from Pete Williams of NBC News: "President Trump has recently said that he wants to see the Justice Department prosecute figures of the Obama administration, President Obama and Joseph Biden, for what he calls crimes. Is that something DOJ will do?"

Barr's answer went on for a full five minutes. He read it with an air of seriousness and gravity, his voice appearing to shake a bit when he started. The words were aimed like a missile directly at the president.

"Over the past few decades, there have been increasing attempts to use the criminal justice system as a political weapon," he said. "The legal tactic has been to gin up allegations of criminality by one's political opponents based on the flimsiest of legal theories. This is not a good development. This is not good for our political life. And it's not good for the criminal justice system. And as long as I am attorney general, the criminal justice system will not be used for partisan political ends. And this is especially true for the upcoming elections in November."

Before turning to the question of prosecuting Biden or Obama, Barr said the treatment of Trump during the Russia investigation was "abhorrent" and that the allegations against him were "false and utterly baseless." It's the kind of thing Trump loved to hear his attorney general say, but then Barr made it clear the Justice Department would not be prosecuting Trump's political opponents in the middle of a presidential campaign. In fact, neither man had ever been the target of the investigation.

"As to President Obama and Vice President Biden," Barr said, "whatever their level of involvement, based on the information I have today, I don't expect Mr. Durham's work will lead to a criminal investigation of either man."

His words were measured, but the message was crystal clear—and not what Donald Trump wanted to hear.

Trump apparently really did expect Barr to begin going after Biden and Obama. Immediately after that press conference, the relationship changed. Trump had been in the habit of regularly calling his attorney general over the phone, often two or three times a day. Barr would often receive calls at home at night, occasionally after ten, when the attorney general was either in bed or getting ready for bed. After Barr effectively ruled out prosecuting Biden and Obama, Trump put him in the presidential cabinet equivalent of a time-out. He still saw Barr at White House meetings from time to time, but the phone calls became less and less frequent.

As the election approached, Trump's frustration with Barr would pop up in interviews the president did on Fox News and various conservative news outlets. He complained that there had been no report released on Durham's investigation and that Barr had not prosecuted Biden's son Hunter for alleged misdeeds related to work in Ukraine and China. In August, Trump again went on Bartiromo's television show and said, "Bill Barr can go down as the greatest attorney general in the history of our country or he can go down as just an average Joe." In Trump's view, the way to be the greatest attorney general ever, of course, was to prosecute Trump's political enemies.

"It's a disgrace. It's an embarrassment," Trump said on Rush Limbaugh's radio show in October after *Axios* reported that Barr would not release anything from Durham's review of the Russia investigation before the election. "See, this is what I mean with the Republicans. They don't play the tough game."

The week before the election, *The Washington Post* ran a story headlined, "Barr tells friends he would like to remain attorney general in second term if Trump is reelected." That was true, but Barr later told me he fully expected Trump to lose.

"I had a view all the way through that the president was going to lose," Barr told me during an interview at his home in McLean, Virginia, more than six months after he left office. "He was making it too much of a base election. God bless him, he turned out his base, but I felt he had to repair the bridges he had burned [with moderate voters] in the suburbs."

When the big day came, Barr dropped by the election-night party at the White House, but left early before Trump arrived. He hadn't seen the president for weeks and had no desire to see him then. When the president started making claims of fraud during the following days, Barr said nothing publicly.

Johnny McEntee, Trump's enforcer and the director of presidential personnel, had his own idea about how to deal with the Department of Justice. He fired the staffer serving as the DOJ White House liaison and installed a conservative activist named Heidi Stirrup in the job. Stirrup was primarily known as an anti-abortion activist who had worked for years as a mid-level staffer for Republicans in Congress. She had no legal experience whatsoever, but she was intensely loyal to Trump—and to McEntee. She would be McEntee's eyes and ears at the Justice Department. Barr's team wanted no part of her and actually managed to delay her arrival for a while by slow-walking her FBI background check, but a few days after the election, the background check was completed and she was cleared to start work.

Stirrup showed up at the Justice Department like she was ready to take charge. Her car was an easy one to spot in the DOJ parking lot;

it was covered with Trump stickers—unusual at a department where even the most political of political appointees try to appear to be above the fray. On her first full day in the office, she went in to meet a senior official on Barr's team. It didn't go well. She began the meeting by yelling at him for not doing anything about what she said was an attempt to steal the election.

"You need to wake up to the fact this election is being stolen!" she screamed. "It needs to be stopped!"

"White House liaison" sounds like a lofty title, but the job is really to act as a messenger. It's not a particularly high-level or powerful job. Every cabinet department has one. The liaison doesn't have any responsibility for setting or implementing policy. They facilitate communications between the agency and the White House. The job certainly doesn't entail yelling at senior department officials about criminal charges. But McEntee had attempted to redefine the role, dispatching people to the cabinet agencies to shake things up and push the leadership to more aggressively serve Trump's personal interests. He didn't want people who would simply be messengers. McEntee wanted people who would boss around the senior officials and report back.

At DOJ, Barr's team saw Stirrup as more than just annoying. Her behavior made them worry she would try to get information on whether they were doing anything to investigate the allegations of fraud coming from the White House, and even report back to the White House on her findings. This would have been highly unethical and cross a bright red line—the White House is not supposed to interfere in criminal investigations.

The next time Stirrup came around to berate the senior official, he asked her if she would like to deliver her message directly to the attorney general, and with that he brought her in to see Barr. Most people who first meet Barr find him intimidating, but not Heidi Stirrup.

"The election is being stolen," she lectured the attorney general.

"You need better people doing these investigations." And she told him she had a list of people, presumably provided by McEntee, that he needed to hire.

"We have to support the president!" she declared.

Now she was yelling at the attorney general. He had never seen this kind of behavior. A physically large and imposing presence, Barr was seventy years old and only the second person in American history confirmed twice as attorney general; before serving in Trump's cabinet, he had been attorney general for President George H. W. Bush in the early 1990s. Barr calmly explained to her the limits of what the Justice Department could do. She left and never saw him again. By the end of the week, Barr ordered her banned from the building. Her pass was deactivated and security was instructed not to let her in the building. She still had the title of White House liaison, but was never again allowed inside the Justice Department.

Barr avoided contact with Trump during the days following the election and said nothing publicly about election fraud. But on November 9, he sent a letter to US attorneys around the country that was interpreted by many to be a sign he might use the Department of Justice to help Trump's crusade to dispute the election. Under long-standing DOJ policy, the Justice Department does not investigate voter fraud until after an election is certified. The theory behind the policy is that DOJ's responsibility is to prosecute crimes, not to get involved in election disputes. So, under the policy, federal prosecutors only get involved after the election is over and the final results are certified.

But in his November 9 letter to federal prosecutors, Barr reversed that policy and said "substantial allegations" of voter irregularities could be investigated before the election was certified if the alleged irregularities "could potentially impact the outcome" of the election in any state. The move was highly controversial, prompting the career prosecutor with responsibility for overseeing investigations related to election fraud, Richard Pilger, to resign in protest. Law professor Stephen Vladeck of the University of Texas said Barr was playing into Trump's strategy of delegitimizing the results of a proper election and called the move "one of the more problematic acts of any attorney general in my lifetime."

But Barr already had concluded it was highly unlikely there were any credible allegations of fraud big enough to tip the scales in the election. After all, he had fully expected Trump to lose and therefore was not surprised by the outcome. He also knew that at some point Trump was going to confront him about it and he wanted to be able to say he had looked into the allegations and there was nothing to them. So, in addition to giving prosecutors a green light to open investigations where there were clear and credible allegations of substantial fraud, Barr began his own unofficial inquiry into the major allegations the president and his allies were making.

"My attitude was it was put up or shut up time," Barr told me. "If there was evidence of fraud, I had no motive to suppress it. But my suspicion all the way along was that there was nothing there. It was all bullshit."

The Department of Justice ended up conducting no formal investigations of voter fraud during the weeks after the election, but Barr's informal review looked at whether there was anything at all to back up what the president was saying. Here are a few of the things he looked at:

BALLOT "DUMPS" IN MILWAUKEE AND DETROIT

Trump talked about this all the time and kept talking about it even after he left the White House. He said he was winning early in the evening (true) and then massive amounts of ballots were brought in late in the evening in the Democratically controlled cities of Milwaukee and Detroit that tipped the scales for Biden. Barr contacted the US attorneys responsible for Michigan and Wisconsin and asked them if there was anything suspicious about the way the votes came in. They looked at the historical data from previous elections and how the voting process worked. It quickly became obvious that there were no mysterious "ballot dumps" and that the vote counting process went just as it did in previous elections—including the election Trump won four years earlier.

In Detroit, for example, ballots were counted at one central location—a large downtown arena called the TCF Center. As "proof" of fraud, Trump's allies pointed to videos showing boxes filled with ballots arriving to be counted at the TCF Center after the eight p.m. deadline for votes to be cast. But with a quick phone call, Barr found out there was a perfectly logical explanation for why this happened. It had to do with how the 662 precincts in Wayne County, home to Detroit, count their votes.

"In every other county, they count the ballots at the precinct, but in Wayne County, they bring them into one central counting place. So the boxes are coming in all night. The fact that boxes are coming in—well, that's what they do." Nothing unusual or illegal. The ballots are turned in at the precincts by eight p.m. and then transported—in boxes—to the place where they are counted.

And there's more—Trump actually did a little better against Biden in Detroit than he did there against Hillary Clinton in 2016. Biden got a thousand fewer votes in the city of Detroit than Clinton received in 2016 and Trump got five thousand more votes there than he did four years earlier. Trump didn't lose Michigan because of illegal ballots cast in Detroit. He lost Michigan because Biden beat him badly in the suburbs.

OUT-OF-STATE VOTERS IN NEVADA

At a press conference in Las Vegas two days after the election, the Trump campaign claimed thousands of people who were not residents of the state voted illegally. "Non-residents have voted," declared Ric Grenell. Grenell had briefly served as the acting director of national intelligence in the Trump administration, but this turned out to be a particularly dumb allegation.

The Trump campaign sent Barr a letter claiming to have a list of 3,062 people who illegally voted after moving out of state. A few days later, the number grew as conservative activist Matt Schlapp declared at another Trump campaign press conference that nine thousand "non-Nevadans" voted. Barr asked the US attorney's office in Nevada to see if there was anything to the allegation. A quick survey revealed that there was nothing nefarious going on.

"They found out that for all but a few, there were legitimate reasons for voting from out of state," Barr told me. "Most of them were military. There was another chunk that were people receiving extended medical treatment outside the state." Others were Nevada residents who were studying out of state.

After sampling several areas around the state, they only found a handful of people who voted from out of state without an obviously legitimate reason.

"So, the number of actual improper voters was *de minimus*," Barr told me.

By the way, *de miniumus*, according to the Merriam-Webster dictionary, means "lacking significance or importance: so minor as to merit disregard."

RIGGED VOTING MACHINES

Barr brought in cybersecurity experts at the Department of Homeland Security and the FBI and received two briefings at the Command Center in the Justice Department headquarters about whether there was any merit to the allegations the machines were used to rig the election.

"We realized from the beginning it was just bullshit," Barr told me, noting that even if the machines somehow changed the count, it would show up when they were recounted by hand.

"It's a counting machine," he said. "And they save everything that was counted. So, you just reconcile the two. There had been no discrepancy reported anywhere and I'm still not aware of any discrepancy."

None of these inquiries amounted to a formal criminal investigation, but Barr spent considerable time chasing down cockamamie allegations because he knew he was going to eventually see Trump, who was going to demand to know why the Justice Department was not doing more to stop the people Trump claimed were stealing the election. Barr was already hearing from Trump's allies. Even Maria Bartiromo, who was making the wild allegations about fraud the centerpiece of her shows on Fox News and the Fox Business Network, called Barr to complain that the DOJ hadn't done anything to stop the Democrats from stealing the election.

"She called me up and she was screaming," Barr told me. "I yelled back at her. She's lost it."

I reached out to Bartiromo to get her response to this. After all, it's highly inappropriate for a journalist to call the attorney general and demand he do something related to a criminal investigation. Bartiromo did not respond, but a Fox News spokesperson did get back to me and denied Barr's account of the conversation on Bartiromo's behalf, adding, "It was Barr who was aggressive with her, yelling and cursing during the call."

Barr also told me he heard from Senate Majority Leader Mitch McConnell in mid-November. McConnell had an entirely different concern. Publicly, McConnell was saying very little about Trump's wild allegations other than he had a right to pursue legal challenges. But McConnell knew that Biden had legitimately won the election and he thought that Trump's baseless and embarrassing claims of fraud were damaging to the country—and to the Republican Party. Trump's refusal to concede was also complicating McConnell's efforts to win back control of the Senate. The two Republican senators from Georgia had runoff elections scheduled for January 5. To McConnell the road to victory was a simple one; Republicans needed to make the argument that with Biden soon to be in the White House, it was crucial to have a Republican-controlled Senate as a check on his power. But McConnell also knew that if he publicly shot down Trump's claims of fraud and declared Biden the winner, Trump would be enraged and likely act to sabotage the Republican senate campaigns in Georgia.

"Look, we need the president in Georgia," McConnell told Barr, "and so we cannot be frontally attacking him right now. But you're in a better position to inject some reality into this situation. You are really the only one who can do it."

"I understand that," Barr said. "And I'm going to do it at the appropriate time."

On the morning of November 23, Barr finally met with Trump. It was their first meeting since before the election. They met in the Oval

Office. Chief of Staff Mark Meadows and White House Counsel Pat Cipollone were there as well. Not surprisingly, the only thing Trump wanted to talk about was election fraud.

"I understand you guys don't think it's your role to go out and look at this," Trump told Barr.

"Mr. President, if we get specific and credible information of fraud, we will go out and look at it," Barr responded, reminding him of the controversial directive he had issued giving US attorneys the green light to investigate credible allegations of election fraud. "I have overruled people at DOJ to give us that latitude. I'm going to use my judgment as to what we're going to look at."

Meadows didn't say much at this meeting, but Cipollone backed up Barr.

"Mr. President, let the department do its work," the White House counsel said. "If there's something to look at, I'm sure they're going to look at it."

Barr pointed out that even as the president and his allies had been claiming massive fraud, none of the lawsuits the campaign's lawyers had filed in court actually claimed fraud.

"They're alleging violation of the rules, and that's for your people to litigate in court," Barr said. "We don't take a position on that. You know, the Justice Department wasn't in there during *Bush v. Gore*."

As for the allegations of fraud, Barr told Trump he fully expected the Justice Department to come under attack for not uncovering evidence.

"You have to expect that all you're going to be hearing from Giuliani and the rest of these people is that Justice isn't looking at stuff," Barr said. "They're out there promising fraud and they're empty-handed. And now people need an explanation of why is there no evidence. Well, their answer is, 'Justice isn't looking at it.' But the problem isn't the absence of Justice, the problem is the absence of evidence."

Barr left the meeting concerned that the president simply was not listening to reason. He didn't appear to be anywhere near the point of conceding he had lost the election. It was past time to begin the complicated process of transitioning to the Biden administration. Before he left the White House, Barr met with Meadows, Cipollone, and a couple of other senior advisors close to the president. Barr later described the conversation to me.

"This is getting serious," he told Meadows and the others. "I mean, how far is he going to take this thing? This is complicating the transition."

Barr told me Meadows and the others assured him Trump was sensitive to the needs of the transition and would soon be changing his tone and laying the groundwork for "a graceful exit."

Hours later there was a positive sign. The administration finally took the first formal step toward a transition. Emily Murphy, the head of the General Services Administration, sent Biden a letter informing him that the transition process would begin. The letter should have been delivered more than two weeks earlier, but now that it was sent, federal agencies could begin working directly with the incoming Biden officials who would also now be able to receive classified briefings.

But within days it became perfectly clear Trump was not conceding the election. In fact, his efforts to overturn the results became more aggressive as he started to reach out directly to Republican leaders in the states whose results he was disputing to get their help. McConnell again called Barr, urging him to come out and definitively shoot down the talk of widespread fraud.

"Bill, I look around and you are the only person who can do it," McConnell told him.

So, on December 1, Barr did what McConnell had urged him to do, making his big break with Donald Trump. After a discussion with his top advisors, some of whom had been urging Barr to publicly contradict Trump's claims about the election, Barr decided he would declare publicly that the Justice Department had found no evidence of widespread election fraud. Instead of holding a press conference or releasing a statement, Barr's team planned to have Barr make the statement during an interview with the Associated Press (AP).

The interview with AP reporter Michael Balsamo happened over lunch in the attorney general's private dining room. Barr and Balsamo were joined by Will Levi, the DOJ chief of staff, and DOJ spokeswoman Kerri Kupec. Balsamo was not told the reason for the interview. When Barr dropped his bombshell between bites of salad, he mumbled his words. Balsamo wasn't sure he had caught exactly what Barr had said.

"Just to be crystal clear," Balsamo said. "Are you saying—"

"Sir, I think you better repeat what you just said," Kupec interjected.

"To date, we have not seen fraud on a scale that could have effected a different outcome in the election," Barr repeated. This time Balsamo heard him loudly and clearly.

Balsamo's story exploded on the AP newswire shortly after lunch ended.

> WASHINGTON (AP)—Disputing President Donald Trump's persistent, baseless claims, Attorney General William Barr declared Tuesday the U.S. Justice Department has uncovered no evidence of widespread voter fraud that could change the outcome of the 2020 election.

The story blew a gaping hole into the president's claims. Nobody seriously questioned Barr's conservative credentials or that he had been among Trump's most loyal and supportive cabinet secretaries.

Barr's conclusion sent the definitive message that the effort to over-turn the election was entirely without merit.

After lunch Barr and Levi had a meeting scheduled at the White House with Chief of Staff Meadows. After meeting briefly with him, they went upstairs to Cipollone's office. As they were meeting, one of the White House counsel's aides knocked on the door and told him the president wanted to see him and then, pointing to Barr, the aide said, "And he is looking for you."

Barr, Levi, and Cipollone together walked downstairs and over to the president's personal dining room near the Oval Office. Trump was sitting at the table. Meadows was sitting next to him with his arms firmly crossed over his chest and White House advisor Eric Herschmann was standing off to the side. The details of this meeting were described to me in vivid detail by several of those present. One of them told me Trump had "the eyes and mannerism of a madman" during the meeting.

With everybody but Trump and Meadows standing, Trump went off on Barr.

"I think you've noticed I haven't been talking to you much," Trump said to Barr, sarcastically adding, "I've been leaving you alone."

Barr thought the comment was reminiscent of a line in the movie *Dr. Strangelove* where the main character, Brigadier General Jack D. Ripper, says, "I do not avoid women, Mandrake, but I do deny them my essence." Trump, Barr thought, was saying that he had been de-nying him his essence.

Trump turned to Barr's comments about election fraud in the AP interview.

"Did you say that?"

"Yes," Barr responded.

"How the fuck could you do this to me? Why did you say it?"

"Because it's true."

"You must hate Trump," Trump said, referring to himself in the third person. "You must hate Trump."

Trump's face was red. Barr thought the president was trying to control himself, but Trump seemed to him angrier than he had ever seen him. As the meeting went on, Trump's anger became more explosive. The news about Barr's AP interview was dominating the news coverage on every cable news channel except the one Trump was watching. The television in the room was tuned to the right-wing, pro-Trump network One America News, which was broadcasting a committee hearing of the Michigan legislature. The hearing featured wild and disproven allegations of massive fraud, including the testimony of a woman named Melissa Carone, who had worked at the counting location in Detroit and told the committee, "Everything that happened at the TCF Center was fraud. Every single thing." The next day, Carone would testify again next to Rudy Giuliani in an appearance widely lampooned because she was slurring her words and appeared to be drunk. Carone later denied she was drunk.

"They saw the boxes going in!" Trump yelled, referring to the discredited stories about boxes of illegal ballots that were brought in to be counted late at night in Detroit.

"You know, Mr. President, there are 662 precincts in Wayne County," Barr said. Trump seemed taken aback that he knew the exact number. "It's the only county with all the boxes going to a central place. And you actually did better there this time around than you did last time."

Barr continued: "You keep on saying that the Department of Justice is not looking at this stuff, and we are looking at it in a responsible way. But your people keep on shoveling this shit out."

As Trump continued to rant about other examples of fraud,

Meadows sat silently, still with his arms crossed, his posture suggesting he agreed with Trump and that he, too, was upset by what Barr had done.

"You know, you only have five weeks, Mr. President, after an election to make legal challenges," Barr said. "This would have taken a crackerjack team with a really coherent and disciplined strategy. Instead, you have a clown show. No self-respecting lawyer is going anywhere near it. It's just a joke. That's why you are where you are."

Interestingly, Trump didn't argue when Barr told him his "clown show" legal team had wasted time. In fact, he said, "You may be right about that."

After going through his litany of claims—stolen ballots, fake ballots, dead people voting, rigged voting machines, etc.—Trump switched to other grievances, exploding at Barr for failing to prosecute Biden's son Hunter.

"If that had been one of my kids, they would have been all over him!" he said.

By the end of the meeting, it was Trump doing almost all of the talking. Why hadn't Barr released the Durham report before the election? Why didn't he prosecute former FBI Director James Comey? He was banging on the table. He said Barr had been worthless.

As Barr left, he was unsure whether he still had a job. Had Trump just fired him? And if not, shouldn't he quit? Why remain attorney general after what the president had just said to him? His status had been left up in the air.

The next morning, Barr received a call from Meadows.

"I think there's a way through this," Meadows told him. He could keep Trump from pulling the trigger and firing him, but he wanted an assurance from Barr that he wouldn't resign.

"Are you willing to stay?" Meadows asked him.

"I'm not going to sandbag you," Barr said. "I will give you a warning if I'm going to leave, and number two, I'll stay as long as I'm needed."

Barr almost immediately began to regret his decision to stay. His statement on election fraud did nothing to deter Trump. The president was listening, almost exclusively, to Giuliani and others outside his administration who were telling him, preposterously, that he was still going to win.

Two days after Barr declared there was no widespread fraud, Trump's allies discovered a video they portrayed as a smoking gun— evidence of voter fraud in Fulton County, Georgia. It was surveillance video of a vote-counting facility in the early-morning hours of election night that purported to show suitcases of ballots taken out from under a table after election monitors had left. The video was played over and over and over again on social media and conservative news outlets. Barr again decided to conduct his own inquiry. Already the Georgia Bureau of Investigation was looking at it, analyzing the video and interviewing witnesses. Barr asked the FBI and the US attorney for Northern Georgia, BJay Pak, to investigate as well. All the investigators came to the same conclusion. The ballots were legitimate. No fraud. Nothing nefarious. Never mind.

On December 14, all fifty states met the deadline set in the Constitution to certify the results of the election. In each state, including the ones Trump was contesting, the results were finalized. Trump was still dug in, but Barr felt it was a good time to leave. He went to the White House to tell the president he planned to resign before the end of the year. It was their first meeting since the explosive confrontation on December 1 where Barr was unsure if he had just been fired.

Barr wanted to leave on his own terms and with a little dignity. To defuse the tension and appeal to Trump's ego in a way to prevent the president from firing him immediately with a tweet, Barr wrote an effusive resignation letter. The letter looked like it could have been written by Trump himself. Barr handed it to him when he got to the Oval Office.

"I am proud to have played a role in the many successes and unprecedented achievements you have delivered for the American people," Barr wrote. "Your record is all the more historic because you accomplished it in the face of relentless, implacable resistance."

The letter praised Trump's record, and played directly into Trump's bitter complaints about how he had been treated by Democrats, saying his efforts "had been met by a partisan onslaught against you in which no tactic, no matter how abusive and deceitful, was out of bounds. The nadir of this campaign was the effort to cripple, if not oust, your Administration with frenzied and baseless accusations of collusion with Russia."

Trump read the letter while Barr was sitting across from him.

"This is pretty good," Trump said with a smile.

The meeting ended on a cordial note, but Bill Barr never again spoke to Donald Trump.

When I went down to interview Trump in Mar-a-Lago after he left the White House, I asked him about Barr's finding that there had been no fraud.

"They say that they looked at all of this," I said to Trump. "They looked at Georgia."

"No, they didn't look," he said.

"They looked at the stuff under the table and they said that was the way the ballots were stored."

"Excuse me," Trump interrupted. "That's nonsense."

"This is what Bill Barr was saying—"

"They didn't do their job, okay?" Trump said to me. "I was very disappointed in the attorney general."

———

Trump went on to repeat many of the very allegations that Barr had explained to him were wrong. He either hadn't listened or just didn't believe what his attorney general had told him. On the other hand, when people told him the election had been stolen from him, he believed them entirely—even when there was no objective reason to trust what they were saying.

After I published an article in *The Atlantic* magazine about what Barr told me regarding Trump's "bullshit" election-fraud claims, Trump went on an all-out tirade against his former attorney general, attacking him in a series of statements and interviews. The day after my article appeared, I got a message from Trump's office saying he would soon be calling me to do a follow-up interview for this book. But at the appointed time, instead of hearing from Trump, I got a call from his assistant Nate Luna, who proceeded to do a dramatic reading of a statement from Trump specifically attacking me.

"Jonathan Karl's story on Slow Moving Bill Barr is made up beyond any level imaginable," the statement began.

But then immediately after saying my story was made up, the statement attacked Barr for the things he said to me that I quoted in the article.

"It takes a very strong and special person to go against the 'mob.' Bill Barr was not that person," Trump said in the statement. "Despite evidence of tremendous Election Fraud, he just didn't want to go there. He was afraid, weak, and, frankly, now that I see what he is saying, pathetic."

When Luna was done with his dramatic reading, I pointed out that the story was not made up. Barr said these things to me. They are on tape. And Trump knew it. That's why he so harshly attacked Barr after I published what Barr said.

———

By the time Barr stepped down as attorney general, Trump was no longer talking to people about just voter fraud. He was hearing even stranger and more dangerous things about how he could remain in power.

"I felt that he was too influenced by these sycophants on the outside who were constantly telling him what he wanted to hear," Barr later told me. "That's one of his weaknesses. He has strengths. You know, in some ways, some presidents can be isolated, and they don't talk enough to people on the outside. He talks too much." Trump keeps talking to people, Barr said, "until he finds someone who's saying something that he wants to hear."

CHAPTER TWELVE

THE BIGGEST LOSER,
PART TWO

As Donald Trump's lawyers suffered a crushing string of legal defeats and public humiliations, he became more and more isolated in the White House. In late November and early December, he would go days at a time without being seen in public—a rarity for a president who craved attention. In the past he could escape his problems in Washington by doing campaign rallies around the country, feasting on the adoration of his supporters no matter how bad things looked back at the White House. But the campaign was over and he was almost never traveling anywhere. He wasn't even playing much golf. He spent most of his days in his private dining room adjacent to the Oval Office watching television, reading newspapers, and making phone calls.

"He would make calls until he heard what he wanted to hear," one friend of the president told me. And while he wasn't talking much to his actual cabinet, he had cobbled together a new group of advisors, most of them outside of the White House, who told him precisely what he wanted to hear. As one Trump ally told me, he assembled "a kitchen cabinet of idiots" or what another Trump friend called a band of "super placaters."

On the day of Giuliani's mortifying press conference at RNC headquarters—the one where black hair dye was running down the sides of his face and outlandish conspiracies were coming out of his mouth—I called up one of Trump's most loyal and important supporters in Congress, somebody who had been talking to the president virtually every day.

"He's a man who knows he lost," this Republican congressman told me. "It's hard on him."

Like so many close to Trump, he was talking about the president of the United States like he was a child, excusing and enabling his inexcusable behavior.

It's hard on him? Really?

Trump was refusing to concede an election he had clearly lost. He was blocking the transition for a president-elect who had clearly won. He was spreading lies and promoting misinformation designed to convince millions of Americans that democracy had collapsed.

It's hard on him?

"Will he ever admit it?" I asked. "Will he ever actually concede?"

It was a question I had been asking of people in Trump's inner circle for two weeks. It was becoming increasingly clear to me that he would never admit defeat. With each loss in court, Trump seemed to be digging in deeper.

"He is getting there," the congressman said, "but then the crazies like Rudy Giuliani call and say, 'You can win!'"

In an attempt to cheer him up, some people close to Trump tried to get him to focus on planning life after the White House. They talked to him about setting up his political organization to play a big role in the 2022 midterm elections and getting his old "TRUMP" Boeing 757 ready to fly around the country for rallies and maybe even embark on a big international tour. There was talk of planning the Trump presidential library. "It's going to look like Graceland," one of the people who talked to Trump about the library told me at the time.

For a while, Trump engaged in some of those conversations and First Lady Melania Trump began making arrangements for their son, Barron, to attend school in Florida starting in January. Jared and Ivanka made plans to move out of their home in the Kalorama section in Washington and into a new place in Miami. But the more hopeless his effort to challenge the election became, the more detached from reality Donald Trump became.

Meanwhile, Sidney Powell's talk of an international conspiracy to rig voting machines was too much for even Fox News host Tucker Carlson, who had been promoting his own brand of crazy talk about election fraud. The night of the press conference at the RNC, Carlson told his audience he had asked Powell to come on the show and share her evidence.

"When we kept pressing, she got angry and told us to stop contacting her," Carlson said at the start of his show. "When we checked with others around the Trump campaign, people in positions of authority, they told us Powell has never given them any evidence, either, nor did she provide any today at the press conference."

One would think even the most hard-core Trump acolyte—and even Trump himself—would have second thoughts after hearing that Sidney Powell angrily refused to give Tucker Carlson a shred of evidence to prove her wild allegations. But nothing would deter Trump and his most fervent enablers. The attitude of those blindly loyal to Trump was summed up in a tweet by Rush Limbaugh's producer, responding to Carlson, "Where is the 'evidence' this election was fair?"

On November 20, Georgia certified Biden as the state's winner after counting the ballots three times—an initial count after polls closed on election night, a machine recount, and a recount of all 4.9 million ballots by hand. In terms of Trump's hopes for challenging the election results, the certified result in Georgia was another nail in a coffin that had already been hammered shut. In announcing the results of the hand recount, Georgia's Republican secretary of state, who had long been a Trump supporter, said, "I live by the motto that numbers don't lie." Brad Raffensperger had done his job as a public official even as he ratified the defeat of the candidate he had supported.

White House press secretaries are public officials, too. But Press Secretary Kaleigh McEnany slandered Raffensperger, calling him "Georgia's corrupt secretary of state." Before the Trump presidency, White House press secretaries at least tried to appear to avoid directly involving themselves in politics. Unlike a spokesperson for a political party or a candidate, a White House press secretary is a public servant whose salary is paid by taxpayers. But this was another norm trashed by the Trump White House. McEnany apparently felt empowered to overtly engage in politics and to lie—calling Raffensperger "corrupt" without any evidence or even a plausible explanation for impugning his integrity—because her predecessors in the Trump White House had done the same thing, although not quite as shamelessly.

Recounts and court challenges are part of the democratic process; Trump legitimately had a right to seek election audits and to go to court in states where he believed the rules had not been followed. In a few instances, it was not entirely unreasonable to argue that changes to election rules had been hastily and improperly made. But when those efforts failed, Trump turned to a new tactic—something so brazenly anti-democratic that no losing presidential candidate—let alone an incumbent president—had ever seriously contemplated. He went directly to Republican-led state legislatures and asked them to throw out election results in their states and choose the winner themselves.

There was a thin thread of a legal basis, sort of, for this effort in Article II of the Constitution, which gives state legislatures the power to determine the manner for choosing their state's electoral votes. But that doesn't mean state legislatures can simply throw out the results of the election. After all, the manner chosen by every single state for choosing electors is a popular election—the people get to vote. If a state legislature chose to throw out the results of the election and substitute its own preference for president, it would not just be violating the fundamental principle of democracy, it would be violating its own laws.

Regardless of the flimsy legal basis for this strategy, on November 20, Trump invited the Republican leadership of the Michigan state legislature to meet with him in the Oval Office so he could ask them to overturn Biden's victory in their state. Michigan Senate Majority Leader Mike Shirkey and House Speaker Lee Chatfield showed up for the meeting along with Jason Wentworth, who was due to soon replace Chatfield as speaker of the house. All of them were strong supporters of Donald Trump and had helped campaign for his reelection. But even before they arrived in Washington, they agreed that, no matter what Trump had to say to them, they would not act to nullify the Michigan election results. They believed, correctly, they had no power to do so. Shortly after the meeting ended, the two Michigan Republican leaders put out a lengthy statement they had prepared before they even walked into the White House. The statement addressed the president's demand they overturn the election and provided a definitive answer.

"The candidates who win the most votes win elections and Michigan's electoral votes," the Republican leaders said in the statement.

Nothing extraordinary about that. That's the way presidential elections in America work. But in the context of everything else that was happening, the statement stood out as a courageous act. The president of the United States had summoned them to Washington. He insisted they had the power to overturn the election. And they flatly denied him.

"We have not yet been made aware of any information that would change the outcome of the election in Michigan," the statement continued, "and as legislative leaders, we will follow the law and follow the normal process regarding Michigan's electors."

The next day Trump was dealt his most devastating legal defeat yet. A federal court in Pennsylvania shot down a lawsuit filed by the Trump campaign to prevent the state from certifying Biden's victory. The opinion was written by Judge Matthew Brann, a member of the conservative Federalist Society, the organization that had helped Trump pick his judicial nominees. His credentials may have made him look like a Trump-friendly judge, but Brann eviscerated the Trump campaign's lawsuit, likening it to "Frankenstein's monster."

The Trump campaign, Judge Brann wrote, was asking the court to "disenfranchise almost seven million voters."

"One might expect that when seeking such a startling outcome," he wrote, "a plaintiff would come formidably armed with compelling legal arguments and factual proof of rampant corruption. That has not happened."

The decision did more than knock down a frivolous lawsuit filed by the president's lawyers. It stood as a scathing indictment of the effort to overturn the election.

"Instead, this Court has been presented with strained legal

arguments without merit and speculative accusations, unpled in the operative complaint and unsupported by evidence," Judge Brann wrote. "In the United States of America, this cannot justify the disenfranchisement of a single voter, let alone all the voters of its sixth most populated state. Our people, laws, and institutions demand more."

Senator Pat Toomey (R-PA), another conservative Republican, responded to the lawsuit by issuing a statement calling on President Trump to recognize the obvious—he lost, and Biden won.

"With today's decision by Judge Matthew Brann, a longtime conservative Republican whom I know to be a fair and unbiased jurist, to dismiss the Trump campaign's lawsuit, President Trump has exhausted all plausible legal options to challenge the result of the presidential race in Pennsylvania," Toomey said.

Toomey continued: "This ruling follows a series of procedural losses for President Trump's campaign. On Friday, the state of Georgia certified the victory of Joe Biden after a hand recount of paper ballots confirmed the conclusion of the initial electronic count. Michigan lawmakers rejected the apparent attempt by President Trump to thwart the will of Michigan voters and select an illegitimate slate of electoral college electors. These developments, together with the outcomes in the rest of the nation, confirm that Joe Biden won the 2020 election and will become the 46th President of the United States."

Toomey concluded his statement by doing something most of his Republican colleagues in Congress had not yet done.

"I congratulate President-elect Biden and Vice President–elect Kamala Harris on their victory," Toomey said. "They are both dedicated public servants and I will be praying for them and for our country."

How did Trump respond to this cascade of defeats coming from fellow Republicans? He denied reality, tweeting, without any factual basis whatsoever, that his "investigators" had "found" hundreds of thousands of fraudulent votes.

"Hopefully the Courts and/or Legislatures will have the COURAGE to do what has to be done to maintain the integrity of our Elections," he tweeted. "THE WORLD IS WATCHING."

It was madness. The courts had struck down his arguments and Republican leaders in the states were consistently telling him they had no power to reverse the election. Still, the effort continued.

On November 25, Rudy Giuliani organized a "hearing" with Republican state senators in Pennsylvania. I put "hearing" in quotes, because it wasn't actually convened at the state capitol. The "hearing" was held in a poorly lit ballroom of the Wyndham hotel in Gettysburg, Pennsylvania, and it had the atmosphere of a Trump campaign rally. Trump had announced he was going to attend, but decided against it at the last minute. Instead, he called in to the hearing while Giuliani and fellow Trump lawyer Jenna Ellis were testifying. Ellis awkwardly held her cell phone up to the microphone so that everybody there could hear.

"This election was rigged, and we can't let that happen," Trump said. It was a call to arms, but his voice sounded tired, depressed, and defeated. "This election has to be turned around because we won Pennsylvania by a lot and we won all these swing states by a lot."

Speaking before the Republican senators, Giuliani presented what seemed to be a damning piece of evidence. He said more vote-by-mail ballots had been counted than had been sent out. And he presented his evidence with stunning specificity, saying that 1,823,148 ballots had been sent out. It was a startling revelation: More votes than ballots!

"But when you go to the count of the final count of the vote," Giuliani said, "there were 2,589,242 mail-in-ballots. What happened?

How do you account for the 700,000 mail-in ballots that appeared from nowhere?"

Back at Trump campaign headquarters, Trump campaign spokesman Tim Murtaugh was wondering the same thing. Shortly after the hearing was over, he reached out to Jenna Ellis to ask her where the numbers had come from. Murtaugh was preparing for a television interview and wanted to be able to cite this explosive new finding, but Ellis said she didn't know where the numbers had come from. So Murtaugh went to the Pennsylvania secretary of state's website to try to find the numbers for himself. What he found was that Giuliani had simply confused two sets of numbers. Yes, in fact, there had been exactly 1,823,148 ballots sent out—but that was for the *primary* election in June, not for the *general* election in November. The correct number—right there on the state's website—for ballots sent out for the general election was 3,087,524. No additional ballots had been magically found or manufactured. There was no mystery. Rudy Giuliani just had his numbers mixed up.

Murtaugh contacted Ellis again and told her what he had discovered.

"You need to get him to stop saying this," Murtaugh told her. "He's made a mistake. It's not true."

"It's too late," Ellis responded. "He's been saying it and he's going to keep saying it."

Driving all of this was Donald Trump's pathological fear of losing. Long before he got into politics, he built his entire brand on being a winner. Even when he was going through his bankruptcies in the 1990s, his creditors kept his personal line of credit flowing so that Trump could keep up his super-rich-guy image even as he was awash in red ink. That was done, an officer in one of the banks he was indebted to told me, because Trump's most valuable asset, by far, was his name. And the name was valuable because he had succeeded in associating it with winning and wealth. If Trump had to ditch the limousines and flamboyantly luxurious lifestyle, the value of his brand would tank.

While most politicians, even those who are fabulously rich, act like they are just like regular working-class people, Trump did the opposite as a candidate. He brought his personal helicopter to the Iowa State Fair and traveled the country in his Boeing 757 with his name emblazoned on the side. While Jeb Bush, the son of one president and the brother of another, ran around pretending to be just a regular guy, Trump proudly embraced an image that he was anything but a regular guy. He was a guy who always wins. He's a guy who is richer than anybody. He's a guy who never loses. The message projected by his image was that if you elect Trump, the country will win because Trump always wins.

It may have been an effective strategy—and it certainly worked during the 2016 Republican primaries. But there's a risky downside to having your success tied to the notion that you are the ultimate winner. If you suffer a loss, it can all come crashing down.

The year before he launched his presidential campaign, Trump explained this clearly and concisely to reporter Michael D'Antonio in an interview for a 2015 book entitled *The Truth about Trump*.

"The most important aspect of leadership is winning. If you have a record of winning, people are going to follow you," Trump said. "If you lose a lot, nobody's going to follow you, because you're looked at as a loser."

By the end of 2020, Trump was losing. A lot. People like Kellyanne Conway, who had told me he would soon come around and accept the loss, were dead wrong. The accumulation of losses was making him desperate. Trump couldn't admit he had lost because he feared that if he did, his adoring fans would go away. As he had told D'Antonio, "If you lose a lot, nobody's going to follow you."

By December, Trump had compounded his loss in the election with a monumental string of losses in court—sixty defeats in cases brought by his legal team and his allies. Rudy Giuliani was running around holding makeshift hearings in the contested states, but they were accomplishing nothing more than Trump's failed personal appeal to the leaders of the Michigan legislature had.

Some of the people who had been closest to Trump were now actively avoiding him. I called one of Trump's most stalwart allies in Congress on December 4, the day before Trump planned to travel to Georgia for a rally billed as a campaign event for Georgia Senators Kelly Loeffler and David Perdue, who both faced runoff elections on January 5. But Trump was showing no interest in the Senate races. His mood had darkened with the accumulation of losses. He was lashing out at his political allies—including the Georgia senators—for not fighting hard enough for him.

"I was thinking of going to Georgia," the congressman told me. "But I don't want to be on the plane with him."

Before making the trip, Trump called Georgia's Republican Governor Brian Kemp early in the morning of Saturday, December 5. He had a demand. Trump wanted Governor Kemp to call a special session of the Republican-controlled Georgia legislature to have a vote on overturning the state's presidential election, sending a slate of Trump electors to Washington instead of the Biden electors chosen by voters. Trump had already directly appealed to four Georgia state senators who agreed to sign a letter demanding such a special session. But it's up to the governor to call a special session. Trump's call resulted in yet another loss.

The next evening, Kemp issued a joint statement with Lieutenant Governor Geoff Duncan flatly rejecting Trump's request, saying that sending a different set of electors "is not an option that is allowed under state or federal law."

The statement added: "Any attempt by the legislature to retro-actively change that process for the November 3rd election would be unconstitutional."

Trump was asking Georgia Republicans to violate the Constitution, just as he had asked Michigan Republicans to do.

The last gasp of this effort came in one of the most absurd legal actions by Trump's allies. Texas Attorney General Ken Paxton filed a lawsuit with the Supreme Court to invalidate the electoral votes from four states Biden won: Georgia, Michigan, Pennsylvania, and Wisconsin. If the sixty-two electoral votes from those states were nullified, Biden's victory would be reversed. Trump cheered on the lawsuit with the single most concise, direct, and revealing tweet of the post-election period:

Donald J. Trump
@realDonaldTrump

#OVERTURN

12/9/20, 10:34 AM

The response from Michigan's attorney general summed up the absurdity of the lawsuit: "Michigan voters will decide the outcome of their elections, not Texas politicians."

But with Trump supporting it, Republican attorneys general from seventeen states signed on to join Texas in the lawsuit. And in the House, Congressman Mike Johnson of Louisiana worked to get fellow Republicans to sign a "friend of the court" brief supporting the lawsuit. Johnson sent an email to all his Republican colleagues in

Congress. The subject line: "Time-sensitive request from President Trump." The president, he wrote, "specifically asked me to contact all Republican Members of the House and Senate today and request that all join."

He added: "He said he will be anxiously awaiting the final list to review."

The implicit threat was obvious—Trump is keeping score and taking names.

Congresswoman Liz Cheney, who at the time was the third highest ranking Republican in the House, considered Johnson a smart lawyer and a good friend. They came into Congress at the same time and had offices close to each other. Cheney called Johnson multiple times to urge him to drop the effort, saying the lawsuit was an affront to the Constitution and filled with disproven allegations of voter fraud. Cheney told me that Johnson acknowledged to her the lawsuit would fail, but he said it was important to give Trump one last chance and that doing so would make it easier for him to concede.

"We've got to show the president we are fighting," Cheney says Johnson told her. "He knows this is the last chance."

Cheney tried to convince her colleagues not to sign on to Johnson's "friend of the court" brief and says House Republican Leader Kevin McCarthy told her he agreed the lawsuit was bad and wouldn't be signing.

"Kevin said to me, 'I just want you to know, I'm not signing the Texas amicus brief,'" Cheney later told me. "He said it gives the federal government too much authority over elections."

When the brief was filed with the Supreme Court on December 10, there were 106 Republican signatures—a big number, but it did not include McCarthy. Cheney was heartened that McCarthy had taken a principled stand even as a majority of House Republicans had not. But a few hours later, Johnson amended the filing and added twenty more names he said had been left off due to a "clerical error"—among the names now included was Kevin McCarthy.

McCarthy denied to me that he told Cheney he would not sign the brief, but he acknowledged that a member of his staff may have told her that. Regardless, he did sign and Cheney now found herself at odds with the entire Republican leadership. With McCarthy's signature, every member of the House Republican leadership, except for Liz Cheney, joined the effort to throw out electoral votes from four states.

The mass appeasement of Trump's demands to support a lawsuit seen by almost all legal experts as frivolous—and a lawsuit aimed at throwing out the votes of millions of Americans—showed that despite the mounting losses, Republicans were still following him. After all the losses, Trump had somehow managed to convince Republicans he was still not a loser.

And then he lost again.

The Supreme Court rejected the Texas lawsuit with a terse statement saying, "Texas has not demonstrated a judicially cognizable interest in the manner in which another State conducts its elections." In other words, Texas has no authority to tell other states how to run their elections.

The rejection was unanimous. If Trump had been expecting the three justices he put on the Supreme Court to bail him out, he was mistaken. It was also a mistake to think Trump would accept defeat once the Supreme Court rejected his "last chance" lawsuit.

With failure of the legal challenges and the failure of his effort to entice Republican-led state legislatures to overturn the election, Trump became even more obsessed with wild conspiracies about the election. Enter Sidney Powell.

Powell was brought onto the Trump legal team by Rudy Giuliani, but her talk of an international conspiracy to rig the election was even wackier than the stuff Giuliani had been peddling in his election-fraud road show. Powell was telling anybody who listened that the CIA was in on the conspiracy and that one of the central players in the massive cover-up was CIA Director Gina Haspel. For a brief moment, Powell's talk was even too crazy for Giuliani, who issued a statement on November 22 saying, "Sidney Powell is practicing law on her own. She is not a member of the Trump legal team." In truth, her influence on Trump was only growing.

Since right after the election, Powell had a reliable platform that ensured she could speak directly to the president: Maria Bartiromo's shows on Fox News and the Fox Business Network. During one typically unhinged interview in late November, Powell told Bartiromo that Trump should fire his CIA director.

"Why Gina Haspel is still there in the CIA is beyond my comprehension," Powell said. "She should be fired immediately."

She said the magic words that guaranteed she'd be welcomed into Donald Trump's inner circle: "We are fixing to overturn the election in multiple states and President Trump won not just by hundreds of thousands of votes but by millions of votes that were shifted by this software that was designed expressly for that purpose."

Bartiromo's response: "Wow!"

Powell's interviews with Bartiromo caught Trump's attention and gave her a direct line into the White House. Late one evening shortly after the election, Director of National Intelligence (DNI) John Ratcliffe got a phone call on his personal cell phone—a number he had only given out to family, close friends, and the White House. When he answered, he was surprised to hear it was Rudy Giuliani and Sidney Powell calling—a late-night conference call of crazy.

Powell started right in saying there was a CIA supercomputer called "HAMMER" that used a software called "SCORECARD" that was used to hack into voting machines and change votes. They said a former CIA officer named Dennis Montgomery had blown the whistle on the whole operation. Powell had already talked about some of this nonsense publicly—on Maria Bartiromo's show, of course. Ratcliffe thought it sounded nuts and wondered how the hell they got his phone number. He politely told them he needed to get off the phone.

"We were talking to Mark [Meadows] and he really wanted us to share this information with you," Giuliani told Ratcliffe.

"As the chief of staff knows, I need to be careful who I speak to," Ratcliffe said, "but I'll follow up with Mark."

Ratcliffe hung up and called Mark Meadows.

"Why are they calling me?" Ratcliffe asked, firmly telling Meadows that he could not be talking to people like Sidney Powell and Rudy Giuliani. He told him that the DNI has no business getting involved in domestic investigations, let alone anything political like this. And besides, the DNI doesn't do investigations. That's what the FBI does.

"I understand," Meadows told him. "I understand."

Ratcliffe did, however, take a look at what Powell was saying and found out there wasn't—and never had been—a CIA supercomputer called "HAMMER." And, further, their CIA "whistleblower" Dennis Montgomery had never actually been an employee at the CIA; instead, he had briefly been a contractor for the agency nearly two decades earlier. His contract with the CIA had been abruptly terminated after he was accused of providing the agency with sham technology.

Despite Ratcliffe's plea to Meadows, the calls from Giuliani and Powell didn't stop. He heard from each of them again in mid-December shortly after the Supreme Court rejected the Texas case. Ratcliffe let the calls—and there were several of them—go to voicemail. He again complained to Meadows, telling the chief of staff, again, that it was not appropriate for him to be involved in anything to do with challenging the election.

This time the duo had a new conspiracy. It had to do with Antrim County, a remote spot in Northern Michigan with fewer than twenty-four thousand residents and a population density of forty-nine people per square mile. Antrim County became a focal point for conspiracy theorists because the solidly Republican county was briefly listed on election night as being won by Biden. It had been an error that was quickly corrected to reflect the true outcome—Trump with 9,748 votes, beating Biden with 5,960. Now Powell was saying the error revealed the rigged voting machine software at work—and that, somehow, it was all controlled by computer servers operating in Europe.

Ratcliffe ignored the calls, but Powell found an audience with the president. Trump brought up the Powell/Giuliani conspiracy with Ratcliffe and asked if he could investigate. When Ratcliffe explained why he couldn't, Trump pointed out that Ratcliffe is the head of the intelligence community and that the FBI is part of the intelligence community.

"Will you at least call the FBI and make sure they are investigating?" Trump asked his director of national intelligence.

Trump apparently didn't want to go directly to FBI Director Christopher Wray with this crazy conspiracy because although Trump talked often about firing Wray, he rarely spoke to him anymore.

Under any normal set of circumstances, the Antrim County conspiracy theory would have never made it beyond a few crackpot websites associated with fringe groups and adherents of the QAnon movement. The reality here was that a human error in a rural and sparsely populated Michigan county had been quickly corrected. But it was somehow spun up to be proof of an international conspiracy to rig voting machines with software controlled by computer systems in Europe. This was truly bonkers stuff, but the president of the United States was asking America's top intelligence official to look into it. And when that official said he did not have the authority to conduct his own "investigation," the president was asking him to get the FBI involved.

So Ratcliffe did what so many others around Trump did in similar situations: He passed on the absurd request for somebody else to deal with, placing a call to FBI Director Christopher Wray. Wray wasn't immediately available, so Ratcliffe reached Deputy FBI Director David Bowdich instead and told him about the president's interest in the conspiracy theory being peddled by Sidney Powell and Rudy Giuliani.

"I'm not trying to get into your business," Ratcliffe told Bowdich, "but I want to be in a position if asked about this to assure folks in the White House that the FBI is aware of this allegation and you are looking into it."

Bowdich already knew about the crazy allegation. He told Ratcliffe not to worry. Antrim County, Michigan, was conducting an audit of the machines and a recount of the ballots. He told Ratcliffe they would know within forty-eight hours if there were any irregularities.

As it turned out, Antrim County's audit was completed on December 17. The results showed no issue with the machines and the hand count was virtually identical with the machine count that had been completed on election night.

Here were the results on election night:

> Trump: 9,748
> Biden: 5,960

And here were the results of the manual recount:

> Trump: 9,759
> Biden: 5,959

Trump's lead increased by twelve votes out of 15,718 ballots cast—not because of some international conspiracy to rig the voting machines, but, as election officials explained, "The slight differences in counts were in line with what is typically seen in hand recounts, as human counters may not award a vote to a pen mark on a ballot oval, where the machine counted it as a vote, or vice-versa."

No surprise. The wacky conspiracy was proved false and did not change the outcome of the election. But it did manage to consume the attention of the White House chief of staff, the director of national intelligence, the deputy director of the FBI, and the president of the United States.

And the truly amazing thing here was that the election had already been finalized—in Michigan and in all fifty states. Under US law—specifically the Electoral Count Act of 1887—each state must certify its election results and assign its electoral votes by the Wednesday after the second Monday in December. In 2020, that date was December 14. Every state abided by the law and assigned its electors according to the results of the presidential election, resulting in 306 electoral votes for Biden and 232 electoral votes for Trump.

The next day, December 15, Senator Mitch McConnell went to the Senate floor and gave the speech he should have given a month earlier but had been trying to avoid because he knew how much it would antagonize Trump. McConnell had never repeated Trump's talk about a stolen election, but he had also never challenged the president's reckless allegations. In fact, one week after the election, McConnell had sarcastically dismissed concerns about the president's flurry of lawsuits and refusal to concede, saying, "Suffice to say a few legal inquiries from the president do not exactly spell the end of the republic." Now he was finally ready to set the record straight.

"Many of us hoped that the presidential election would yield a different result, but our system of government has processes to determine who will be sworn in on January twentieth," McConnell said. "The electoral college has spoken. So today, I want to congratulate President-elect Joe Biden."

McConnell also congratulated Vice President–elect Kamala Harris and noted the historic significance of her election.

"Beyond our differences, all Americans can take pride that our nation has a female vice president–elect for the very first time," he said.

After finishing his speech, McConnell turned and walked out of the Senate chamber to his office about thirty yards down the hall. Almost immediately after he got back to his office, McConnell's chief of staff told him the president of the United States was on the phone and wanted to talk to him.

McConnell later told me the president started yelling at him as soon as he answered the phone. He told me he could not remember his exact words, but that his rant was filled with expletives.

"I let him take a breath at some point," McConnell told me. "And I said, well, the electoral college is the final word."

Trump hung up on McConnell. It was the last time the two men spoke.

CHAPTER THIRTEEN

OVERTURN

With the electoral college votes certified in all fifty states, Senate Majority Leader Mitch McConnell set out to prevent an embarrassing last-ditch effort by Trump diehards in the House to disrupt the final ceremonial step in the presidential election: the counting of electoral votes in a joint session of Congress on January 6. Trump's expletive-ridden reaction to McConnell's speech congratulating Joe Biden on his election victory made it obvious that Trump wasn't going to go quietly or gracefully.

A few hours after making his speech on December 15 and telling Trump directly that the electoral college had spoken, McConnell convened a conference call of all Republican senators. His message was firm and direct. He wanted Republican senators to accept the reality that the election was truly over and Biden was the president-elect. As was almost always the case with McConnell, this principled stand was made with cold political calculation. Under the rules governing the counting of electoral votes, if even a single Republican senator joined House Republicans in objecting to any state's electoral votes on January 6, the ceremonial counting would be interrupted by a debate and a vote on whether to accept that state's certified results. McConnell warned this would be a "terrible vote" that would further divide Republicans by forcing them to go on the record voting against Trump. As McConnell had just told the world in his speech on the Senate floor, the electoral college had spoken and Biden had won. Why set up a politically uncomfortable vote for a lost cause? Nobody on the call spoke up to disagree.

McConnell's plea to drop the objections should have been an easy one, given what was going down at the White House, where the president's efforts to challenge the election results were completely detached from reality. Trump seemed to actually believe the utterly unfounded conspiracy theory about rigged voting machines and was saying that federal investigators needed to take possession of the machines. When it became clear that Attorney General Bill Barr's Justice Department had no intention of doing that—after all, Barr had concluded the allegation of rigged machines was "bullshit"—Trump's attention turned to the Department of Homeland Security.

In mid-December, Rudy Giuliani reached out to Ken Cuccinelli, who was serving as acting deputy secretary of Homeland Security, and urged him to seize control of voting machines in the contested states. Cuccinelli was a hard-line conservative who had supported and helped implement some of Trump's most controversial policies on immigration, but he told Giuliani that DHS had no authority to seize voting machines owned by the states. The effort didn't stop there.

Director of Presidential Personnel Johnny McEntee, who had no authority whatsoever over such things, made his own call directly to acting Secretary of Homeland Security Chad Wolf.

"The president is upset," McEntee told him. "He doesn't understand why you haven't gotten control of the voting machines."

Wolf told McEntee the same thing Cuccinelli had told Giuliani:

The Department of Homeland Security had no authority to seize voting machines.

Then on December 18 came a meeting so bizarre, long, and out of control that it may go down in history as the strangest meeting Donald Trump, or any other president, ever had at the White House.

The first report of the meeting came in a straightforward news story the next day by *New York Times* reporters Maggie Haberman and Zolan Kanno-Youngs. Here was the lede paragraph:

> President Trump on Friday discussed naming Sidney Powell, who as a lawyer for his campaign team unleashed conspiracy theories about a Venezuelan plot to rig voting machines in the United States, to be a special counsel overseeing an investigation of voter fraud, according to two people briefed on the discussion.

The story was an alarming one. Powell's talk about rigged voting machines was so nutty that it prompted Rudy Giuliani to deny she was part of the Trump campaign's legal team. Now Trump was talking about making her a special counsel? Even more alarming, the *Times* reported that Trump's former national security advisor, retired Lieutenant General Michael Flynn, was at the meeting and that Trump asked him about a kooky idea Flynn had floated just a day earlier about imposing martial law and deploying the military to force a rerun of the election. What the hell was going on? According to the article, White House Counsel Pat Cipollone and other White House aides pushed back hard against the ideas Powell and Flynn were proposing, adding that the meeting "stretched on for a long period of time."

It sure did. As it turned out, Powell and Flynn spent more than five hours at the White House, and as strange and troubling as *The New York Times*' description of the meeting was, the reality was more preposterous and more frightening. The first indication that there was more to the story came in a tweet from a man named Patrick Byrne who said he, too, was at the meeting:

Patrick Byrne
@PatrickByrne

My involvement is I was in the room when it happened. The raised voices included my own. I can promise you: President Trump is being terribly served by his advisers. They want him to lose and are lying to him. He is surrounding [SIC] by mendacious mediocrities.

12/20/20

Byrne also posted a photo he had taken of himself in an empty hallway in the White House complex. In the photo, he is wearing a hooded black ski parka with patches of unshaven stubble on his chin and lip. Byrne had not previously been tied in any way to the Trump campaign and had never met Donald Trump, but, like Sidney Powell, he had been peddling elaborate conspiracies about the election. Byrne is no ordinary crackpot. He is a highly successful businessman, founder of the publicly traded company Overstock.com. He is also highly educated, with degrees from Dartmouth and Cambridge and a Ph.D. in philosophy from Stanford. More recently, though, he had become a proponent of conspiracies about a "deep state" controlling the US government—and stealing the election.

Byrne later wrote his own detailed account of the meeting. It's an outlandish tale about how he, Sidney Powell, and Michael Flynn decided to make a spontaneous visit to the White House at 6:15 p.m.

on December 18, how they managed to get two unnamed Trump staffers to clear them into the White House complex, and how, once they
got inside the gate, they worked their way closer and closer to the
Oval Office, where, by 7:30, they found themselves welcomed by President Trump, who had not seen Flynn since he had fired him back in
February 2017. Byrne described how Flynn told the president he could
deploy the National Guard to oversee a rerunning of the election in
the states Trump lost and how Sidney Powell suggested he could declare a national emergency and seize voting machines in those states.
He detailed how he urged Trump to bring Powell into the White House
as a special counsel and how three White House lawyers rushed into
the Oval Office along with Chief of Staff Mark Meadows when they
heard what was going on. Byrne said one of the lawyers, but he wasn't
sure which, was White House Counsel Pat Cipollone, who attempted
to intervene by telling the president that he didn't have the authority to
do anything that had just been proposed by Flynn and Powell.

"This guy is lying to you through his teeth," Byrne said he told
Trump, referring to Cipollone. "They want you to lose."

Byrne's outlandish tale continued to describe a shouting match
taking place in front of the president with Byrne and Flynn standing
shoulder-to-shoulder facing off against the White House lawyers
with Byrne thinking that if Pat Cipollone took a step closer, "I was
going to bury my knuckles in his throat." Making the story sound
even more way-out and implausible, Byrne said the president broke
up the argument and asked the group to reconvene thirty minutes
later in the living room of the White House residence, which they
did, with Rudy Giuliani joining the group for another contentious
session that lasted until after midnight. In Byrne's improbable story,
a White House usher served the group Swedish meatballs as they
argued about overturning the presidential election.

The most outlandish thing about Patrick Byrne's tale is that it is true. None of the participants have disputed the basic outline of what he described. In fact, those who have spoken to me about it, including those who believe Byrne is completely out of his mind, say the significant details are largely accurate—although Byrne never could get it straight which of the three lawyers was Pat Cipollone. The other two White House lawyers at the marathon meeting were Senior Advisor Eric Herschmann and Staff Secretary Derek Lyons.

After Byrne wrote his version of what happened, Jonathan Swan and Zachary Basu of *Axios* wrote a riveting account of the meeting that added details Byrne left out, including this comical description of Byrne yelling at Herschmann:

> "You're a quitter," he said. "You've been interfering with everything. You've been cutting us off."
>
> "Do you even know who the fuck I am, you idiot?" Herschmann snapped back.
>
> "Yeah, you're Patrick Cipollone," Byrne said.
>
> "Wrong! Wrong, you idiot!"*

That, too, was consistent with Byrne's story. He said he didn't know which lawyer was the White House counsel. Byrne also wrote that as Trump left the Oval Office to go up to his living room, he said to Byrne, "You know, in two hundred years there probably has not been a meeting in this room like what just happened."

No doubt about that.

When it was all over it was left unclear whether Trump was actually going to appoint Sidney Powell as a special counsel. If he had, it would have almost certainly led to the immediate resignation of Pat Cipollone as White House counsel. It was also unclear what exactly

---

*"Inside the Craziest Meeting of the Trump Presidency," Jonathan Swan and Zachary Basu, *Axios*, February 2, 2021.

her job would be. Under the regulations governing special counsels, only an attorney general or acting attorney general can make the appointment. And Trump's attorney general sure as hell wasn't going to appoint Sidney Powell to anything.

Three days after the out-of-control White House meeting, Bill Barr had his last press conference as attorney general. He was, of course, asked about the report Trump was considering seizing voting machines and appointing Powell special counsel.

Barr said there was "no basis now for seizing machines by the federal government," and he said he would not name a special counsel to investigate allegations of a stolen election.

"If I thought a special counsel at this stage was the right tool and was appropriate," he said, "I would name one, but I haven't, and I'm not going to."

Barr had no problem slamming the door shut on the election follies, but House Republicans were not deterred by the bizarre turn Trump's efforts to challenge the election had taken. Trump die-hards in Congress set out to add a new element to the madness swirling around the president by plotting to challenge the election results when Congress convened to count the electoral votes—exactly what Senator McConnell was trying to avoid. And Trump was starting to hype yet another new element to the coming showdown over the ceremonial counting—a major protest led by his supporters. His first tweet on this subject came on December 19, the day after the Oval Office meeting with Sidney Powell and Michael Flynn. "Big protest in D.C. on January 6th," he tweeted. "Be there, will be wild!" That appears to be the first public mention of a protest that day.

While McConnell was trying to hold the line with Republican senators, momentum was building among Republicans in the House to challenge the electoral results in all six states where Trump was refusing to admit he lost. And in stark contrast to McConnell, House Republican Leader Kevin McCarthy was refusing to say where he stood, saying in an interview with Maria Bartiromo, "We'll wade through and see what happens."

On December 21, Trump had another marathon meeting about election fraud in the Oval Office with a group of people telling him he could still win.

This time it was a group of far-right House Republicans including Representative-elect Marjorie Taylor Greene (R-GA), Representative Matt Gaetz (R-FL), Representative Mo Brooks (R-AL), Representative Louie Gohmert (R-TX), Representative Jim Jordan (R-OH), and Representative Paul Gosar (R-AZ). It was a who's who of Trump's most fanatical supporters. Rudy Giuliani was there as well. This time the focus was on January 6 and getting Republicans on board to challenge the electoral votes in the six states Trump was contesting: Arizona, Georgia, Michigan, Nevada, Pennsylvania, and Wisconsin. Trump also had the group meet with Vice President Pence, who, of course, would be presiding over the vote count.

When the meeting was over, Chief of Staff Meadows announced it on Twitter: "Several members of Congress just finished a meeting in the Oval Office with President @realDonaldTrump, preparing to fight back against mounting evidence of voter fraud. Stay tuned."

A short while later, a similar message was posted by Marjorie Taylor Greene—the incoming congresswoman best known for being an adherent of the QAnon conspiracy movement. She tweeted a video of herself walking out of the White House and offering a summary of the meeting.

"Just finished with our meetings at the White House this afternoon," Greene said. "We had a great planning session for our January

6 objection. We aren't going to let this election be stolen by Joe Biden and the Democrats. President Trump won by a landslide."

Meanwhile, McConnell's effort to keep Senate Republicans from joining Trump's lost cause continued.

"It's not going anywhere," Senator John Thune (R-SD), a member of McConnell's leadership team, said to a group of reporters on Capitol Hill. "In the Senate, it would go down like a shot dog. I just don't think it makes a lot of sense to put everybody through this when you know what the ultimate outcome is going to be."

But this was looking like a futile effort. Senator-elect Tommy Tuberville (R-AL) had suggested he would join House Republicans in their objections, which would ensure the debate and votes McConnell wanted to avoid would happen.

Noticeably absent from the discussions on any of this was Kevin McCarthy. The House Republican leader was still avoiding taking any public position on the effort but he had privately let McConnell know that he, too, wanted to avoid a showdown of electoral objections on January 6. And in a call with Trump and Mark Meadows, McCarthy flatly told Trump the effort was doomed to fail because even if senators joined the objections and forced a vote, the vote would fail overwhelmingly.

"I don't think you are right about that, Kevin," Meadows interjected.

This was a strange thing to say. Nobody—nobody—thought there would be the votes in Congress to overturn the election, especially considering Democrats controlled the House, and in the Senate, Mitch McConnell and a bunch of other Republicans had already recognized Biden's victory.

But Meadows went on to offer an entirely incorrect description of what would happen. He said that the vote on whether to throw out any state's electoral votes would not be a simple majority vote. Instead, Meadows told Trump, it would be one vote per congressional delegation. And because Republicans controlled twenty-six of the fifty state delegations, Trump could prevail.

McCarthy told Meadows he was entirely incorrect (which he was). Rejecting a slate of electors would require majority votes in both the House and Senate.

"I just don't think that's right, Kevin," Meadows said.

As the discussion continued, McCarthy got the text of the Electoral Count Act of 1887, which, as the name suggests, sets the rules for counting electoral votes. He read the relevant section of the law out loud over the phone. It clearly says that the only way a state's electoral votes could be invalidated is if a majority of both the House and the Senate voted to reject them. And that, obviously, was not going to happen.

The record had been corrected, but it did nothing to slow the drive to contest the electoral votes on January 6. On December 30, Senator Josh Hawley (R-MO) became the first senator to announce he would join the House in objecting. The messy debate McConnell wanted to avoid was going to happen on January 6. As for McCarthy, whatever he privately thought of Trump's lost cause, he was not going to cross him publicly. He knew if he did, he would incur Trump's wrath and likely face a rebellion among the large group of House Republicans who had shown they would stand with Trump no matter what.

But there was something else driving McCarthy's actions. Like so many others around Trump, McCarthy seemed to believe that if he stayed close to the president, he could curtail his most destructive behavior. I had heard this kind of rationale over and over again in the Trump White House. In *Front Row at the Trump Show* I wrote that in the first year of the Trump presidency I had heard at least a half dozen senior officials say some variation of this: *If you think what's*

happening is out of control, you should see the things we stop from hap-
pening.

By year four, I had heard that from dozens of people in the administration and could see that rationale play out in the actions of many
others. It's quite possible some of those people did protect the country from some of Trump's most destructive impulses by staying close
to him. Defense Secretary Mark Esper and Joint Chiefs Chairman
Mark Milley, for example, walked across Lafayette Square with Donald Trump during one of the most shameful moments of his presidency following the killing of George Floyd. But the two men also
may have prevented Trump from invoking the Insurrection Act and
sending active-duty troops onto the streets of American cities—
something that could have been far worse than the ill-fated photo op
in front of St. John's Church. Attorney General Bill Barr echoed
Trump's attacks on the Russia investigation and overruled career
prosecutors in ways favorable to Trump's political allies, but he also
likely prevented Trump from firing FBI Director Chris Wray and
slammed the door shut on the idea of using the Justice Department
to help overturn the election. Even Dr. Anthony Fauci did what he
needed to do to avoid antagonizing Trump so he would remain a
member of the coronavirus task force and have at least some impact
on the federal response to the pandemic.

These were not trivial things. As bad as things got, there are people
who aided and abetted the Trump presidency who also can convincingly argue *it could have been worse.*

It's unclear whether it would have made any difference if McCarthy
had done what McConnell did and publicly broken with Trump. But
it was increasingly clear that if the goal was to limit the president's
destructive behavior regarding the election challenges, the effort had
been an abysmal failure. Even after Barr and McConnell broke with
Trump, even after the Supreme Court unanimously rejected the last

big legal challenge, even after the electoral college voted, McCarthy refused to publicly acknowledge the election was over. He did not publicly criticize Trump's assault on the integrity of American democracy.

Trump's destructive behavior around this period wasn't limited to the election nonsense. On Christmas Eve, he threatened to veto a $900 billion pandemic relief bill that had been negotiated by Treasury Secretary Steven Mnuchin—a bill to provide economic relief to millions of Americans and fund the federal response to the pandemic. Trump said he objected because of a provision in the bill to provide $600 in direct payments to middle- and lower-income Americans. He said he wanted payments of $2,000. But the $600 figure had been proposed by his own treasury secretary. Trump also suggested he might not sign a bill to fund the rest of the government, raising the possibility of a government shutdown in the middle of the greatest public health crisis in more than a century.

This was dangerously erratic behavior. Secretary Mnuchin had been negotiating on behalf of Trump and regularly kept him updated as the bill was finalized and passed—with big, bipartisan majorities—in the House and Senate. When it passed on December 21, Mnuchin called the bill "fabulous" and put out a statement saying, "I want to thank President Trump for his leadership."

But six hours later, with no warning to Mnuchin, Trump put out his own statement on Twitter, calling the bill "a disgrace."

Two days later, he was threatening a veto and a government shutdown—actions that risked triggering an economic meltdown during the final weeks of his presidency. McCarthy was in a California hospital getting wheeled into an operating room for elbow surgery when he got a call from Trump saying he was going to veto the bill. McCarthy pleaded with him not to do it, but had no time to argue with him—he was about to go under general anesthesia.

McCarthy and Senator Lindsey Graham spent the Christmas holiday on the phone with Trump trying to convince him to back down. Senator McConnell was not part of the discussions. Trump was so furious that McConnell had recognized Joe Biden as president-elect that he still refused to talk to him. Incredibly, this meant the president was now refusing to speak to the leaders of both the Senate and the House (it had been more than a year since he last talked to Speaker of the House Nancy Pelosi). As one person close to the negotiations with Trump told me at the time, "It's like dealing with a child."

After three days of intense back-and-forth that began in earnest on Christmas Day—conversations where the president repeatedly changed the subject to manic talk about Democrats stealing the election—Trump finally relented. During a conference call with McCarthy, Mnuchin, and Graham on the evening of December 27, Trump agreed to back down and sign the bill. Even after the call was over, nobody could be sure he wouldn't change his mind again until he actually signed the bill into law, which he did later that night.

One disaster was averted. But the entire episode was a reminder that Trump—more erratic and self-destructive than he had ever been—was still president and, as bad as things were, had the ability to make things much worse. He had lost and, as most of the country knew, was clearly going down. Who else would he bring down with him?

CHAPTER FOURTEEN

ANY MEANS NECESSARY

n New Year's Day 2021, a well-known Trump supporter issued a message over Twitter suggesting that Vice President Mike Pence could soon face execution by firing squad.

Lin Wood
@LLinWood
Replying to @Courie85 @VP and 2 others

If Pence is arrested, @SecPompeo will save the election.
Pence will be in jail awaiting trial for treason. He will face
execution by firing squad. He is a coward & will sing like a
bird & confess ALL.

1/1/21, 1:02 PM

The message was especially alarming because it came from a lawyer who had direct ties to President Trump. His name was Lin Wood. He had met with Trump at the White House in April 2020 and since the election had spoken with him multiple times about the legal effort to challenge the election results. Wood didn't work for Trump, but he had filed numerous lawsuits on behalf of his bid to overturn Joe Biden's victory. He had been recruited to the Trump cause by the president's son Donald Trump Jr., who had invited Wood to speak at a press conference with RNC Chairwoman Ronna McDaniel in Atlanta just days after the election. Wood also had appeared with Sidney Powell and Michael Flynn at numerous pro-Trump "Stop the Steal" rallies since the election. And now he was talking about Vice President Pence facing the firing squad. Wood didn't specify Pence's crime, but he was obviously referring to Pence's refusal to say he would follow Trump's unconstitutional demand that he should somehow act to overturn the election when he presided over the counting of electoral votes on January 6.

In light of Lin Wood's association with Trump, I reached out to White House Press Secretary Kayleigh McEnany to ask what the president thought of one of his allies calling for Pence's arrest and execution. I received no response. As Wood's threatening tweet spread rapidly across social media and cable television, there was no comment whatsoever from the White House or the Trump campaign. Finally, more than seven hours later, Trump campaign lawyer Jenna Ellis responded with a tweet on her personal Twitter account.

Jenna Ellis
@JennaEllisEsq

To be clear: I do not support the statements from Attorney Lin Wood. I support the rule of law and the U.S. Constitution.

1/1/21, 8:33 PM

Notably, Ellis said *she* didn't support Lin Wood's statements. Remarkably, nobody would say whether President Trump supported them. It was an ominous start to the new year.

Trump was not taking a New Year's Day break from social media. In fact, he was furiously tweeting all day long about his plans for January 6.

"The BIG Protest Rally in Washington, D.C., will take place at 11.00 A.M. on January 6th," he tweeted about an hour after Wood called for Pence's execution. "StopTheSteal!"

Shortly after that, Trump retweeted Senator Josh Hawley's announcement that he would be challenging Biden's electoral votes when Congress convened, with Vice President Pence presiding, for the ceremonial counting of electoral votes on January 6.

"Massive amounts of evidence will be presented on the 6th," Trump tweeted along with Senator Hawley's statement. "We won, BIG!"

Senate Republican Leader Mitch McConnell had been furious when Hawley became the first senator to say he would join House Republicans in objecting to electoral votes. Hawley's action now meant there would be extended debate and votes on challenging Biden's victory. On a New Year's Eve conference call with Republican senators, McConnell, with unusual anger in his voice, demanded that Hawley justify his decision and posed a series of questions that came down to this: Why was he forcing a vote where his colleagues would have to choose between publicly defying Donald Trump or defying the Constitution by overturning the election?

Hawley didn't answer.

McConnell asked him again to defend his decision to support Trump's lost cause and, in the process, put his Republican colleagues in such an awkward position.

Still no answer.

Another senator on the call said that maybe Hawley was having technical difficulties. But it soon became clear there were no technical difficulties. Hawley wasn't there. He had blown off the call, ignoring McConnell's pleas, and then not bothered to join the call to defend his decision.

Now that Hawley had forced a debate and vote on Trump's lost cause, McConnell was determined to keep other senators from voting with Hawley to effectively undo a presidential election. McConnell's efforts here were complicated by his own actions. He had waited until nearly six weeks after the election to publicly recognize Biden's election victory, allowing Trump's misinformation about voter fraud to fester and take hold among many Republican voters. And even after that, he was much more forceful about shooting down the claims of election fraud in private than he was in public. But now McConnell was on a mission. He felt Trump's lost cause was hurting the Republican Party.

"My first choice would have been to not have the vote at all," McConnell later told me. "But if we had to have the vote, I wanted to have as few of my members as possible [vote yes]."

The last time there had been a vote on rejecting electoral votes, it was Democrats doing the objecting. After the 2004 election, Senator Barbara Boxer (D-CA) had joined a group of House Democrats in objecting to George W. Bush's victory over John Kerry in Ohio. At the time, McConnell unleashed on Boxer, saying her objection was "shameful" and an "assault on our traditions." He said a vote to object would "trample on the proud republican government our founding fathers bequeathed us."

Boxer's crusade, though, was a lonely one. The Senate rejected her challenge by a vote of 97–1.

Now it was Republicans doing the rejecting, but McConnell's

views had not changed. He wanted to see Hawley every bit as isolated in his objection as Barbara Boxer was with hers.

"What I said in my conference was this is the most important vote I will have ever cast in the thirty-six years I've been here," McConnell told me. "This goes right into the question of the resilience of our democracy."

The Republican leader in the House was taking no such stand. In fact, Kevin McCarthy would not even say where he stood on the issue McConnell said was the most important vote he'd ever taken. In a New Year's Day conference call of House Republicans, Liz Cheney made an impassioned argument against objecting, echoing many of the same points McConnell was making to Senate Republicans. When she was done speaking, McCarthy spoke up to clarify that Cheney, who was still the third-ranking Republican in the House, was giving her personal opinion and not speaking on behalf of the Republican leadership.

At that point, Representative Adam Kinzinger (R-IL) spoke up and directly asked McCarthy how he thought Republicans should vote. Kinzinger was one of the few Republicans in the House who often criticized Trump. He agreed with Cheney that it would be unconstitutional and undemocratic for Congress to overturn a presidential election and he wanted to hear McCarthy take a stand. Did the Republican leader think House Republicans should vote to overturn the certified votes of the electoral college? Kinzinger warned it was dangerous to tell people the election was stolen and that he feared it would lead to violence.

McCarthy ignored Kinzinger's warning about violence and brushed off the demand he take a position, saying members of Congress would have to decide for themselves, "unless you all want to give me your voting cards." Of course, there were many other issues where McCarthy had told Republicans exactly how he wanted them to vote. That's what party leaders do; they lead the party. But in response to another member, McCarthy again refused to say what he personally thought about objecting to certified electoral votes, sarcastically adding, "Look, if you guys want to give me your voting cards, I am happy to vote for you."

Irritated by McCarthy's second mention of voting cards, Representative Anthony Gonzalez (R-OH) shot back.

"Kevin, stop telling us we're trying to give you our voting cards," Gonzalez said. "That's bullshit. We have a right to know where you stand on this."

The next day, January 2, was a beautiful Saturday in Washington—a sunny day, blue skies, and temperatures above freezing. I went out to take a walk on the National Mall and saw Kevin McCarthy doing the same. I went over to talk to him and we walked together for a bit. Behind us was the US Capitol building, where the stage for the January 20 inauguration had already been built. Ahead of us were the Washington Monument and Lincoln Memorial.

I asked McCarthy what kind of speech he was going to give when Congress convened on January 6 for the official counting of the certified electoral votes. Would he finally acknowledge that Joe Biden had won the election and was the legitimate president-elect of the United States? When he didn't directly answer my question, I pointed out that he had an opportunity to make a powerful statement about the integrity of our democracy. He was the leader of the House Republicans and had been one of Trump's most important allies in Congress. If he came forward and said it was time to stop the talk about a stolen election and if he recognized Biden as president-elect, it would matter. Mitch McConnell had done it. Bill Barr had done it. And that morning, every living former secretary of defense—including five who had served under Republican presidents and two who had served under President Trump—published a jointly written letter in *The Washington Post* warning that the baseless challenges to the election results were dangerous and needed to stop.

"Our elections have occurred," the former defense secretaries wrote. "Recounts and audits have been conducted. Appropriate challenges have been addressed by the courts. Governors have certified the results. And the electoral college has voted. The time for questioning the results has passed; the time for the formal counting of the electoral college votes, as prescribed in the Constitution and statute, has arrived."*

But a large group of House Republicans was not taking that advice or heeding that warning. They were the biggest group of holdouts and Kevin McCarthy was their leader. He had the opportunity to give them a cold dose of truth. The blowback from Trump and from his cult-like supporters in Congress might be severe, but it would be the right thing to do. And if he did it forcefully and convincingly, others would follow him.

Exaggerating to make a point about the historical weight of the moment, I nodded toward the monuments along the National Mall—memorials to political leaders remembered precisely because they did things that were both important and difficult to do.

"Who knows," I said, "if you do the right thing, maybe there will be a statue of you out here someday."

McCarthy laughed.

"Where's the statue for Jeff Flake? Where's the statue for that guy from Tennessee?" he said, referring to the former Republican Senator Bob Corker who, like former Republican Senator Jeff Flake, had stood

---

*Liz Cheney played a key role in this as well, helping her father, Dick Cheney, himself a former secretary of defense, to organize the effort and reaching out to the other former defense secretaries to sign on.

up to Trump during Trump's first two years in office. As McCarthy saw it, both men gave big speeches condemning Trump's actions and were rewarded with political obscurity. They became pariahs within the Republican Party. Nobody talks much of Flake and Corker anymore. McCarthy believed they ultimately accomplished little by taking on Trump. Their speeches didn't change Trump's behavior—in fact, they may have egged him on to be more outrageous.

In McCarthy's view, he had accomplished much more by staying close to Trump than those Republicans who had defied him. Just a week earlier, for example, he had convinced Trump to abandon his Christmas Eve threat to veto the $900 billion relief bill. McCarthy believed that if he didn't have a relationship with him, Trump might have gone through with the veto threat and triggered a disastrous government shutdown to go along with it. That could have resulted in an economic meltdown and hardship for millions of Americans counting on government help.

And then there was the pure politics of it all—internal House Republican politics. McCarthy was now within just five seats of becoming Speaker of the House. That's because House Republicans fared much better than Trump in 2020, picking up fifteen seats even as Trump lost to Biden. McCarthy could see the speakership within his grasp in 2022. But if he crossed Trump, he figured he'd face an insurrection and could be voted out as leader. History could wait. His chance to be Speaker could not. Whatever Kevin McCarthy thought of Trump's lies and his lost cause and the damage it all was doing to our democracy, he wasn't going to do anything that would risk his chance to be the next Speaker of the House.

While McCarthy dodged questions about whether he would join the objectors, Donald Trump spent his Saturday morning at the White

House watching cable news. At ten, his television was tuned to *Cavuto Live* on Fox News. Host Neil Cavuto was taking the day off, but guest host David Asman had a live interview with Georgia Secretary of State Brad Raffensperger, whom Asman introduced as a lifelong Republican. Although Raffensperger told Asman that Biden had truly won in Georgia and that the result was confirmed with multiple recounts, he said that as a Republican, he wished Trump had won.

Minutes after the interview ended, a caller left a voicemail on the media line for the office of the Georgia secretary of state.

"This is Molly Michael at the White House," the message said. "President Trump would like to talk to Mr. Raffensperger."

When Raffensberger's press secretary, Walter Jones, listened to the message, he thought it was a prank. After all, the call came into a phone number listed on the secretary of state's website for general media inquiries. It was a line reporters called, not a line the president of the United States would use. And they were getting a lot of crazy calls because the president's allies had been attacking Raffensperger for weeks, going back to November when White House Press Secretary Kayleigh McEnany referred to Raffensperger as Georgia's "corrupt secretary of state" on Fox News. Trump had even called Raffensperger an "enemy of the people." Jones figured there was no way this was a real call, but he passed the information on to Georgia's Deputy Secretary of State Jordan Fuchs.

Fuchs also doubted the call was really from the White House, but she reached out to White House Chief of Staff Mark Meadows to see if Trump was really trying to reach Raffensperger by calling a general number for media inquiries. Meadows answered right away and was not in a good mood. Yes, Trump had seen Raffensperger on Fox News and he wanted to talk to him. Meadows said it wasn't the first time the White House had tried to reach out to Raffensperger on behalf of the president. In fact, Meadows said, the White House had reached out a total of eighteen times since the election and had not received a call back.

Fuchs was surprised to hear the message was real and even more surprised to hear Meadows's complaint about those eighteen unreturned messages. She remembered that Raffensperger had received some text messages from somebody claiming to be the White House chief of staff, but the texts came from a private Gmail account. He had been getting all kinds of threatening messages and certainly didn't think the White House chief of staff would be sending him text messages from a Gmail account. They all had assumed the messages were fake.

Raffensperger now got the message and knew it was real. The president wanted to talk to him, but Raffensperger wasn't sure it was a good idea to talk to the president. After all, Trump's campaign was actually in the process of suing the Georgia secretary of state over the way he had handled the election. Meadows assured him it would be a productive conversation and Raffensperger agreed to take the call as long as his lawyer and his deputy could be on as well. It was set up for three p.m.

Raffensperger is a low-key guy, a civil engineer who, until the 2020 election, was unknown to most people, even in Georgia. He had never spoken to Donald Trump or any other president before. Prior to the call, Raffensperger told his wife he thought it was "pretty cool" that he'd be talking to Trump and, although he didn't have good news for him about the election, he was determined to treat him with respect. Despite the circumstances of the call, he considered it an honor to be getting a call from a president of the United States. He also knew he needed to protect himself, so he directed his staff to record the call.

The call would become a key piece of evidence in Trump's impeachment trial and is one of the clearest examples of presidential abuse of power ever captured on tape. For his part, Raffensperger believed Trump made the call because he had seen him on Fox News that morning talking about being a Republican and saying he had been hoping Trump would win the election.

As the call begins, Trump says he had been going over "the numbers" in Georgia and, "it's pretty clear we won." It's obvious from the start that he doesn't really have any evidence because he begins by talking not about votes, but about his rallies.

"We won very substantially in Georgia," he says. "You even see it by rally size, frankly. We'd be getting 25,000–30,000 people at a rally, and the competition would get less than a hundred people."

For more than twelve minutes, the call is a Trump monologue. He goes on and on running through a series of disproven and baseless allegations—dead people voting, illegal ballots, forged absentee votes, etc.—and then gets to the point and makes his demand.

"I just want to find 11,780 votes, which is one more than we have [to get]," he tells Raffensperger. He repeats the number several more times. It's exactly one more than the number of votes he would need to overturn Joe Biden's victory in the state.

As he rambles on about how he probably won the state by hundreds of thousands of votes, he keeps returning to that number, asking Raffensperger to "find" just enough votes to overturn the results.

Eventually Meadows, who is also on the call, chimes in to give Raffensperger a chance to talk and tries to steer the conversation to safer—noncriminal—ground and asks if "in the spirit of cooperation and compromise" there could be an agreement to look more closely at the allegations of fraudulent votes.

As Raffensperger begins to answer, explaining how the allegations had already been examined and disproven, Trump interrupts and says he is not looking for a closer examination of the allegations. He just wants the votes he needs to win. He says the number again, this time precisely the number to win: 11,779 votes.

"We're giving you minimal, minimal numbers. We're doing the most conservative numbers possible."

"Well, Mr. President, the challenge that you have is the data you have is wrong," Raffensperger answered, speaking calmly and respectfully.

Over the course of the rest of the call, which went on for more than an hour, Raffensperger calmly refutes the allegations of fraud. As Trump repeats misinformation, Raffensperger answers with facts.

For example, regarding the number of dead people voting—Trump was claiming thousands—Raffensperger says, "The actual number were two. Two. Two people that were dead that voted. So that's wrong."

Realizing that Raffensperger isn't going to go along with his demand, Trump resorts to threatening him, suggesting he might be guilty of a "criminal offense" for not reporting all the fraud.

"That's a big risk to you," Trump tells Raffensperger. "That's a big risk."

The call might never have been made public if Donald Trump hadn't told the world about it the next morning in a tweet that lied about what Raffensperger had said.

Donald J. Trump
@realDonaldTrump

I spoke to Secretary of State Brad Raffensperger yesterday about Fulton County and voter fraud in Georgia. He was unwilling, or unable, to answer questions such as the "ballots under table" scam, ballot destruction, out of state "voters", dead voters, and more. He has no clue.

1/3/21, 8:57 AM

To correct the record, one of the people on the call released a recording to *The Washington Post*. Now everybody could hear that Raffensperger did answer the president's allegations. And more than that, everybody could hear the president asking the Georgia secretary of state to overturn the election by "finding" exactly the number of votes he needed to beat Biden in Georgia—and ominously suggesting he could be guilty of a criminal offense if he didn't.

The call was a shocking display of presidential bullying, but it had absolutely no effect on the determination of House Republicans to make their own attempt to overturn the election results. In fact, on the evening of January 3, Kevin McCarthy defended those who planned to object without, once again, saying what he planned to do.

"I think it's right that we have the debate," McCarthy told *The Hill*. "I mean, you see now that senators are going to object, the House is going to object—how else do we have a way to change the election problems?"

Again there was a stark contrast between McCarthy and Liz Cheney. Earlier that day, Cheney had sent a detailed twenty-one-page memo to all her Republican colleagues. The memo, which she had written with her husband, Philip Perry, a prominent Republican lawyer, argued that objecting to electoral votes would "set an exceptionally dangerous precedent, threatening to steal states' explicit constitutional responsibility for choosing the president and bestowing it instead on Congress." Such action, Cheney wrote, "is directly at odds with the Constitution's clear text and our core beliefs as Republicans."

The Cheney memo was quickly overshadowed by other events, but it represented the most thorough and substantive effort by a prominent Republican to convince fellow Republicans to abandon Trump's lost cause. "Democrats have long attempted, unconstitutionally, to federalize every element of our nation—including elections," she argued. "Republicans should not embrace Democrats' unconstitutional position on these issues."

She pointed out that governors in all six states had certified the results of their elections and transmitted those results to Congress. All that was left to do was to count the electoral votes. As for the allegations of fraud in each of those six states, Cheney's memo detailed the ways state and federal courts had repeatedly shot down the allegations made by the Trump campaign. The courts had ruled over and over again there was simply no evidence to support the president's claims.

For Donald Trump it was a very busy weekend dedicated to overturning the election. He had been claiming for weeks that the election had been stolen from him. That was all a lie. But as the time was running out on his presidency, he set out to steal the election for real. This was a multidimensional effort. He was pushing his Republican allies in Congress to disrupt the counting of votes, pressuring local officials to undo results on the state level, trying to get an assist from the Supreme Court, and demanding his vice president use power he didn't really have. But there was one other move he attempted that weekend that almost nobody knew about at the time.

While Trump was reaching out to Raffensperger and turning the screws on his vice president, he was also secretly conferring with an obscure environmental lawyer at the Justice Department named Jeffrey Clark about taking over as acting attorney general and using the power of that office to overturn the election. The scheme, which was first reported by *New York Times* reporter Katie Benner three days after Trump left office, was among the most brazen attempts by Trump to cling to power. I have spoken to multiple officials with direct knowledge of what happened who confirm Benner's account and described additional details about this extraordinary episode.

At the time, Clark was head of DOJ's Environment and Natural Resources Division and also had been serving as the acting head of the Civil Division. One of his colleagues described him to me as "a slightly awkward, dorky lawyer" who had an expertise in environmental law and no experience whatsoever in election law. He was an unlikely person to join Trump's crusade and to attempt to stage a coup at the Justice Department, but that's exactly what happened.

Clark was unknown to Trump until sometime in December when Representative Scott Perry (R-PA), a member of the right-wing House Freedom Caucus, told the president about him and said that Clark believed the election had been stolen and that the Justice Department should do something about it. After that, Trump reached out to him and Clark promised to push the DOJ leadership to more aggressively investigate claims of fraud. I am told by two sources familiar with Clark's action that he had added a new conspiracy theory to the mix. He believed that wireless thermostats made in China for Google by a company called Nest Labs might have been used to manipulate voting machines in Georgia. The idea was nuts, but it intrigued Trump, who asked Director of National Intelligence John Ratcliffe to look into it.

In a meeting in late December, Clark—who had told nobody at DOJ about his conversations with Trump—shocked the senior leadership at the Justice Department by proposing to force Georgia to effectively reverse Biden's victory in the state. In an email to acting Attorney General Jeffrey Rosen and Deputy Attorney General Richard Donoghue dated December 28, 2020, Clark presented a five-page document he had drafted to put officials in Georgia on notice with a demand to convene a special session of the state legislature to deal with election fraud.

"He drafted a letter," one of the officials who reviewed Clark's proposal told me shortly after Trump left office, "which would call upon the Georgia legislature to come back in special session and inform them that the Department of Justice had found serious irregularities that had affected the outcome of the election, so therefore they should come back in and appoint new electors."

In August 2021, the Justice Department turned Clark's emails and his draft letter over to the House Committee on Oversight and Reform. The draft letter, which was addressed to Georgia's Republican governor and the Republican leaders of the Georgia House and Senate, makes it clear that Clark intended to take the same action in other states as well.

"The Department of Justice is investigating various irregularities in the 2020 election for President of the United States," Clark's draft letter to the Georgia officials said. "The Department will update you as we are able on investigatory progress, but at this time we have identified significant concerns that may have impacted the outcome of the election in multiple States, including the State of Georgia."

In the email accompanying the letter, Clark urged Rosen and Donoghue to send the letter to Georgia officials as soon as possible, but he also acknowledged that he hadn't yet fact-checked what he had written.

"Personally, I see no valid downsides to sending out the letter," Clark wrote. "I put it together quickly and would want to do a formal cite check before sending but I don't think we should let unnecessary moss grow on this."

The senior leadership at DOJ shot down Clark's call for the Justice Department to pressure Georgia or any other state to overturn their election results.

"There is no chance that I would sign this letter or anything remotely like this," Donoghue responded in an email to Clark. "While it may be true that the Department 'is investigating various irregularities in the 2020 election for President' (something we typically would not state publicly) the investigations that I am aware of relate to suspicions of misconduct that are of such a small scale that they simply would not impact the outcome of the Presidential Election."

Rosen concurred, writing, "I confirmed again today that I am not prepared to sign such a letter."

But Clark didn't stop there. When acting Attorney General Rosen and the senior leadership at DOJ shot down the idea, Clark secretly took it to Trump and presented himself as the person willing to do what the others had refused to do. In the early afternoon of Sunday, January 3, Clark informed Rosen that Trump had decided to put him in charge of the Justice Department and that Rosen was out as acting attorney general. Rosen said he needed to hear it directly from the president and a meeting was scheduled for six p.m. at the White House.

Rosen told senior leaders at the DOJ about what was happening, prompting an emergency conference call of the top dozen officials at the Justice Department. There was unanimous agreement among all of them. If Trump went through with the plan to install Clark as the acting attorney general, they would all resign. About ninety minutes after that call ended, Rosen went to the White House along with Assistant Attorney General Steven Engel. Engel had a good relationship with Trump, but it was his role to deliver the message on behalf of the rest of the leadership that they would all resign if Trump went through with his plan.

In the Oval Office, Trump had Rosen and Clark sit side by side and directly across from him at the Resolute desk. It was set up like an episode of *The Apprentice*. He wanted to hear again from Clark what he would do if he were made acting attorney general, and he wanted to hear from Rosen why he should keep his job.

The Oval Office was packed with lawyers. In addition to Rosen, Clark, and Engel, White House lawyers Pat Cipollone, Pat Philbin, and Eric Herschmann were there along with White House Chief of Staff Mark Meadows. The meeting lasted for well over two hours, but it quickly became apparent that ousting Rosen was going to backfire. Rosen told Trump that DOJ had no legal authority to do what Clark was proposing. And Engel told Trump if he followed through with his plans, there would be mass resignations that would make it impossible for Clark to do his job, as well as create a massive public relations disaster.

"Trump began to see that Clark was not going to be his white knight," one of those at the meeting told me.

The Justice Department coup edition of *The Apprentice* ended with Rosen keeping his job. As the meeting wrapped up, Trump looked over to the awkward and dejected Jeffrey Clark and asked Rosen, "What's going to happen to him now?"

Rosen assured Trump there were no hard feelings and that Clark would not lose his job.

"You're the only one who can fire him," Rosen said. "He's a presidential appointee."

Trump's delusions of using the Justice Department to ride to the rescue of his defeated campaign were over. And in Trump's mind, there was really only one way left for him to stay in power. In Trump's mind, it was now all up to Mike Pence.

CHAPTER FIFTEEN

HANG MIKE PENCE

A few days after Christmas 2020, Vice President Mike Pence's chief of staff called Jared Kushner with an unusual request. The vice president's office almost never asked Kushner for anything, but now Chief of Staff Marc Short really needed something. He wanted Kushner to have an intervention with the president. Trump had become convinced Pence could single-handedly reverse the results of the presidential election and turn Joe Biden's victory into a win for Trump. The idea was preposterous, but members of Trump's legal team—the same legal team that had lost dozens of court challenges—had convinced him it was true. Now the president was setting expectations among his most fervent supporters that Pence had the power to guarantee four more years of the Trump presidency. The vice president's advisors feared Trump's belief in Pence's power to overturn the election was more than just wrong. It was dangerous.

It all came down to the role, as defined by the Constitution, that Vice President Pence would play on January 6, 2021, when he would be presiding over the last formal step of the presidential election. On that day, Congress would come together for a joint session of the House and Senate to officially count the electoral votes that had already been cast and certified by all fifty states. Once the counting was complete, it would be up to the vice president to formally declare the winner of the presidential election. Vice presidents had played this role, with a few exceptions, since John Adams presided over the counting of the electoral votes that reelected George Washington in 1793. At times, the ceremony has been a bit awkward. On January 6, 1961, the House chamber erupted in applause after Vice President Richard Nixon announced John F. Kennedy's victory—and Nixon's own defeat. On January 6, 2001, Vice President Al Gore presided over the counting of George W. Bush's victory in the contested 2000 presidential election Gore believed he would have won if the Supreme Court had not stopped a recount in the state of Florida. And, most recently, Vice President Joe Biden presided over the counting of the electoral votes that handed Donald Trump his victory on January 6, 2017.

Trump had been frequently reminded of the role Pence would play when Trump tuned into his favorite television program, *Fox & Friends*, the unabashedly pro-Trump morning show on Fox News. The Lincoln Project, an anti-Trump group run by Republicans opposed to Trump, had been relentlessly running an ad during the show's commercial breaks with the sole purpose of driving a wedge between Trump and his loyal vice president.

"The end is coming, Donald," the ad's narrator says. "Even Mike Pence knows. He is backing away from your train wreck, from your desperate lies, and clown lawyers. When Mike Pence is running away from you, you know it's over."

The commercial ran almost exclusively in Washington, DC, where Trump could see it at the White House, and in West Palm Beach, Florida, where it could be seen at Trump's Mar-a-Lago resort. It was deviously effective in upsetting Trump and making him question Pence's loyalty. The final words of the ad looked ahead to January 6—telling Trump something he likely did not know:

"Oh, there's one last thing, Donald. On January 6, Mike Pence will put the nail in your political coffin when he presides over the Senate vote to prove Joe Biden won. It's over, and Mike Pence knows it."

The ad touched on something that had been obvious to just about anybody watching Trump's desperate and failing attempts to challenge the election results: Mike Pence was nowhere to be seen. The vice president had kept a low profile since the election and when he did make public appearances, he steered clear of Trump's fact-free allegations that the election had been stolen with massive voter fraud.

Now Trump's renegade band of lawyers was telling him Pence could do what they had failed to do in court. All he had to do, they said, was to use his power as the presiding officer of the official counting of the electoral votes to reject the votes from the six states Trump's legal team had been attempting, with no success, to contest in court. Trump immediately embraced the idea. He first brought it up with Pence in mid-December, shortly after all fifty states certified their electoral votes. At first Pence, never one to challenge Trump, told the president he didn't think he had that power, but he promised to look into it, and he asked his chief lawyer in the vice president's office, Greg Jacob, to study the issue. Not surprisingly, Jacob came back with a conclusion that Pence had no constitutional authority to reject electoral votes and flip the election results. His role was ceremonial.

Donald Trump refused to accept that answer. When Pence explained it to him, it seemed as if the president had not heard him. Trump just kept telling Pence he was counting on him—that he was expecting him to "do the right thing."

On December 29, Representative Louie Gohmert, one of Trump's most ardent supporters in Congress, went so far as to file a bizarre lawsuit in federal court against Pence with the aim of forcing him to use his power to reject electoral votes from states Trump was contesting. The lawsuit was an absurdity, but Pence's allies believed it wasn't actually Gohmert's idea. They believed Trump himself was behind the lawsuit and had asked the congressman to file it. And, in fact, the lead attorney on the lawsuit was none other than Sidney Powell, who was also advising Trump.

The idea that Pence could overturn the election had become a Trump obsession. Pence had failed to talk him out of it and was being sued by one of Trump's congressional supporters, and now somebody else needed to convince the president the idea was a fantasy.

That's why Marc Short called Jared Kushner. Short believed Kushner was smart enough to understand Trump was flat-out wrong. Kushner had privately been telling friends he knew the election was over. He clearly knew there was nothing Mike Pence could do to change it.

"Please talk to the president," Short said to Kushner. "He listens to you. Explain to him that the vice president's role in counting electoral votes is entirely ceremonial. He has no power whatsoever to reject any state's electoral votes."

"You know, I'm really focused on the Middle East right now," Kushner responded. "I haven't been involved in the election stuff since Rudy Giuliani came in."

"But this is a big problem," Short said. "The president is being misled. Please talk to him."

"I really don't want to get involved," Kushner responded. "My focus is on Middle East peace."

Short was disappointed, but not surprised. Kushner had been a central player in the Trump campaign and one of the president's most trusted advisors. But one of the reasons Kushner had been such a powerful figure in the Trump White House was that he steadfastly avoided lost causes and almost never took a stand he believed would upset his father-in-law. Kushner had his fingerprints all over some of the Trump administration's successes—from the trade deal with Mexico and Canada to criminal justice reform to the Abraham Accords that normalized Israel's relations with some of its Arab neighbors—but he was nowhere to be seen when things were going wrong.

Chief of Staff Mark Meadows was no help, either. He had been blocking the vice president's staff from meetings. For their part, Pence's aides began to suspect Meadows was actually part of the problem. Evidence for this came in the form of an email Meadows sent to the vice president's senior staff on December 31, an email that has never before been made public.

The subject was: "Constitutional Analysis of the Vice President's Authority for January 6, 2021, Vote Count." The email included a document written by Trump campaign lawyer Jenna Ellis.

The Ellis memo noted that there had been challenges to the election results in six states—Arizona, Georgia, Michigan, Pennsylvania, Nevada, and Wisconsin—and argued that when each of those six states came up for a count on January 6, Pence could declare that the electoral votes were in dispute and the states needed to clarify whether they intended to send electoral votes for Biden (as they all had) or for Trump (as Trump's lawyers had argued they should).

The analysis seemed to assume that each of those states had sent two slates of electoral votes—one for Biden and an alternative batch for Trump. This was not the case. All of the states in question had only sent and certified electoral votes for Biden.

Ellis then outlined a detailed process designed to result in a Trump victory.

"The Vice President should require a response from each state legislature no later than 7pm Eastern Standard Time on January 15th

2021," Ellis wrote. "If any state legislature fails to provide a timely response, no electoral votes can be opened and counted from that state."

If the votes from the states Trump was contesting were not opened and counted, Biden would be deprived of an electoral majority. Ellis's memo addressed that next.

"The Constitution provides that if no candidate for president receives a majority of electoral votes that Congress shall vote by state delegation," she continued. "This will provide two and a half days for Congress to meet and vote by delegation prior to January 20 at noon for the inauguration."

Under such a scenario that inauguration could be a second one for Trump. Because if enough of Biden's electoral votes were not "opened and counted," the president, according to the Constitution, would be chosen by Congress under a system where each state delegation casts a single vote. At the time, Republicans had a majority in twenty-six of the fifty state delegations—enough to make Donald Trump the victor.

In the memo forwarded by Mark Meadows to the vice president's office, Jenna Ellis was making the case Pence could in fact do exactly what the president wanted him to do. He could overturn the certified results of the presidential election in enough states to hand Trump the victory.

She portrayed this not just as something Pence could do but something Pence *must* do to abide by his solemn constitutional duty.

"This is a meritorious request because the Vice President has taken an oath to uphold the Constitution," she wrote. "He is not exercising discretion nor establishing a new precedent. He is simply asking for clarification from the constitutionally appointed authority."

The next day, New Year's Day, the vice president's chief of staff received another missive from the West Wing. This time it came in the form of an unsigned document sent in a text message from Johnny McEntee. McEntee was the now thirty-one-year-old personal assistant who had been put in charge of the Presidential Personnel Office. Now he was informing the vice president's office that Pence had unquestioned authority to overturn the election. Here is the memo, which also has never before been made public, in its entirety:

JEFFERSON USED HIS POSITION AS VP TO WIN

- The Constitution sets precise requirements for the form in which the states are to submit their electoral votes.
- In 1801, the ballots of all states were in perfect conformity except Georgia's.
- Georgia's submission dramatically failed to conform to the requirements.
- VP Jefferson presided over the counting of the ballots even as he was one of the candidates.
- Had the defective ballots been rejected, Jefferson would have most likely lost the election.
- Senate tellers told Jefferson in a loud voice that there was a problem with the Georgia ballots.
- Rather than investigating, Jefferson ignored the problems and announced himself the winner.
- This proves, that the VP has, at a minimum, a substantial discretion to address issues with the electoral process.

And that was it. McEntee was no constitutional scholar and no historian, but he was telling Pence that Thomas Jefferson had used his power as vice president to win—and that Pence should do the same.

After all, Thomas Jefferson was the author of the Declaration of Independence and one of those guys on Mount Rushmore. If it was okay for him to use his power as vice president to get himself elected president after the election of 1800, how could it not be okay for Pence to use his power to reelect Donald Trump now?

Not surprisingly, McEntee's bullet-point description of Jefferson's actions was deeply flawed. But to Trump, it was the gospel truth. He brought it up with Pence several times over the days leading up to January 6.

When I met with Trump at Mar-a-Lago nearly two months after he left the White House, he was still repeating Johnny McEntee's talking points about how Jefferson had used his position as vice president to ensure his victory in the 1800 presidential election.

"There would be nothing wrong with doing what Thomas Jefferson did, he kept the votes," Trump told me. "So Mike, in theory, could say, well, I'm going to keep the votes because it's all mixed up, it's wrong, you made a mistake, we're going to keep the votes."

"If Mike Pence did what you wanted, do you think you would still be in the White House?" I asked him.

"I think we would have won, yeah," he answered. "Unfortunately, Mike was not Thomas Jefferson. It's too bad."

"Can you ever forgive him for that?" I asked.

"I don't know," Trump said. "Because I picked him. I like him. I still like him. But I don't know that I can forgive him."

The bitterness months later was shocking. The way Trump saw it, Pence had deprived him of the thing he wanted most. He could have guaranteed his triumphant reelection. Instead, he had deprived him of a second term.

This was all madness. There's no other way to put it. Just consider what really happened with Jefferson.

In the election of 1800, Thomas Jefferson, who was then vice president, won a narrow victory over President John Adams. In the electoral college, the vote was seventy-three to sixty-five. As the Constitution dictates, it was up to Jefferson, in the vice president's role as president of the Senate, to preside over a joint session of Congress for the official counting of the votes certified and sent to Congress by the states.

Article II of the Constitution sets forth specific instructions for the states to follow when preparing their electoral votes. Here's the exact language:

"And they shall make a List of all the Persons voted for, and of the Number of Votes for each; which List they shall sign and certify, and transmit sealed to the Seat of the Government of the United States, directed to the President of the Senate."

The counting back then proceeded much like it is done now. As each state was called, the envelope containing the votes was opened, handed to the vice president, and the results were announced and added to the handwritten tally. Just as it is today, the process was a formality. The states had each already announced the winners. Everybody knew which states Jefferson had won and which states Adams had won, and, as a result, everybody knew Jefferson had won the election. Nobody—not Adams, not Adams's supporters—contested that fact. But the Constitution stipulates that those electoral votes need to be opened and officially counted in a joint session of Congress before the results are official.

When the state of Georgia was called and its certificate handed to Jefferson, he was notified by Congress's tellers—that is, the congressional staff who keep track of the votes—that there was a problem with the way the state's certificate was prepared. It contained a list of names for the electors, but did not specify whether they were for Jefferson or Adams. It also wasn't properly signed by state officials.

The leading experts on this little-noted episode in American history are historians Bruce Ackerman and David Fontana who, nearly two decades before the election of 2020, searched the National Archives to find the original electoral certificate that Georgia sent to Congress. They also searched for and found records about the election certification in Georgia's state archives. Here's how Ackerman and Fontana describe what happened when it came time to count Georgia's vote:

"As each state was called, Jefferson opened the envelope and passed the ballot to the tellers. When he opened the Georgia ballot, the tellers looked at it and told him, in a tone loud enough for others in the room to hear, that there was a problem with it. They handed it back to Jefferson for re-examination. Jefferson then proceeded as if nothing remarkable had happened. Georgia's votes were included in the running total."

Trump had been told the lesson of this story is that Georgia's electoral slate was in dispute and Jefferson exercised the power to decide whether to accept them. By accepting the flawed electoral certificate, he ensured his own victory.

But there is a massive hole in this argument. There may have been a technical problem with the way Georgia's paperwork had been prepared, but nobody doubted Jefferson won Georgia.

"Until Jefferson opened the Georgia envelope, he had every reason to believe that he and [running mate Aaron] Burr had won that state's electoral votes," Ackerman and Fontana wrote in 2005: "that's what the newspapers had been reporting. Moreover, the members of Georgia's congressional delegation—two of whom were Federalists—were present on the vote-counting day. Surely they would have raised a noisy objection if they believed their state's votes had been placed in the wrong column. Moreover, Jefferson's guess about the Georgia electors' true intentions proved to be correct. We have gone on a fact-finding mission to the Georgia archives, and have found that the defects in the state's ballot were merely the result of frontier lawyering. There is no doubt that the electors intended to vote for the Republican ticket."

So, no, Jefferson didn't overturn election results in Georgia to make himself president. He won the election. And nobody doubted it.

And if that is not enough to show the absurdity of Trump's argument, there's another factor. After the 1800 election, Congress passed, and the states ratified, the Twelfth Amendment to the Constitution, which made the limited role played by the vice president, in their role as president of the Senate, explicit: "The president of the Senate shall, in the presence of the Senate and House of Representatives, open all the certificates, and the votes shall then be counted."

That's it. In legal parlance the word "shall" is a command, something required by law. The vice president has no power to reject votes. He has a command to open the envelopes and allow the counting to proceed. Case closed.

The process was clarified one more time in the Electoral Count Act of 1887, which was passed in the wake of the disputed 1876 election, where several states sent competing sets of electoral votes. In that case, the law outlines the process to be taken. If there is an objection from at least one member of the House and at least one member of the Senate, Congress is to vote on which set of electoral votes will be counted. Once again: there is no role for the vice president to make that determination. He is a master of ceremonies, not a judge.

But Trump wasn't hearing the arguments. All he was hearing was the fact that Pence would be presiding over the counting of the votes—and the falsehood that he could fix it and bring about the elusive Trump victory.

———

As January 6 approached, Pence continued to see Trump every day. Invariably the subject of the electoral vote counting would come up. Pence would tell the president he believed his role in counting electoral votes was strictly ceremonial, that only Congress, with a majority vote, could reject them. White House Counsel Pat Cipollone told Trump the same thing—over and over again. But Trump disregarded the views of the top lawyer in the White House and ignored Pence's protestations. He looked at his vice president and he was confident he would do what he had always done: he would be loyal to Trump. According to multiple sources who witnessed these interactions during the first days of January, the meetings were not particularly contentious. Pence didn't push back too hard. And Trump just kept saying, "You know, the top constitutional scholars tell me you can do it."

On Monday, January 4, Pence flew on Air Force Two to Georgia, where he spent the first part of the day campaigning for the state's two Republican senators, who each faced a runoff election the following day. He had not said anything publicly about the idea he could overturn the election that coming Wednesday. But when Pence took the stage at Rock Springs Church in Milner, Georgia, he did raise expectations for what could happen when Congress came together to count electoral votes.

"I know we all got our doubts about the last election," Pence said. "I want to assure you I share the concerns of millions of Americans about voting irregularities. And I promise you come this Wednesday [January 6], we'll have our day in Congress."

He wasn't repeating the wild allegations about massive voter fraud. He wasn't saying he could overturn the election. But he was raising expectations that something big could happen on January 6. What he meant was that Congress would have a chance to debate the electoral votes in those states that were challenged by a member of the House and Senate. There's no doubt, however, that many of those Trump supporters listening to him say "we will have our day" would be expecting more. When he said those words, the crowd erupted in thunderous applause.

As Pence flew back to Washington that afternoon on Air Force Two, Trump's secretary sent word that the president wanted to see him as soon as he arrived.

The request didn't specify the reason for the meeting, but Pence knew it would be about January 6, so he asked Greg Jacob, the counsel for the vice president's office, to join him and Marc Short at the meeting. The meeting lasted nearly ninety minutes. Before it was over, the whirring engines of Marine One could be heard as the presidential helicopter landed on the South Lawn to take Trump on the first leg of his trip to Georgia, where he was scheduled to have his own rally at eight p.m. for the Republican Senate candidates. A group of White House reporters and photographers could be seen outside, assembled to cover the president's departure on Marine One.

Inside the Oval Office, the president was joined by a lawyer named John Eastman. He was a late addition to Trump's legal team who started advising the president on his legal strategy in mid-December, after Trump and his allies had already lost dozens of court challenges. Eastman was a former clerk for Supreme Court Justice Clarence Thomas and a professor at Chapman University in California. He had briefly ignited a controversy in August 2020, when he wrote an essay in *Newsweek* suggesting that Kamala Harris—who was born at 9:28 p.m. at Kaiser Hospital in Oakland, California, on October 20, 1964—was ineligible to be vice president because her parents were not born in the United States and therefore, Eastman argued, Harris was not a "natural-born" American citizen. In the essay, Eastman said that at the time of her birth, Harris "owed her allegiance to a foreign power or powers—Jamaica, in the case of her father, and India, in the case of her mother." This racist claptrap was widely denounced. Not even Trump, who had infamously questioned Barack Obama's citizenship, had made such an absurd claim. *Newsweek* quickly apologized for publishing the article, saying, "the essay inevitably conveyed the ugly message that Senator Kamala Harris, a woman of color and the child of immigrants, was somehow not truly American" and was being used "as a tool to perpetuate racism and xenophobia."

Now, four months after writing that article, Eastman was there in the Oval Office sitting with the president and vice president.

In addition to Eastman, Trump had his secretary call another lawyer recently added to the Trump legal team, Mark Martin, and put him on speakerphone. Martin was the dean of Regent University School of Law in Virginia and the former chief justice of the North Carolina Supreme Court. He had been asked to offer his legal advice to the president by fellow North Carolinian Mark Meadows, and Trump had recently taken to describing him as "my Constitutional expert." Noticeably absent at this meeting was the man whose job it was to provide the president with legal advice. Cipollone had told Trump point-blank that the vice president didn't have the power to reject electoral votes. Trump excluded him from the meeting.

As with Trump's previous discussions with Pence on this issue, the meeting was not overly heated or contentious. In fact, Trump let his lawyers do most of the talking. Pence had already told Trump that his counsel, Greg Jacob, had researched the issue and concluded the vice president simply didn't have the power to reject electoral votes— and that the only way that could happen would be with a majority vote of Congress.

"These are esteemed legal scholars, Mike," Trump said. "And they are telling me you can do it."

And with that, Eastman brought up what he claimed were two

historical examples of vice-presidential influence over election re-sults. First was the discredited theory that Jefferson's action in 1801 to accept Georgia's flawed certificate of electoral votes somehow dem-onstrated Pence had the authority to reject electoral votes he deemed flawed or questionable. The second example the lawyers brought up was more recent and involved Richard Nixon.

It was from 1961, when then–Vice President Nixon presided over the counting of electoral votes from the 1960 presidential election. The election in Hawaii, which had only recently become a state, was in dispute. Nixon won by a mere 171 votes, but Kennedy was granted a request for a recount. The recount had not been completed before the deadline for submitting Hawaii's three electoral votes, so the state sent two slates of electoral votes—one envelope for Nixon and one for Kennedy.

As it turned out, Kennedy had enough electoral votes to win re-gardless of what happened with Hawaii's three electoral votes, so when it came time to open and count the envelope containing Ha-waii's electoral votes, Nixon announced he would count the slate for Kennedy instead of the one for him. After he asked if there was any objection—and there was none—the votes were counted for Kennedy.

This little episode of American presidential history was cited by Trump's "esteemed legal scholars" as evidence that a vice president can determine whether to accept a state's electoral votes.

Pence reminded Eastman and Martin that he was a lawyer, too, as he and his counsel calmly explained the flaws in that reasoning. First, in the case of Hawaii's 1960 recount, the state sent two sets of elec-toral votes. In the current situation, each state had only sent one set of electoral votes and all of those were properly certified. Second, Nixon didn't take the action on his own. He asked if there was any objection. There was none. If there had been one, the issue of resolving which slate of votes to accept would have been determined by a vote of Congress, not Nixon.

They could have made another point: Nixon wasn't attempting to overturn the results of a presidential election when he accepted Kennedy's electoral votes; he was being gracious. Those three electoral votes wouldn't change the outcome; instead of going through the process of contesting them, he simply gave the votes to Kennedy.

Regarding the Jefferson example, Pence pointed out that nobody had disputed Jefferson won Georgia and, regardless, the rules governing the vice president's role had been changed twice since then—once by the Twelfth Amendment and again by the Electoral Count Act of 1887. In other words, Jefferson didn't do what Trump and his new lawyers said he had done, and even if he had, it wouldn't matter because the rules had changed since then.

The meeting broke up and Trump took off for his first rally in Georgia. When he took the stage before thousands of supporters in Dalton, Georgia, Trump bitterly complained about election fraud and accused Democrats of trying to steal the election. But he said Mike Pence could still save the day.

"I hope Mike Pence comes through for us, I have to tell you," Trump said at the Georgia rally. "I hope that our great vice president comes through for us. He's a great guy. Of course, if he doesn't come through, I won't like him quite as much."

He said it with a smile, but it was a threat. He was telling his supporters everything would be okay—he could still win—if "our great vice president comes through for us." He had just dramatically turned up the pressure on Mike Pence.

The next day, January 5, Pence was scheduled to have lunch with Trump. Shortly before the meeting was to start, Trump issued a short tweet saying publicly what he had been saying privately to Pence for several days:

> **Donald J. Trump**
> @realDonald Trump
>
> The Vice President has the power to reject fraudulently chosen electors.
>
> 1/5/21, 11:06 AM

When Pence and Short showed up at the Oval Office, Chief of Staff Meadows cut them off and said Short could not go in.

"This is a one-on-one meeting," Meadows said.

Trump and Pence did not end up eating lunch together and the meeting didn't last long. The vice president told his senior advisors that he again explained to the president that his role the following day would be purely ceremonial.

That afternoon, *The New York Times* ran a story that, for the first time, reported Pence had told Trump he did not believe he had the power to block the certification of Biden's victory. The article said Pence had delivered that message during their weekly lunch. In fact, the message had been delivered repeatedly by Pence for days—although he had done so only privately.

As the results of the Georgia Senate race came in that night—embarrassing defeats for the two Republican Senators—Trump issued a statement denouncing the *New York Times* report as "fake news."

"The Vice President and I are in total agreement that the Vice President has the power to act," Trump said in his written statement.

The statement was a lie. Pence did not agree with him, and Trump knew it.

Hours later, Trump was still up, fuming about his vice president.

"If Vice President @Mike_Pence comes through for us, we will win the Presidency," he tweeted at one a.m., just after the calendar turned to January 6. Hours later, Trump was up again and tweeting at his vice president, saying he had it in his power to turn the election results around by rejecting electoral votes in states Trump was contesting.

"All Mike Pence has to do is send them back to the States, AND WE WIN," Trump tweeted at 8:17 a.m. on January 6. "Do it Mike, this is a time for extreme courage!"

On that fateful morning, Pence looked over the lengthy statement he and his staff had written to explain what he was about to do. In some ways, it was a perfectly ordinary statement, explaining why Pence intended to do what every other vice president who had presided over the counting of electoral votes had done.

"It is my considered judgment," the statement said, "that my oath to support and defend the Constitution constrains me from claiming unilateral authority to determine which electoral votes should be counted and which should not."

If that were not the case, he pointed out, the vice president would be exercising the power to single-handedly choose the president.

"Our Founders were deeply skeptical of concentrations of power and created a Republic based on separation of powers and checks and balances under the Constitution of the United States," Pence wrote. "Vesting the Vice President with unilateral authority to decide presidential contests would be entirely antithetical to that design."

In other words, giving a single person that kind of power would be antidemocratic—and anti-American.

The statement was two and a half pages long. Part of it echoed some of Trump's baseless claims of election fraud, claiming there were "significant allegations of voting irregularities" and arguing members of Congress had the right to challenge the results. He promised, as the presiding officer, he would ensure a full debate on those allegations. But he would not do what the president had demanded.

The facts outlined in the statement may have been perfectly ordinary and uncontroversial to anybody but the most deranged Trump partisan, but for Pence the act of putting out the statement was beyond extraordinary. In all his time as vice president, he had never once publicly disagreed with President Trump. Not once. This would be the first time.

Before getting in his vice-presidential motorcade to go to the Capitol building, and before releasing his statement, Pence spoke once more by telephone with Trump. Days later the *New York Times* offered what seemed to be a sensationalist description of the call. According to the *Times* report, which was written by three of the newspaper's best reporters—Maggie Haberman, Peter Baker, and Annie Karni—Trump crudely cajoled his vice president to do what he was demanding by saying, "You can either go down in history as a patriot or you can go down in history as a pussy."

Could he really have said those words? At the time, the White House press office flatly denied the story. Some Pence aides said they did not know if that was said but also told reporters they doubted it was true.

I mean, really, would the president of the United States call the vice president on the day he was to preside over the official certification of election results and say he would be a "pussy" if he followed the Constitution? That would be preposterous, right?

No. Not preposterous if that president is Donald Trump.

When I met with Trump in Mar-a-Lago to interview him for this book, I asked him if that *New York Times* report was true.

"There was a report, excuse my language—" I said.

"Go ahead," Trump said.

"—not mine, it was in the report—"

"Yeah."

"—that you talked to [Pence] that morning and you said, 'You can be a patriot or you can be a pussy.' Did you really say that or is that an incorrect report?"

"I wouldn't dispute it," he answered.

"Really?"

"I wouldn't dispute it," he repeated. "I also said, 'You can be Thomas Jefferson or you can be no Thomas Jefferson, and you turned out to be no Thomas Jefferson.'"

Not only was Trump not denying the remark, he seemed, months later, proud of it. Proud of the crude words he had unleashed on his ever-loyal vice president.

For Pence, that conversation on the morning of January 6 was the most painful he had ever had with Trump. He had incurred the wrath of the president whom he had always stood behind. He had stood behind Trump even when he didn't want to, even when it hurt him politically, even when he was morally opposed to his actions. He may have been the most loyal vice president in the history of American vice presidents.

And even as he was about to commit what Trump would consider an act of betrayal, Pence sought to be deferential and submissive to Trump's ego. Pence instructed his staff to delay the release of his statement announcing that he would defy Trump's unlawful command and would instead faithfully preside over the counting of the electoral votes. Trump had a speech later that morning—a speech that would go down as one of the most notorious speeches in the history of the American presidency—and Pence did not want his statement disagreeing with the president to go out until after Trump was finished speaking. But Trump's speech started late and went long. He was still speaking as the time came for Pence to take his seat in the House chamber and to begin presiding over the counting of the votes. Shortly after Pence banged the gavel to start the session, the microphones captured him turning to an aide off to the side.

"Is my statement out?" Pence can be heard asking.

"Yes, it is," the aide responded.

There was no turning back now. Pence had a choice between loyalty to Trump and loyalty to the Constitution. He chose not to break the law, and, for that, Trump would forever consider him a coward and a traitor.

CHAPTER SIXTEEN

DAY OF INFAMY

Before the mob of Trump supporters broke through the barricades, beat back police officers, and bashed their way into the US Capitol on January 6, 2021, there was little sense inside the building of the looming disaster. In the House and Senate chambers, there are no televisions. There are no windows facing outdoors. For Congresswoman Liz Cheney, the first indication that something could go dreadfully wrong came when she received a call from her father as she was in the House chamber waiting for the joint session of Congress to open and the counting of electoral votes to begin. Former Vice President Dick Cheney was watching television at home and he didn't like what he was seeing. President Trump was speaking to a large and unruly crowd in an area outside the White House called the Ellipse, and he had just singled out Cheney's daughter. To the elder Cheney the remarks sounded threatening, especially given how riled up the crowd seemed to be.

"We've got to get rid of the weak congresspeople, the ones that aren't any good, the Liz Cheneys of the world," Trump said as the crowd applauded wildly. "We've got to get rid of them."

The former vice president was worried about his daughter's safety. He knew that she planned to give a speech that would further enrage Trump and his already angry supporters protesting outside. The speech she had written was a forceful condemnation of exactly what Trump was demanding—that Congress overturn Joe Biden's victory in the presidential election by voting to reject the electoral votes in the six states Biden had won. He had read his daughter's speech and agreed with every word of it. But with Trump invoking her name and telling his supporters to march down to the Capitol and "fight like hell," Dick Cheney thought she should delay her speech and wait for things to calm down.

On the other side of the Capitol building, senators were gathering to walk through the Capitol rotunda and across to the House chamber. It's a ritual that precedes every joint session of Congress. This was a day filled with symbolism and tradition. Three dark and shiny mahogany boxes had been brought in by the parliamentarian's office to be carried along as the senators walked over to the House. The boxes looked like relics from a time long past—each one held shut by wide leather straps with brass clasps and locked with a skeleton key. They contained documents sent in by certified mail from all fifty states: the signed and sealed electoral votes to be opened and counted during the joint session of Congress. As he made his way to the Senate chamber, Senator Roy Blunt (R-MO) got his first indication that something unusual was going on when an aide informed him that Trump had just announced in his speech that he would be marching with his supporters to the Capitol building. Blunt, who as chairman of the Senate Rules Committee had responsibility for overseeing the day's events and for the inauguration that would take place two weeks later, wondered why the president would be coming to Capitol Hill— and where, exactly, he would be going.

"I thought it was the case that the president can come on the

Senate floor anytime he wants to, but the president can come on the House floor only when invited," Blunt told me. Speaker of the House Nancy Pelosi was obviously not going to be inviting him to the House. "So if he was going to come to one of the two chambers, that would be the Senate."

When Mike Pence arrived at the Capitol, Trump was still giving his speech outside the White House. On his ride from the vice presidential residence, Pence caught a glimpse of some of the tens of thousands of Trump supporters who had traveled to Washington from all over the country. They were there because they believed the election was stolen and they were determined to stop the final certification of Joe Biden as president-elect. And now Trump was telling them that the fate of the presidential election was entirely in Pence's hands.

"If Mike Pence does the right thing, we win the election," Trump told the crowd outside. "All Vice President Pence has to do is send it back to the states to recertify and we become president and you are the happiest people."

The drumbeat from Trump was relentless. His speech went on for more than an hour. He directed most of his ire toward Republicans who he felt had betrayed him. Not just Liz Cheney, but also former Attorney General Bill Barr, who he said had "changed" because he didn't want to look like Trump's "personal attorney." He lashed out at the Supreme Court for rejecting his legal challenges, suggesting the justices *he had nominated* "ruled against Trump" because they were concerned about how they would be received "in the social circuit." He lashed out at Georgia's Republican governor, calling him a "disaster" and suggesting he was a wimp because he weighed only 130 pounds. He slammed Mitt Romney for congratulating Biden on his victory. He attacked Republican Senate leader Mitch McConnell and other "pathetic Republicans." But over and over again he came back to the subject of Mike Pence and how on this day he was the one and only person who could make everything right. Pence, Trump said repeatedly, was the one who could undo all those Republican betrayals and reverse the travesty of the "stolen election."

"Mike Pence is going to have to come through for us, and if he doesn't, that will be a sad day for our country."

At times, Trump spoke as if he were having a conversation directly with Pence.

"Mike Pence, I hope you're going to stand up for the good of our Constitution and for the good of our country," Trump said. "And if you're not, I'm going to be very disappointed in you. I will tell you right now. I'm not hearing good stories."

Each mention of Pence drew a loud response from the crowd. Trump was obsessively focused on his vice president, and now the crowd was, too.

But Trump knew exactly what Pence was going to do. And before he was done speaking, so did everyone else. The vice president had just released his statement explaining that his role was ceremonial and he had no power to reject any of the certified votes in those mahogany boxes.

At one p.m., as Pence stood facing the House chamber with the senators lined up behind him to walk over to the House, police were dealing with a security threat: an unexploded pipe bomb had just been discovered outside the headquarters of the Republican National Committee located just a few blocks away. The discovery of the bomb didn't disrupt the proceedings inside the Capitol building, but soon the Cannon House Office Building across the street had to be evacuated because of its proximity to the RNC's headquarters.

Congressman Cedric Richmond (D-LA) was one of those who was

forced to evacuate his office in the Cannon building. Richmond had been a co-chairman of Joe Biden's presidential campaign and would be leaving Congress in two weeks to serve as one of Biden's top advisors in the White House. He rushed out of his office and over to the Capitol, where he set up to work in an area adjacent to Statuary Hall known as the Lincoln Room. Before the expansion of the Capitol in 1857, the space was home to the House Post Office, and was a refuge for then-Representative Abraham Lincoln, whose desk was several feet away. In the Capitol, you are always surrounded by history. On some days that is more obvious than others. This was one of those days.

The Lincoln Room isn't large, but it has windows with a great view looking west over the Capitol steps toward the Washington Monument and the Lincoln Memorial. Richmond could see what his colleagues inside the House and Senate chambers could not see. There was a large and growing crowd of Trump supporters, many of them waving large blue flags with TRUMP emblazoned on them, moving toward the Capitol. He was surprised by the size of the crowd, but he was even more surprised to see the relative ease with which they moved closer and closer to the building. He could see the police trying to hold the line as the crowd moved in on the security perimeter. They pushed forward, taunting the officers, pushing them, throwing things. Soon the crowd vastly outnumbered the police and the officers retreated and tried to hold the line once again a little closer to the Capitol building. Richmond watched, appalled at what he was seeing. The mob was in control. And while the officers tried to hold the line, they did not draw their weapons.

Before long, he saw a group of Trump supporters break through the police line and climb a tower next to the inaugural platform that had been built for the television crews. The Capitol had not been breached yet. The mob was not yet inside, but they were coming and were already occupying the location of the upcoming Biden inauguration. Richmond's reaction wasn't fear. It was anger.

"I was just watching it thinking, there's no way police would be taking this shit from Black people," Richmond told me. "If they were Black, if they were Hispanic, police would have unloaded on them."

As Richmond watched protestors push past police officers and up the steps of the west front of the Capitol, debate was underway in the House and Senate over the first objection filed by Trump's allies—an attempt to disqualify the votes from the state of Arizona.

Mitch McConnell rose to speak. He was unaware that Capitol Police were engaged in a violent confrontation with Trump supporters on the east and west sides of the Capitol. Some of the tools the police had to control the crowds—including bicycle-rack barricades, riot shields, and helmets—had been captured by the mob and were being used as weapons by them. Video of the assault on the side of the Capitol facing the National Mall shows Officer Daniel Hodges crying out in agony as the mob pinned him against a door leading into the building. Rioters beat him with his own gas mask and baton, bloodying his face and making him think he was going to die. "Men alleging to be veterans told us how they had fought for this country and were fighting for it again," Hodges later recounted. "One man tried to start a chant of 'Four more years.'"

McConnell did not know about all that, but he was angry that Trump's antics had contributed to Republican defeats the previous night in two Senate runoff elections in Georgia. He angrily criticized the attempt by his fellow Republicans to undo the certified results of a presidential election Trump had lost, portraying it as an act of betrayal. If Congress did that, McConnell warned, it would send democracy itself into a "death spiral."

"The voters, the courts, and the states have all spoken," McConnell said. "If we overrule them, it would damage our republic forever."

———

Despite what Trump had told his supporters, he did not join them in their march to the Capitol. He was back, safely and securely, in the White House, watching television, ecstatic about the large crowd that had turned out for him. He told aides in the West Wing it was the largest crowd he had ever spoken to. About a million people were out there, he said. That was a gross exaggeration, but the crowd was huge and they were doing just as he asked, marching up to the Capitol to protest the counting of the electoral votes. Angry to see what McConnell was saying, Trump tweeted a video of the speech he had just given outside the White House. In that speech, Trump told his supporters to "peacefully and patriotically make your voices heard," but the men and women in red hats storming the Capitol steps were not responding to the one time in the speech he used the word "peacefully." They were responding to Trump's battle cry.

"We fight like hell," Trump had just told them. "And if you don't fight like hell, you're not going to have a country anymore."

Inside the Senate chamber, Senator Blunt was still pondering the logistics of a surprise visit from the president, when his phone went off with a text message from an aide. Phones are technically forbidden on the Senate floor—a rule often flouted—and as Rules Committee chairman, Blunt didn't like openly breaking the rules. Nevertheless, he took his phone out of his pocket and read a disturbing message.

"Rioters have seized the west media tower," the message read.

That was exactly what Cedric Richmond had witnessed. The pro-Trump crowd had somehow managed to get onto the large stage outside the Capitol that had been built for the January 20 presidential inauguration—an area that was supposed to be tightly secured and closed off to the public. A minute later, Senator Blunt got another message.

"Police are fighting rioters on the inaugural platform."

Within another minute or so, the lead Secret Service agent responsible for protecting Vice President Pence rushed in and whisked Pence, who had been presiding over the debate, out of the chamber and into a room directly behind it. At that moment, the only other person inside that room was Myles Cullen, a photographer who had worked for the vice president for nearly four years. Pence's aides and his family were nearby in another room behind the Senate floor. The agent briefly went out into the hall to confer with Capitol Police and the Senate sergeant at arms.

"We have to take you out of here immediately," the agent told Pence when he came back to the room.

"I'm not going anywhere," Pence said.

"Sir, we really need to take you out of here right now," the agent said.

"I told you, I am not going anywhere," Pence said, firmly and angrily, his voice rising.

Cullen had worked as Pence's photographer for as long as he had been vice president. He told me it was the first time he had seen Pence yell at anybody.

"I'm going to stay here and I am going to do my job!"

While Pence argued with the man responsible for protecting his life, the Senate session was abruptly shut down. The C-SPAN cameras were turned off. Senate staff frantically started closing and locking all the doors—including the doors to the balconies above the Senate floor. The locks on these doors are old and not particularly functional. They must be manually turned and are certainly not strong enough to keep out a mob.

It is at this moment, as Pence was refusing to leave, that Capitol Hill police officer Eugene Goodman took a series of actions that likely prevented January 6 from turning into a bloodbath much worse than it already was.

Officer Goodman's heroics are well documented. In surveillance video, he can be seen sprinting toward the Senate chamber from the direction of the Capitol rotunda. This happens just moments after the first rioters broke into the building through a smashed window one flight below. On the video, Goodman can be seen passing Senator Romney, warning him to turn back and take shelter with the other senators. As a prime target of Donald Trump, Romney would have been a prime target of the rioters. Goodman's warning prevented Romney from walking right into the incoming mob and may have saved his life.

As rioters poured into the building—the first of them climbing through smashed windows on the first floor and then breaking open the doors for others to come in—Vice President Pence remained in the room behind the Senate chamber for what must have felt like the longest thirteen minutes of his life. For a minute or two he was alone with his photographer and his lead Secret Service agent, Tim Giebels. Eventually Second Lady Karen Pence, their daughter, and Pence's brother Greg* were brought into the room along with Pence's chief of staff Marc Short and his military aide. Although the vice president had made it perfectly clear he was not going to leave the Capitol building, Agent Giebels convinced him that it was not safe for them to stay in that room. The door lock was flimsy and the rioters were coming down the hallway. They had to move. As they left the room, Trump made his first public comment since the Capitol was

---

*Greg Pence was not just the vice president's brother, he was also a Republican member of Congress from Indiana, and he was among those Republicans voting to reject some of Joe Biden's electoral votes. Representative Pence voted to object to the electoral votes from Pennsylvania, and he cast that vote after the Capitol riot.

breached. Instead of issuing a plea for calm or an order to stand down, Trump leveled an attack on Pence—an attack that would further inflame the anger of the rioters toward the vice president.

"Mike Pence didn't have the courage to do what should have been done to protect our Country and our Constitution," Trump said in a tweet posted eleven minutes after the first rioters broke into the Capitol and Pence was removed from the Senate chamber by the Secret Service.

On surveillance video taken ninety seconds after that tweet was posted, Pence can be seen rushing down the stairs behind the Senate chamber along with his wife and daughter. On the video you can also see photographer Myles Cullen walking behind him along with Pence's military aide, who is carrying what looks like a suitcase—the so-called nuclear football containing the codes necessary to launch a nuclear attack. Like the president, the vice president always travels with the nuclear football.

As Pence went down the back staircase, Officer Goodman ran down a nearby public staircase on the other side of the Senate chamber. In the narrow and short hallway on the bottom of that staircase, Goodman had his first direct confrontation with rioters. It's a crucial moment that was captured on camera from several angles. Goodman can be seen with his back to the staircase he just ran down. He's facing the rioters, trying to hold them back. Just behind the rioters, less than twenty yards away, was a little-used stairwell leading to the basement of the Capitol and a network of tunnels leading to the Senate office buildings blocks away.

The timing here is critical. Once Pence and his family walked down the stairway behind the Senate to the ground floor, they had to run over to the stairwell that Officer Goodman was now facing to get to safety in the basement below. The only reason the rioters could not see what was happening over by that stairwell to the basement was because they were looking toward Goodman, yelling at him and trying to push him back. The taunts of the rioters make it perfectly clear this was not just a case of wanton destruction. These people were on a mission.

"Where are they counting the votes?" the rioters demanded. "Where are they counting? Where are they counting?"

Their mission was the one Donald Trump had just spoken about at the rally outside the White House—preventing the counting of the electoral votes that would make Joe Biden's victory official. For the moment, at least, the rioters had succeeded. The Senate was shut down. The counting of the electoral votes had stopped.

As Goodman held back the mob, the most important thing he was doing was buying time. Upstairs in the Senate chamber, the sergeant at arms announced that everybody in the chamber was to be evacuated to a secure room in the Hart Senate Office Building located nearly a half mile away through the tunnels under the Capitol. The only way to get to those tunnels was to get to that stairwell Pence had just used.

As the senators lined up to evacuate a Capitol building that was being overrun by angry Trump supporters, Donald Trump had other concerns. Watching the television coverage back at the White House, Trump placed a call to Tommy Tuberville, who had just been elected to the Senate after a career as a football coach and had been among the first Republican senators to say he would vote to overturn the election. Trump was calling Tuberville, but he inadvertently dialed the mobile phone of Senator Mike Lee (R-UT). Lee answered and passed his phone over to Tuberville, who later described the call to reporters.

"I said, 'Mr. President, they've taken the vice president out. They want me to get off the phone, I gotta go,'" Tuberville said, adding that he was "probably the only guy in the world who hung up on the president of the United States."

As the senators started to leave the chamber, one of the Senate parliamentarians made a fateful decision instructing other staffers to grab the mahogany boxes—the boxes that contained the certified electoral votes from all fifty states—and to bring them along with the senators as they made the escape through the tunnels below. If those boxes had fallen into the hands of the rioters and the electoral votes had been stolen or destroyed, it's unclear how the counting could have resumed. The process of finalizing the presidential election is strictly defined in the Constitution and the Electoral Count Act. The electoral vote certificates must be originals and they must be signed and sealed by government authorities in each of the fifty states. Congress had no copies, and even if they did, only originals can legally be counted. State legislatures across the country would likely have had to reconvene. The electoral college would have had to vote again—but even that was not a certainty because the deadlines for certifying electoral votes had all passed. There would have been chaos, with no clear solution outlined in the Constitution.

The only reason that didn't happen is because those mahogany boxes were saved—rushed out of the chamber along with the senators.

The only reason the mob downstairs didn't see the senators and the boxes make their escape is because Officer Goodman was keeping the rioters' attention—and their anger—focused on him. In video taken of Goodman holding back the crowd, you can actually see senators in the hallway behind the rioters rushing down the stairwell to the basement. The senators, some of them in their eighties, moved slowly. One of the police officers escorting them down the stairs gently urged them to pick up the pace.

"Time is not our friend," one police officer told Senator Blunt as he made his way toward the underground tunnels.

Walking backward, Goodman lured the rioters up to the second floor where he knew there would be several more officers to help him hold the rioters back, at least for a little longer.*

"He's one person, we're thousands!" one of the rioters yells as Goodman runs up the stairs calling on his radio for reinforcements on the second floor.

Goodman led the rioters to a line of fellow officers just outside one of the main doors to the Senate chamber. A belligerent man with a beard who had been leading the assault started yelling at the police officers. He was wearing a wool ski hat and a black T-shirt emblazoned with a large *Q*—signifying the QAnon conspiracy movement, which supported Trump and also had been labeled by the FBI as a domestic terror risk.

"Go arrest the vice president," the man in the Q T-shirt demands of the officers. "Go arrest him. We want justice."

In a doorway at another section of the Capitol, a mob of about two hundred rioters starts chanting for Pence's execution.

"Hang Mike Pence! Hang Mike Pence! Hang Mike Pence!"

As if to make it clear the threat was not an idle one, protestors had erected a gallows outside, complete with a hangman's noose.

Over in the House chamber, Liz Cheney still had her speech in her hands. Despite her father's warning, she had decided go forward with it. The top four House leaders, including Speaker of the House Nancy Pelosi and Republican Leader Kevin McCarthy, were taken off the floor and brought to more secure locations, but the House remained in session for fifteen minutes after the Senate shut down. The debate in the House over rejecting Arizona's electoral votes continued until the rioters were banging on the doors, trying to break into the House

---

*Goodman's actions luring the rioters up the stairs were dramatically captured on video by Igor Bobic, a reporter for the *Huffington Post*, who calmly documented it all despite the obvious danger to himself.

chamber. As the doors were barricaded shut, Representative Jamie Raskin (D-MD) called over to Cheney.

"Look at this," Raskin said, showing her an image on his phone. "They've brought a Confederate flag into the rotunda." There were a few dozen lawmakers inside the House chamber as rioters assaulted the doors, trying to break in. Representative Markwayne Mullin (R-OK), a former professional mixed-martial-arts fighter, barricaded the main entrance to the chamber with a desk as the rioters kept banging against the doors. The lawmakers had no idea how many were outside trying to break in, but the banging was so loud that at one point it was mistaken for gunfire. Mullin later described his experience to *Politico*, saying he was trying to hold back the attackers long enough to give his colleagues time to escape.

"The idea was just to try to delay," Mullin said. "I honestly didn't believe we were going to keep them out of the chamber. I was one hundred percent convinced that we were going to pile up at the door."

Mullin grabbed two wooden stands used to hold up hand-sanitizer dispensers and broke them in two, handing the pieces to fellow lawmakers to be used as weapons if the rioters broke into the chamber. One of those he handed the makeshift weapon to was Representative Troy Nehls (R-TX), a former sheriff who saw combat in Iraq and Afghanistan as a member of the U.S. Army Reserve.

As the rioters banged against the doors with flag poles, shattering one of the glass windows, security officers inside the chamber drew their weapons.

"Is it worth it?" Mullin shouted at the rioters through the shards of glass. "You almost got shot. You almost died. Is it worth it?"

The closest the House chamber came to being breached was when rioter Ashli Babbitt, an Air Force veteran and QAnon adherent, attempted to charge through a smashed window leading into the

Speaker's Lobby, which is connected to the House chamber. She was killed with a single shot fired by a Capitol Police officer inside.

House members were being evacuated as Babbitt was shot, rushing down a stairway behind the House chamber just steps away from the shattered window that she was attempting to charge through. There were also more than a couple dozen House members in the balcony above who had a much more harrowing escape. They were escorted past rioters by Capitol Police—after they took off the pins that identify them as members of Congress. The House members were all led down to the tunnels below the Capitol and over to a large secure room in the Longworth House Office Building across the street.

While senators were evacuated to the Hart building and House members were taken to the Longworth building, the top leaders were taken to a military post two miles from the Capitol called Fort McNair, which is equipped with a facility that is designed to be used as an alternative location for Congress in the event of a terrorist attack on the Capitol. As he got into a large black SUV for the drive to McNair, Kevin McCarthy called Donald Trump. The call gave McCarthy remarkable insight into one of the enduring mysteries about January 6—what the hell was Donald Trump thinking and doing as his supporters violently overwhelmed police officers and invaded the US Capitol?

Shortly afterward, McCarthy talked about his call with Trump in interviews with ABC, Fox News, and CBS from his secure location at Fort McNair. In each of these interviews, McCarthy said he urged Trump to make a televised address to the nation, condemning the violence and calling on the rioters to stand down.

"I begged him to go talk to the nation," McCarthy told George Stephanopoulos on ABC about an hour after he talked to Trump. "I called back. This has got to stop."

That was what McCarthy said publicly about his call, but privately he gave a more thorough account to some of his colleagues. Trump, McCarthy told others, was dismissive when he told him to get out and call off the rioters. In fact, according to what McCarthy told others about the call, Trump seemed to defend the rioters. One of the people McCarthy spoke to about the call was Representative Jaime Herrera Beutler (R-WA).

She said McCarthy told her the president said this about the rioters: "'Well, Kevin, I guess these people are more upset about the election than you are.'"

McCarthy has never publicly disputed this account of his conversation, and I have spoken to multiple other people who talked to McCarthy on January 6 and say he told them essentially the same thing—that Trump was justifying the actions of the rioters and telling McCarthy that the rioters cared more about the election than he did.

McCarthy told others that he yelled at the president.

"Who do you think you are talking to?" McCarthy told Trump, according to a source whom McCarthy later talked to about the conversation. "I just got evacuated from the Capitol! There were shots fired right off the House floor. You need to make this stop."

Still, Trump pushed back.

"They are more upset than you because they believe it more than you, Kevin," Trump said, referring to the false allegation that the election had been stolen.

While Trump was justifying their actions, the rioters were spreading out through the Capitol building. They smashed their way into Speaker Pelosi's offices. One rioter posed for pictures with his feet on her desk and left behind a handwritten note in all caps: WE WILL NOT BACK DOWN. Several of Pelosi's terrified staff barricaded themselves inside a small conference room as rioters attempted to break down the door.

Rioters broke into the House parliamentarian's office, ransacking the place, apparently in search of the electoral vote certificates. They defaced a sign honoring civil rights icon John Lewis. They went into Kevin McCarthy's suite of offices and stole a portrait of Joseph Rainey, the first Black member of the House of Representatives.

Cedric Richmond was one of the many people stuck inside the Capitol because they had not been evacuated before the mob took over. As the rioters filled Statuary Hall, Richmond locked himself inside the Lincoln Room. He could see the rioters outside and hear the commotion inside. He had also plotted an escape route. There was a secret trapdoor in the floor of the Lincoln Room. Richmond liked to show it off when he gave visitors tours of the Capitol. The door led to a tiny, dark circular staircase—the entrance to the old congressional post office, which was now walled off and used by custodians to access air-conditioning ducts. The hidden staircase is said to have been used by the British when they invaded the Capitol during the War of 1812. Richmond had no idea where it led, but he thought it would be his escape route if the rioters broke in.

With his eye on the trapdoor, Richmond couldn't believe how long the rioters were able to roam throughout the corridors of the Capitol. It seemed to go on forever. It seemed like they were being allowed to stay as long as they wanted. "It was almost like, 'Let's let them stay in the Capitol until they get tired and leave on their own,'" Richmond recalled. I spoke to him about his experience months later in an interview at his office in the West Wing, where he was working as one of President Biden's top advisors. As we spoke, Richmond was still angry that the mob spent a good two hours in the building before the police began forcing them to leave. He also told me that while the rioters were still in the building, he received a call from then

President-elect Biden and gave him a firsthand account of what he had witnessed. The two men spoke for about ten minutes as the riot was going on, both of them agreeing Biden's goal of unifying the country had just gotten much more difficult.

Across the hall on the Senate side of the Capitol, Mitch McConnell's staff was barricaded inside his offices, located along the main corridor connecting the House and Senate. Rioters tried hard to break in, and as they tried, Robert Karem, a McConnell aide, called the Pentagon in a desperate appeal for help. Karem, who had recently served as an assistant secretary of defense, got ahold of Kash Patel, acting Defense Secretary Chris Miller's chief of staff.

Karem described the scene and pleaded with Patel to send help.

According to two sources who were told about the call, Patel brushed him off, suggesting the situation at the Capitol was not his responsibility.

Another McConnell aide, Andrew Ferguson, urgently called a friend who had recently left the Justice Department, pleading for help. The former official called Deputy FBI Director David Bowdich and told him there were people in McConnell's office worried their lives were in danger. Bowdich dispatched two SWAT teams from the FBI's Washington Field Office to attempt to evacuate McConnell's staff, and eventually they succeeded in getting some of them out.

The rioters broke into the Senate chamber rather easily, vindicating the Secret Service's urgent move to get Vice President Pence out of the place. The rioters climbed up to the chair where Pence had just been presiding, posing for pictures and leaving a handwritten warning for Pence.

"It's only a matter of time," the note said. "Justice is coming."

While the congressional leadership was out at Fort McNair, Vice President Pence remained inside the Capitol complex. He agreed to retreat to the underground tunnels, but he refused to leave Capitol

Hill. Instead, he was taken to a loading dock located beneath one of the Senate office buildings. I have reviewed unpublished photos taken by Pence's photographer during the approximately five hours he remained down there.* The photos show Pence in a barren garage. There were no windows and no furniture. This was a loading dock with concrete walls and a concrete floor. The vice presidential motorcade had been taken down there, but for the first couple hours, Pence refused to go inside his vehicle. He was concerned that if he did, they would drive him away from Capitol Hill. The last thing he wanted the world to see was his motorcade fleeing the Capitol building.

In a couple photographs, you can see Pence's chief of staff Marc Short showing the vice president his phone. One of the things Short showed him was Trump's tweet saying he had no courage. Pence seems to be grimacing as he looks at Short's phone, but I'm told Pence never really reacted to Trump's taunt—not even privately. The congressional leaders had fled and Pence remained. Trump had incited his supporters to go after Pence. Now there were mobs in the Capitol chanting, "Hang Mike Pence." If there was ever a day Pence had shown courage, this was the day. But Trump called him a coward.

Aboveground, rioters had spread throughout the Capitol building. On the fourth floor they banged on the door of Room S-407—a room used in the past for classified briefings for senators. Now there was a

---

*The photographs provide a remarkable visual account of the vice president's harrowing experience during the riot. On the evening of January 6, Pence posted three pictures on his personal Twitter account of himself with members of the Capitol Police shortly before he returned to the Capitol. But Pence, through a spokesperson, refused to allow me to publish any of the photos taken of him during the siege. These are pictures taken by the official vice presidential photographer. The photographer's salary was paid by US taxpayers. The images are public property. I assume that once the congressional committee investigating January 6 becomes aware of them, the photos will be subpoenaed and ultimately made public, as they should be.

sign on the door that made it a target of the rioters: "Joint Congressional Committee on Inaugural Ceremonies." Inside were ten members of the Joint Committee's staff. These were people responsible for planning the presidential inauguration just two weeks away—the inauguration the rioters were trying to prevent from happening.

As they heard rioters in the hallway outside, the people in S-407 used tables and chairs to barricade themselves inside. They gathered documents related to the inaugural plans and locked them up. Because it had long been used for classified briefings, S-407 has ample resources for securing sensitive documents. Listening to the commotion outside in the hallway, they wondered what they would do if the rioters broke in. There is no escape hatch in the floors of this room. They had no weapons to defend themselves.

One of the inaugural staff members, a retired military officer, quickly developed a plan. On a table inside the room, he noticed eight hammers, each of them positioned on a display like a trophy. The hammers had been meant to be given out as souvenirs for the congressional leaders of the Inaugural Committee after something called the "First Nail" ceremony, an event that happens every four years in September to commemorate the beginning of the construction of the inaugural platform. But this year, nobody got their souvenir because the First Nail ceremony had been canceled, yet another event scrapped because of COVID-19. So the ceremonial hammers were gathering dust in the staff office, now ready to be used against invading rioters.

Throughout the Capitol, there were people locked in rooms and closets, hiding from the rioters. Senator Patty Murray (D-WA) was hiding in a small office near the Senate floor with her husband, terrified as she heard rioters in the hallway outside banging on her door and screaming, "Kill the infidels!" As they sat silently on the floor, worried they might be heard by the rioters, Murray's husband kept his foot on the door, fearful that rioters, who were just inches away on the other side of the door, would try to break in. Talking about her husband, Senator Murray later said, "The terror I saw in his eyes was something I have not seen, and we have been married almost forty-nine years." They remained stuck inside the room for more than an hour before the Capitol Police were able to get there and bring them to where the other senators where sheltering in the Hart building.

As rioters swarmed the area outside the House chamber, Representative Bruce Westerman (R-AR) retreated into Kevin McCarthy's office. When the rioters started coming in, Westerman retreated further into a small private bathroom, grabbing a Civil War sword that had been on display near McCarthy's desk. Westerman locked the bathroom door and clutched the antique sword in his hands. The weapon had belonged to a Union soldier, and now it was poised to be used against rioters, at least one of whom was carrying around a large Confederate battle flag.

Back at the White House, Donald Trump remained in his private dining room adjacent to the Oval Office, watching it all unfold on television. McCarthy wasn't the only one calling him and pleading for him to say something to stop his marauding supporters inside the Capitol. Chris Christie tried calling both the White House and Trump's personal cell phone. Trump didn't take the call. He didn't want to hear any of it. He saw the day as a triumph. The way he saw it, his supporters had come into Washington from all over the country because they believed he had truly won the election and they were willing to fight for him. Trump had often complained that the people around him—the people who worked for him—weren't fighting hard enough for him. You couldn't say that about the people who had come to see him speak outside the White House and marched up to Capitol Hill. They were fighters. And they were fighting for him.

———

Deputy National Security Advisor Matt Pottinger had been in a meeting outside the White House and didn't learn about the riot until he got back to his office shortly before three p.m. He was horrified as he watched the riot playing out on the television in his West Wing office. He was shocked to see that instead of condemning the violence, President Trump had sent out a tweet calling his vice president a coward. When he heard an unconfirmed report that there was a delay in sending the National Guard to help take back the Capitol, he rushed over toward the Oval Office to find out what was going on. In the so-called outer oval located right next to the Oval Office, Pottinger saw several junior aides milling around. He could see Trump wasn't there. He was still in his private dining room watching television while the Capitol was being ransacked by his supporters. As Pottinger stood there in disbelief, other senior officials came in and out, including White House Counsel Pat Cipollone and his deputy and a senior advisor to Vice President Pence. They all looked anguished, but nobody could tell him what was going on and why President Trump wasn't doing anything to stop the rioting. After several minutes, Chief of Staff Mark Meadows rushed by. Pottinger stopped him and asked if it was true that the White House was blocking the deployment of the National Guard. Meadows said the report was false.

"I have given very clear instructions to get the Guard over there to control the situation," Meadows told him, and then rushed back in to see Trump.

Pottinger cannot recall the precise time of that conversation, but he says it was sometime between three and four p.m. The absence of the National Guard was inexplicable. Although there is no evidence the president actively delayed the Guard's deployment, there is also no evidence he did anything to speed it up. Pottinger was so upset by what he was witnessing that after he saw Meadows, he went back to his office and wrote a letter of resignation. Enough was enough. He could no longer work in the Trump White House.

At 3:36, White House Press Secretary Kayleigh McEnany tweeted, "At President @realDonaldTrump's direction, the National Guard is on the way along with other federal protective services. We reiterate President Trump's call against violence and to remain peaceful."

Like so many things Kayleigh McEnany said while she was press secretary, this was entirely untrue. Acting Defense Secretary Chris Miller later testified that he did not approve the plan to deploy the National Guard until 4:32—nearly an hour after McEnany's tweet. And contrary to McEnany's assertion that the guard was deployed at Trump's "direction," Trump didn't direct anything. Miller told Congress that Trump did not call him at all on January 6. The acting defense secretary did, however, hear from Vice President Pence, who called him from his secret location by the loading dock below the Capitol complex and urged him to immediately send the Guard. According to Army records, the National Guard did not begin deploying until 5:02 and didn't arrive at the Capitol until 5:20—a full three hours after rioters breached the building.

While the Capitol was being overrun, Trump wasn't taking action to speed up the deployment of the National Guard. He was arguing with his aides in the White House. Meadows urged him to put out a video statement calling on the rioters to stand down. Another person who saw the president during this time tells me that Trump's longtime aide and former caddie, Dan Scavino, was also urging him to make a statement. On at least two occasions while the riot was underway, Meadows reached out to Ivanka Trump, who was in her second-floor office in the West Wing, and pleaded with her to come down and talk to her father, which she did. At about four p.m., President Trump agreed to make a video, but the process was painful and frustrating. An aide who was with him told me Trump had to tape the message several times before they thought he got it right. Looking back at the message that was finally sent out it's hard to imagine how bad the rejected versions must have been.

"I know your pain, I know you're hurt," Trump said in the message aimed directly at his supporters who were still rummaging through offices in the Capitol. "We had an election that was stolen from us. It was a landslide election, and everyone knows it. Especially the other side. But you have to go home now. We have to have peace. We have to have law and order."

He was finally telling his supporters to go home, but he wasn't condemning their actions. In fact, as the message went on, it was clear that what he was really condemning, yet again, was the election.

"It's a very tough period of time," he said. "There's never been a time like this where such a thing happened where they could take it away from all of us—from me, from you, from our country. This was a fraudulent election. But we can't play into the hands of these people. We have to have peace. So go home. We love you. You are very special."

We love you. You are very special.

That was Trump's message to the people who had just beaten police officers, broken into the Capitol, and screamed out for the execution of Vice President Pence.

We love you. You are very special.

If this was deemed an acceptable message, what was in the messages that were rejected? A White House aide who was there as the president taped it told me that in the earlier rejected versions, Trump neglected to call on his supporters to leave the Capitol. He complained about the election. He empathized with their anger, but he didn't call on them to go home.

At 6:01, as the National Guard worked with the police to finally secure the Capitol, Trump offered another message on Twitter, again justifying the actions of the rioters.

"These are things and events that happen when a sacred landslide election victory is so unceremoniously & viciously stripped away from great patriots who have been badly & unfairly treated for so long," he tweeted. "Go home with love & in peace. Remember this day forever!"

Remember this day forever!

One of the few people around Trump while all this was going on was White House Counsel Pat Cipollone. According to a source close to Cipollone, he came close to resigning but stayed on because he was worried things could get even worse if he left. Cipollone tried in vain to get Trump to publicly condemn the riot, telling him that if he didn't, he risked being removed from office—either through impeachment or by a vote of his cabinet declaring him mentally unfit under the Twenty-Fifth Amendment.

By 6:14, the last of the rioters had been ejected from the Capitol and a security perimeter had been established around the building. The congressional leaders were at their emergency getaway two miles away on the Fort McNair military base. Most of the Senate was still in the Hart Senate Office Building. Most of the House members were in the Longworth House Office Building. Mike Pence remained underground at the loading dock below the Capitol.

Almost all of them agreed they needed to get back as soon as possible to resume what Trump's rioters had disrupted, and to finally make the results of the presidential election official.

CHAPTER SEVENTEEN

MADNESS

Shortly after Donald Trump sent his Twitter message imploring his supporters to "Remember this day forever," congressional leaders decided they would return to the Capitol building at eight p.m. and resume the process of certifying the presidential election. January 6 was not over yet. Before Congress reconvened, the Secret Service and Capitol Police conducted a search of the Capitol building to make sure none of the rioters left behind bombs or other explosive devices, but there was no time to repair the damage done by rioters or to clean up the mess they left behind. Members of the House returned to a building littered with shattered glass, pilfered documents, and other debris. There was a faint stench of pepper spray and spent fire extinguishers in the air. A bust of former President Zachary Taylor was defaced with a red substance that appeared to be blood.

Shortly before members of Congress returned to the ransacked Capitol, Trump lawyer Rudy Giuliani placed a call to a phone he thought belonged to Senator Tommy Tuberville. Giuliani actually dialed the phone of Senator Mike Lee, but, just as happened with

Trump's call earlier in the day, he thought he was calling Tuberville. The call went straight to voicemail.

"Senator Tuberville—or should I say Coach Tuberville?" the message began. "This is Rudy Giuliani, the president's lawyer. I'm calling you because I want to discuss with you how they're trying to rush this hearing and how we need you, our Republican friends, to try to just slow it down."*

After all the terrible events that had transpired over the previous six hours—the storming of the Capitol by Trump supporters, the chants calling for Mike Pence's execution, the evacuation of the House and Senate—the president's lawyer was still scheming to stop the congressional proceedings and reverse the outcome of the presidential election.

"I know they're reconvening at eight o'clock tonight," Giuliani's message continued, "but the only strategy we can follow is to object to numerous states and raise issues so that we get ourselves into tomorrow—ideally until the end of tomorrow."

The president's lawyer wanted to further prolong the agony and continue fighting the lost cause that had culminated in an invasion of the US Capitol building, but many of Trump's allies in Congress had decided enough was enough. It was time to give up the unfounded claims of voter fraud and to congratulate Joe Biden, the winner of the election and the legitimate president-elect of the United States. Several senators who had planned to object to Biden's electoral votes abandoned those plans, and when the Senate reconvened, Senator Lindsey Graham, the president's golfing buddy and most vocal ally in the Senate, rose to give an impassioned speech saying it was time to move on.

"Trump and I, we've had a hell of a journey. I hate it to end this

---

*A recording of the message was obtained by the online publication *The Dispatch* and published on the evening of January 6, 2021.

way. Oh, my God, I hate it," Graham said. "All I can say is count me out, enough is enough."

At the end of his speech, Graham uttered the words he and so many other Republicans had been refusing to say since November: "Joe Biden and Kamala Harris are lawfully elected and will become the president and the vice president of the United States on January the twentieth."

Over in the House, Liz Cheney had spent the hours since the evacuation trying to convince Republicans that it was time to stop trying to overturn the election. The Capitol building had been assaulted for the first time since the British tried to burn the place down during the War of 1812. The rioters didn't just invade the Capitol building, they attacked American democracy. It was time to bring the country together. She spoke with Kevin McCarthy shortly before Congress reconvened and felt reassured when he told her that he planned to give a speech calling for unity. She believed he was going to call for Republicans to abandon the plan to object to Biden's electoral votes.

At the same time, Frank Luntz, a longtime advisor to House Republicans and a close friend of McCarthy's for more than twenty-five years, came to the Capitol and camped out in McCarthy's conference room. Visibly shaken by the day's events, Luntz told Republicans that the riot was more significant than they realized. He pleaded with them to drop their objections to Biden's election victory and to adopt a tone of unity and reconciliation. Few Republicans took his advice, and some, including McCarthy's top advisors, angrily pushed back against the idea they should change their position on challenging the election because of the riot.

As McCarthy rose to speak, Cheney sat in the chamber to listen. McCarthy began his speech by condemning the violence they had all just witnessed, calling it "the saddest day" he'd ever experienced as a member of Congress. But as the speech went on, it became clear that not only was McCarthy not calling on Republicans to drop the election challenges, he himself would continue to object. Before McCarthy finished his speech, Liz Cheney stood up and walked out of the chamber in disgust. She felt McCarthy had misled her. And she was horrified that even after all that had gone down, the leader of the House Republicans continued to do Donald Trump's bidding. He was still fighting Trump's lost cause.

As Cheney walked out of the chamber, she still had with her the speech she had written and intended to deliver before the riot forced the evacuation of the House and Senate chambers. She never did have a chance to deliver the speech on January 6, but she carried it with her as she fled the Capitol and when she returned hours later, using the back pages of the speech to take notes along the way. Reading the speech, an excerpt of which is made public for the first time here in this book, you can see why her father was fearful it would enrage Trump's most fervent supporters.

"We are bound by a solemn oath, given before God, to preserve, protect, and defend the Constitution. We cannot comply with that oath only when it is convenient politically. Our oath is not given to any specific president, and it does not bend or yield to popular sentiment, mob rule, or political threats," Cheney planned to say. "What the Constitution requires here is not a mystery. . . . Congress does not have secret unwritten constitutional authority to overturn presidential elections, impose our will, contradict state law, or contradict the rulings of the courts. If we assert that we do, we are creating a tyranny of Congress."

As the joint session of Congress reconvened, Donald Trump had to watch the proceedings on television without his favorite tool for communicating with his supporters. Shortly before members of Congress returned to the Capitol, Trump's Twitter account was suspended for the first time. It was a devastating blow. Trump had nearly ninety million followers. He often said he might never have been elected without

Twitter, and he might have been right about that. But Twitter declared that Trump's tweets praising the rioters contained "repeated and severe violations" of its civic integrity policy and posed a "risk of violence." Twitter warned that if the offending tweets were not removed, the temporary suspension of his account would become permanent.

Trump's Twitter account wasn't the only thing that was silenced. Many of the most formidable voices in his administration had gone dark, too. His son-in-law, Jared Kushner, was flying back to the United States from Saudi Arabia when the riot began. His plane landed at Joint Base Andrews at about four p.m., but he went straight home, later telling people the Secret Service had told him it would be dangerous to go to the White House. He made no public statement about the riot. Chief of Staff Mark Meadows was at the White House but he didn't make a public statement condemning the riot, either. Trump's daughter Ivanka did make a statement on Twitter, saying, "The violence must stop immediately." But after facing a backlash because she addressed the message to "American Patriots," she deleted it.

Ivanka later tried to portray herself as someone who disagreed with the efforts of her father and his allies to overturn the election, but she never took a public stand against those efforts and there is no evidence she took a stand privately, either. As for her husband, Jared Kushner, on January 7 he told a Republican congressman that he had been avoiding Trump and the Oval Office since the riot. "We'll just get in a fight if I go over there," Kushner told the congressman.

A few days after the riot, Ivanka and Jared had a dinner party at their home in Washington, DC. Among those who attended were Larry Kudlow and Brooke Rollins, who were still working as senior officials in the Trump White House. Kevin Hassett, who had served as one of Trump's top economic advisors until the summer of 2020, was also there. One of those who attended the dinner told me the conversation centered on the idea of creating a new think tank to promote free-market economics in a way that would appeal to Democrats. Kudlow spoke wistfully about the Democrats who had supported Ronald Reagan's tax cuts in the 1980s and how President John Kennedy cut taxes almost as much as Reagan. Remarkably, there was no mention of the fact that a mob had just stormed the Capitol days earlier, ransacking the offices of Democratic leaders and trying to prevent the certification of Joe Biden's election victory. There was no mention whatsoever—by Jared and Ivanka or any of their guests—of January 6.

"It was the elephant in the room," one of the dinner guests told me.

There were some Trump administration figures who did speak out. Acting Secretary of Homeland Security Chad Wolf, who was traveling in Qatar, issued a statement on Twitter condemning the rioters less than an hour after the Capitol was breached. Bill Barr was no longer the attorney general, but he put out a statement more forceful than any issued by a current member of the Trump cabinet, saying, "The violence at the Capitol Building is outrageous and despicable. Federal agencies should move immediately to disperse it." The next day Barr put out a second statement, putting blame for the riot squarely on Trump. "Orchestrating a mob to pressure Congress is inexcusable," Barr said. "The President's conduct yesterday was a betrayal of his office and supporters."

Mike Pompeo was the most prominent member of the Trump administration to issue a statement condemning the riot. Although by the time he sent out his statement, the riot was essentially over.

"The storming of the US Capitol today is unacceptable. Lawlessness and rioting—here or around the world—is always unacceptable," Pompeo tweeted at 6:16 p.m., nearly four hours after rioters breached the Capitol. "Let us swiftly bring justice to the criminals who engaged in this rioting."

Treasury Secretary Steven Mnuchin was traveling in Israel (in a time zone that is seven hours later than Washington, DC) on January 6. After going out for dinner in Jerusalem, he returned to his hotel room and watched the riot unfold on television. As a former business executive who knew Trump for years before he became president, he was perhaps the only person in the cabinet who had the stature to challenge Trump. But Mnuchin didn't call the president on January 6 and he didn't say anything publicly to condemn the riot until the following day, when he had a joint press conference with Israeli Prime Minister Benjamin Netanyahu.

But Mnuchin did have conversations with other members of the cabinet that night and the next morning on a step much more dramatic than issuing a statement. According to a source familiar with the conversations, Mnuchin talked to other members of the cabinet about attempting to remove Trump from office by invoking the Twenty-Fifth Amendment. It would have been an extraordinary and entirely unprecedented move. The Twenty-Fifth Amendment was added to the Constitution after the assassination of President John F. Kennedy and was drafted so that an incapacitated president could be replaced, but it also vaguely left open the possibility that a mentally impaired president could be removed. Doing so would require a majority vote of the cabinet.

Among the cabinet officials Mnuchin spoke to that night was Secretary of State Pompeo. Neither man has talked publicly about the call. I asked both Pompeo and Mnuchin whether they discussed removing Donald Trump by invoking the Twenty-Fifth Amendment. I asked if they favored that step. For months, neither man would give me an on-the-record answer. Neither would say whether, on January 6, they thought Donald Trump might have been mentally unfit to continue serving as president of the United States.

Mnuchin continues to decline to answer those questions. But as I was finishing writing this book, I finally heard back from a spokesman for Pompeo who had previously refused to say anything on the record. The response came the day after I asked Donald Trump and one of his political advisors to respond to my reporting about the January 6 call between Pompeo and Mnuchin. I told Trump's advisor that Pompeo had not denied his discussions on the subject of the Twenty-Fifth Amendment despite my repeated inquiries.

A few hours later I got this response from Pompeo's spokesman: "Pompeo through a spokesman denied there have ever been conversations around invoking the Twenty-Fifth Amendment."

The spokesman declined to put his name to the statement.

Pompeo portrays himself as a Trump loyalist, one preparing for a possible run for president by appealing to Trump's core supporters. For Pompeo, the idea that he would consider, even for a moment, that Donald Trump might have been mentally unfit to be president and should be removed from office would be politically devastating.

No evidence has emerged to suggest Vice President Pence was involved in any of the discussions surrounding the Twenty-Fifth Amendment or that he engaged in any requests that he get involved. But there were at least two cabinet secretaries who did ask Pence to convene a cabinet meeting after the Capitol riot. A source with direct knowledge of the request told me this, but would not reveal which members of the cabinet made the request. Pence's office responded by saying the vice president had no authority to call a cabinet meeting, referring the request to White House Chief of Staff Mark Meadows. The meeting never happened.

The question of removing Trump this way, however, quickly became moot. A source close to Pompeo told me the secretary of state asked for a legal analysis of the process for invoking the Twenty-Fifth Amendment. The analysis determined that it would take too much time, considering that Trump only had fourteen days left in office and any attempt to forcefully remove him would be subject to legal challenge. By the next day, two of the cabinet members who might have supported the move were gone. Transportation Secretary Elaine Chao and Education Secretary Betsy DeVos resigned on January 7. In her letter of resignation to Trump, DeVos called the riot at the Capitol "unconscionable" and said, "there is no mistaking the impact your rhetoric had." She told Trump that "impressionable children are watching all of this, and they are learning from us." As for Chao, she wrote a letter to her staff explaining why she resigned, calling the riot a "traumatic and entirely avoidable event" that "deeply troubled me in a way I simply cannot set aside."

Speaker of the House Nancy Pelosi and Democratic Senate Leader Chuck Schumer called Pence on the morning of January 7 to ask him to invoke the Twenty-Fifth Amendment. He waited a full five days to respond, writing a letter to Speaker Pelosi saying, "Under our Constitution, the 25th Amendment is not a means of punishment or usurpation. Invoking the 25th Amendment in such a way would set a terrible precedent."

In a telephone interview shortly before this book went to press, Trump told me that he was unaware of any discussion about the Twenty-Fifth Amendment. "I didn't hear it at all," Trump said, "and if I did, people would have been fired very quickly." He added that some members of his cabinet told him in writing that the idea they would act to remove him through the Twenty-Fifth Amendment was "total bullshit." I asked to see those written statements, but none were shown to me.

While the discussions did happen, the idea that Trump's cabinet would vote to remove him was, in fact, ludicrous. Trump's first-ever cabinet meeting in 2017 began with each cabinet member except then Defense Secretary Jim Mattis making obsequious statements praising

Trump's leadership. Not much had changed since then. There had been a few isolated voices who would challenge him from time to time, but those officials were gone. This was never going to be a group of people who would stand up to him and publicly declare he was mentally unfit to be president.

National Security Advisor Robert O'Brien issued Twitter statements on January 6 condemning the violence and praising Pence for showing courage during the riot. But like most of his Trump administration colleagues, he did not speak to the president on that day. On the morning of January 7, O'Brien went into the Oval Office to see Trump and have him sign some papers. He was among the first senior officials to see the president face-to-face after the riot. So, what did O'Brien say to Trump about the horrific events that had just transpired? The topic didn't come up. Trump didn't say a word about what happened and O'Brien didn't mention it, either.

The debate in Congress over the election challenges had dragged on until the early-morning hours of January 7. Shortly after midnight, Liz Cheney went up to Mike Pence in Statuary Hall as he was walking from the Senate chamber over to the House.

"As an American, I just want to say thank you for what you did," Cheney told him. "It was really important. It was courageous."

Pence looked her in the eye and seemed to nod slightly, but he didn't say anything to her. He knew there would be massive blowback for what he had done and apparently he did not want to be seen or overheard talking to the Republican congresswoman who had taken such a high-profile stand against Donald Trump's effort to overturn the election.

By 3:39 a.m., the counting was over and the last objections had been rejected. It fell to Vice President Pence to announce the final, certified, and irrevocable results of the presidential election—306 electoral votes for Joe Biden, 232 electoral votes for Donald Trump.

Pence's actions that day and into the early-morning hours of January 7 were both courageous and ordinary. He did what every other vice president who had presided over the counting of electoral votes had done. He followed the rules and did the only thing he could have done without breaking the law. The only reason this ordinary action was courageous was because to abide by the law, he had to defy a president who had so incited his supporters that they were demanding Pence's execution. Pence did the only thing he could legally do, and, under these extraordinary circumstances, that was an act of courage. It was particularly remarkable because Pence had been so unfailingly loyal to Trump for the entire four years of his presidency.

Unlike the top congressional leaders who had been evacuated during the riot to a location two miles away, Pence stayed within the Capitol complex throughout it all. Pence's life had been in danger, but Trump didn't bother to call to check on him—not once while the riot was underway and not at all that night. In fact, Trump didn't check in with Pence the next day, either. Or the day after that. It wasn't until January 11, five days after the riot, that Trump finally talked to his vice president. The two men met for ninety minutes in the Oval Office. The White House said the two were meeting to discuss "the week ahead." After the meeting was over, an unnamed senior administration official told reporters the two men talked about the Trump administration's accomplishments and "pledged to continue to work on behalf of the country for the remainder of their term." Amazingly, even then the subject of the Capitol riot and the threats to Pence's life did not come up.

Twitter unlocked Donald Trump's account on the evening of January 7, after he agreed to delete his tweets glorifying the violence and to post a video message finally condemning the attack. In the video message, Trump, reading from a teleprompter, called the riot a "heinous attack on the United States Capitol" and acknowledged, for the first time, "a new administration will be inaugurated on January twentieth." In light of what had just happened, the message marked progress, but even here Trump did not mention Biden by name or congratulate him on his victory.

Trump's return to Twitter was short-lived. By the next morning, he was back to complaining about the election.

"The 75,000,000 great American Patriots who voted for me," he tweeted, "will not be disrespected or treated unfairly in any way, shape or form!!!"

An hour later came his last tweet ever: "To all of those who have asked, I will not be going to the Inauguration on January 20."

Twitter responded with what the company called a "permanent suspension" of Trump's account, explaining that, in the context of what happened at the Capitol, the tweets violated its glorification of violence policy. In a lengthy explanation, the company said that Trump's statement that he would not be attending the inauguration was being interpreted by his supporters as a message that he still didn't consider Biden's victory legitimate. And, further, the tweet "may also serve as encouragement to those potentially considering violent acts that the Inauguration would be a 'safe' target, as he will not be attending."

But there was a reason behind that tweet that only Trump and a handful of others knew. It was something unknown to the Twitter executives who decided to ban Trump's account.

In the course of reporting for this book, I learned that shortly before Trump posted his message saying he would not be attending the inauguration, he had been informed that he would not be invited.

Republican Senate leader Mitch McConnell told his top aide that after all that happened on January 6, they could not allow Donald

Trump to attend the inauguration. This is according to a source with direct knowledge of the conversation. McConnell felt he could not give Trump another opportunity to disrupt the peaceful transfer of power. McConnell wanted to get a letter together from the top four congressional leaders informing Trump that he had been disinvited. Kevin McCarthy opposed the idea, arguing it would be an important message of unity to have Trump attend the ceremony as Biden took the oath of office. But McConnell was determined to disinvite Trump regardless of whether McCarthy would sign the letter. A senior advisor to McConnell informed Mark Meadows about McConnell's desire to disinvite Trump. McCarthy also alerted the White House about McConnell's plan to disinvite Trump. The letter was never written, because before it could be drafted, Trump sent out his tweet saying he wouldn't be attending. Trump apparently wanted people to think it was his decision alone to become the first outgoing president after an election to fail to attend an inauguration since Andrew Johnson skipped the inauguration of Ulysses S. Grant in 1869.*

Banned from Twitter and largely out of public sight, Trump's final days were uncharacteristically quiet. On January 13, the House voted to impeach him for inciting the riot, but even as that debate unfolded, Trump was on the sidelines. Ten Republicans voted to impeach him, the highest number of House members ever to vote to impeach a member of their own party. Liz Cheney was one of the first Republicans to publicly say she would vote to impeach. In announcing her decision, she said Trump was responsible for what happened on January 6.

"The President of the United States summoned this mob, assembled the mob, and lit the flame of this attack. Everything that

---

*I attempted to ask Trump about this during our final interview for this book, but he hung up on me before I could ask the question, telling me the interview was a waste of time.

followed was his doing," she said in a statement announcing her decision to impeach. "There has never been a greater betrayal by a President of the United States of his office and his oath to the Constitution."

The vast majority of Republicans voted against impeachment. But many of those who still stood by him also criticized his behavior. As he announced his decision to vote against impeachment, Kevin McCarthy said Trump shared blame for what happened.

"The president bears responsibility for Wednesday's attack on Congress by mob rioters," McCarthy said. "He should have immediately denounced the mob when he saw what was unfolding."

It was a disastrous downfall for President Trump. His final days were marked by a violent and failed insurrection that he had inspired. Members of his cabinet discussed declaring him mentally unfit. He became the first president ever to be impeached twice. Even some of his most loyal allies were condemning his actions. Yet even in those dark final days, he wasn't giving up his lost cause.

On January 15, Trump agreed to meet with Mike Lindell, the founder of a company called MyPillow. Lindell had been one of those pushing the wackiest conspiracy theories about the election and was still, even a week after the riot, talking about overturning the election. He was granted a meeting with Trump in the Oval Office to talk about the steps he believed could be taken immediately to keep Joe Biden from becoming president. In a picture taken by *Washington Post* photographer Jabin Botsford, Lindell can be seen walking out of the West Wing after the meeting holding a bunch of papers. Some of the words are clearly visible, including a line at the bottom saying "martial law if necessary."

CHAPTER EIGHTEEN

TRANSITIONS

I was on the White House North Lawn shortly before noon on January 20, 2021, when I saw the last person left from the original Trump White House team.

He was standing behind me just minutes before Joe Biden took the oath of office and gave his inaugural address on Capitol Hill. Donald Trump had just landed at Palm Beach International Airport after taking his final trip aboard Air Force One. Almost all of the Trump staff were gone, but the White House was abuzz with activity. The place was filled with reporters there to witness and document history as the curtain officially dropped on the Trump presidency and the Biden team arrived to set up their offices in the West Wing.

Chris Liddell will forever hold the record as the longest-serving official in the Trump White House. For another twenty minutes or so he would be the deputy White House chief of staff for policy. He had worked on the Trump campaign in 2016 and then on the Trump transition. His work at the White House began on January 20, 2017— the first day of the Trump presidency. But if Liddell was the longest-serving senior White House official, he may also have had the lowest public profile of them all. Brought into Trump's orbit by Jared Kushner, Liddell was one of the wealthiest and most successful people in the West Wing, with a résumé that included several years as the chief financial officer at Microsoft and a stint as the vice chairman and CFO of General Motors.

Liddell was a subject of some fascination in the news media of New Zealand, where he was born and raised, but his only social media presence was a private Instagram account. During the depths of the economic downturn, while most of the country was in lockdown because of the COVID-19 pandemic, Liddell posted photos of his Corvettes—one was vintage, from the 1950s, the other a top-of-the-line recent model—variously parked at the White House and in front of his $5 million mansion in the Kalorama neighborhood of Washington, where both Ivanka Trump and Barack Obama were neighbors. But fewer than a hundred people, including a handful of his White House colleagues, were invited to follow his Instagram account and could see all that.

For most of his tenure, Liddell worked quietly in the background, and in the final months of the Trump presidency, he was almost invisible. There was good reason for that. He was the head of something called the White House Transition Coordinating Council—in other words, he was the White House official responsible for working with President-elect Joe Biden's team on ensuring a smooth transition of power. It was something the Trump administration was required by law to do, even as President Trump was doing everything in his power to prevent the transition to the Biden presidency from happening.

As the clock ran out on the Trump era, Liddell walked along the driveway between the White House and the stretch of the North Lawn where the television reporters broadcast our reports. Nobody seemed to notice him or have any idea who he was. After I caught a glimpse of him, I took off the microphone clipped to my suit jacket and briefly abandoned my camera position so I could talk, for the last time, with someone currently working as an official in the Trump White House. He was looking at the building, as if he was trying to capture the moment in his mind. The forty-fifth president and virtually everybody else who had worked for him were gone; the forty-sixth president was not yet sworn in. I asked him what he was thinking. As usual, he wasn't very talkative.

"Four years—for better or worse," he said.

Then he asked me to take a picture of him in front of the White House, capturing an image of the final moments of the Trump presidency.

Not long before I snapped that photograph, Liddell had greeted the first Biden officials to the White House, including incoming Chief of Staff Ron Klain and incoming National Security Advisor Jake Sullivan. It was still Trump's White House, but the forty-fifth president left shortly after eight a.m., taking his last trip on Marine One, and shortly after that, the Biden team started moving in. Liddell wasn't known by many in the outside world, but he was known by some of the incoming Biden officials. In the immediate aftermath of the election, he was the only senior Trump administration official regularly speaking with the Biden team. While the president was vowing to "stop the steal" and overturn Biden's election victory, Liddell was quietly taking steps aimed at ensuring a smooth transition to the Biden presidency. Because of the president's refusal to concede, this was something of a clandestine operation that Liddell ran out of his small office on the second floor of the West Wing. He kept Chief of Staff Mark Meadows informed about what he was doing, but he never once talked to Donald Trump about it. Not once.

This wasn't a brave act of courage on Liddell's part, although considering all else that was going on around him, it may have seemed that way. Liddell was required by law to help President-elect Biden's team prepare to take over. The law that required this is the Presidential Transition Act (PTA) of 1963, which stipulates that an incumbent administration take a series of specific actions designed to ensure a smooth transfer of power. After the 2000 Florida recount, the law was amended to begin transition preparations before the election, in order to make an orderly transition even in the event of a lengthy dispute over the election results.

Under the PTA, the White House must create a transition council six months before the general election. The council's job is to provide resources for what it calls the "principal contenders" for the presidency—in practice, the major party nominees. Even before Election Day, the incumbent president must provide resources for their opponent to begin preparing for a transition in the event they win. The candidate gets federal office space, a budget for staff and expenses, and the authority to ask the FBI to perform background checks for people likely to serve in key positions in the administration.

Liddell volunteered for this job in early 2020 and it was given to him by Meadows in April 2020. It was an assignment nobody else really wanted, but it was also a job for which Liddell was uniquely qualified. Eight years earlier, Mitt Romney had tapped Liddell to be the executive director of his presidential transition team after he won the 2012 Republican presidential nomination. Liddell had helped lead the Romney Readiness Project, preparing a list of candidates for four thousand presidential appointees and an agenda for Romney's first two hundred days. Romney lost, of course, and nothing became of Liddell's plan, but he later wrote a book about the process. Liddell knew what it takes to prepare for a presidential transition.

On September 3, 2020, two months before an election Donald Trump had already said he could not lose, the Trump administration signed an agreement with the Biden campaign that provided the first federal resources for the Biden transition—including office space large enough for one hundred employees at the Commerce Department building, located right next to the Ellipse on 1401 Constitution Avenue, NW. It was a step required by law and Liddell made sure it happened. The Biden team was pleasantly surprised the agreement was signed on time and without a hitch. But even as that happened, it was already clear Trump had no interest in any transfer of power. He had long been telling supporters that there was no way he could lose the election—that is, unless it was stolen from him. Then on September 23—just twenty days after his administration set aside a piece of prime Washington real estate for the Biden campaign to use to prepare to set up his administration in the event he won—Trump was asked a very simple and direct question by White House reporter Brian Karem.

"Will you commit here today [to] a peaceful transferal of power after the November election?"

Since the dawn of the American republic, there has been only one answer to that question. In this case, the transfer would be either to a Biden presidency or, if Trump won, to a second Trump term.

But in a foreshadowing of what was to come, Trump offered a noncommittal answer.

"Well, we're gonna have to see what happens."

The answer was chilling. "We're gonna have to see what happens"?* And then Trump made it worse, telling the world why if he lost the election, he might not agree to leave office peacefully.

"You know that I've been complaining very strongly about the ballots, and the ballots are a disaster."

---

*During one of his presidential election debates with Hillary Clinton in 2016, Trump was asked by moderator Chris Wallace if he would accept the results of that election. He didn't give an answer back then, either, telling Wallace, "I will tell you at the time." The implications for saying something like that were much greater when he was president. If he had lost in 2016, he would have had no responsibility for transferring power as he did in 2020.

Ultimately, Donald Trump did walk out of the White House voluntarily. Democracy prevailed. He did not need to be dragged out. The inauguration happened on schedule and without incident. The system worked.

But it's not that simple. This was a close call. There was nothing inevitable about what happened on January 20. The peaceful transition of power ultimately happened, in large part, because honorable people defied Donald Trump's wishes and helped make it happen.

Georgia's secretary of state, Brad Raffensperger, was a Republican who endorsed Trump and voted for him. Trump demanded he "find" enough votes to overturn the results in his state. He threatened him. Raffensperger refused. What if he hadn't? There was no guarantee Raffensperger would do the right thing.

Trump demanded Republican leaders of the state legislatures in Pennsylvania and Michigan overturn the elections in their states by sending to Washington Trump electoral votes instead of electoral votes for Biden, who actually won their states. They didn't do it. What if they had tried?

Trump told his secretary of Homeland Security he wanted him to seize voting machines in states he lost—a demand made first by Trump and later through his young enforcer, Johnny McEntee. Acting Secretary Chad Wolf had no authority to do that and he refused. But what if he had tried?

Judges, some of them conservative Republicans Trump had nominated, rejected lawsuits aimed at overturning the elections. What if they went along with Trump's power grab and ruled in his favor as Trump clearly believed they would?

Trump bluntly demanded that the Supreme Court—with a clear

conservative majority thanks to the three justices he nominated—intervene and save his presidency. In the end they unanimously rejected his final appeal. What if the conservative majority in the Supreme Court acted the way Trump expected them to act?

What if Bill Barr had followed the president's orders and mobilized the considerable resources of the Department of Justice to overturn the election? Barr had seemed willing to stand by the president on just about everything, but in the end, he incurred Trump's wrath by not only failing to do what Trump demanded, but by publicly declaring there was no evidence of widespread voter fraud. What if Barr had not stood up to Trump?

Barr's successor, Jeffrey Rosen, held the line, too. And when Trump tried to fire Rosen, nearly a dozen senior Justice Department officials threatened to resign. What if they had done what Trump wanted them to do?

And, finally, Mike Pence defied Trump by refusing to upend the final certification of the election results on January 6. What if he instead brought down the gavel and said he was rejecting the electoral votes Trump and his congressional allies wanted rejected?

None of these people had the authority to do what Trump demanded, but there is no guarantee the orderly transfer of power on January 20 would have happened if they had tried.

It may also be said of these people that they saved our democracy by refusing to break the law. Some of them paid a steep price for doing the right thing. Brad Raffensperger, for example, became a target of death threats that continued months after the election and that were focused not just on him but also his family. People who believed Trump's lies about the election somehow got Raffensperger's wife's phone number and bombarded her with threatening and pornographic messages. The pressure was intense, but he stayed focused and did what the law required him to do. "Sometimes a person has to stand up and be counted," Raffensperger told me. "I'll stand up and be counted because I stood on the truth."

The system held. Democracy prevailed. But there were many steps along the way where we were perilously close to a complete breakdown, a true constitutional crisis. Ultimately, I don't believe Trump could have held on to power for long. I say this because people at the highest levels of federal law enforcement and the US military had made it clear they would not go along with an illegal effort by Trump to stay in power. Acting Attorney General Jeffrey Rosen had rejected the schemes to seize voting machines and to force state legislatures to reconsider their electoral votes. Trump almost fired him, but he didn't. That meant Rosen was still in charge of the vast law enforcement resources of the Justice Department. And there was the message Joint Chiefs Chairman General Mark Milley had delivered to anchors from the five major television networks right before the election: the military would not be part of any attempted coup. If Trump had tried to stay in power, it would have been ugly, but he would have been removed from office—by force, if necessary.

Ultimately, he left office peacefully and without incident on January 20 primarily because he had failed, and failed spectacularly, in each and every attempt he had made to prevent Joe Biden from becoming president.

Chris Liddell played his part, too. Like many others around the president, he never believed the mad allegations of fraud. He knew the election was over by the time all the major news organizations, including Fox News, declared Biden the winner on the Saturday after the election. He did what the law required him to do but what the president he served had no interest in getting done. His actions helped keep a deeply problematic transition from turning into all-out calamity.

Even so, the transition was damn near disastrous. Biden's transition team was not permitted to meet with officials in federal agencies until a full twenty days after the election, when the Trump-appointed head of the General Services Administration (GSA) belatedly issued something called a letter of ascertainment that instructed federal agencies to begin working with the president-elect's team. This is a legally necessary step that usually happens as soon as there is a clear winner in the election, but in this case it didn't happen until November 23. And even after that, elements of the Trump administration failed to cooperate.

Trump's Office of Management and Budget did not provide the Biden team basic information on federal spending. The office of Trump's top trade negotiator, Robert Lighthizer, refused to provide information on the status of ongoing trade negotiations. The Pentagon was slow to provide information and delayed critical briefings for incoming Defense Department officials.

But Liddell did his part to keep the wheels turning toward a Biden presidency. During the first few weeks after the election, he did it in part by hiding his work from President Trump's win-at-all-costs enforcers. Normally the Presidential Personnel Office, for example, plays a key role in the transitions, but Liddell did not have a single conversation with PPO Director Johnny McEntee about the Biden transition. The only transition conversations he had with McEntee, in fact, were conversations before the election about plans for a second term if Trump won.

In a more normal world, Liddell would have asked McEntee to notify all four thousand political appointees in the federal government to submit their letters of resignation (postdated January 20) shortly before the election. These are letters that are necessary so whoever is president on January 20 can put their own team in place without going through the process of firing anybody. Liddell didn't dare make that request out of fear McEntee would have then taken efforts to shut down the transition process. Liddell ended up sending out a notice asking for resignation letters on his own—but he didn't do it until January 7, the day after the Capitol riot, when Liddell was so disgusted he almost put in his own letter of resignation, effective immediately.

Liddell decided to stay, not out of loyalty to Trump, but out of fear of what Trump might do over his final thirteen days in office, and fear of what would happen to the transition if he walked away.

By the time January 20 came, most people in the Trump West Wing were already gone. Jared Kushner and Ivanka Trump had packed up their offices days earlier. Press Secretary Kayleigh McEnany had left for Florida less than a week after the Capitol riot. Top economic advisor Larry Kudlow was gone.

There were others who stuck around and, like Liddell, worked in good faith to ensure as smooth a transition as possible under the extraordinarily unusual circumstances. One of those who played a key role was Tony Ornato, a Secret Service officer who served as deputy chief of staff for operations during the last year of the Trump presidency. After the GSA issued the letter of ascertainment, Ornato began working to make sure the Biden team would have everything they needed when they came into the White House on January 20. Ornato knew firsthand how complicated presidential transitions are; as a Secret Service officer he had taken part in two of them—in 2009 when Barack Obama replaced George W. Bush and in 2017 when Donald Trump replaced Obama. This time, Ornato was asked by Chief of Staff Mark Meadows to take the steps necessary to ensure a smooth handoff to the Biden team, but like Liddell, Ornato never once discussed any of it with President Trump.

From December until early January, Ornato was in regular contact with Jennifer O'Malley Dillon, who had served as Joe Biden's campaign manager and had been chosen to serve as the deputy chief of staff for operations in the Biden White House. The two of them worked out the complicated choreography of the official transfer that takes place at noon on January 20.

This was an especially complicated hand-off because of the challenges posed by the ongoing pandemic. New coronavirus infections hit an all-time high on January 17. Along with everything else that comes with taking over the federal government and all its sprawling agencies during a pandemic, Dillon had to ensure the White House itself was a safe place for the new president and his team. After all, the Trump White House had been a pandemic hot zone where many officials, including Trump, had been infected. Ornato helped Dillon arrange to get vaccines for as many senior officials as possible and to get an accounting of all the nonpolitical staff at the White House who had been vaccinated. They also arranged for an extra-thorough cleaning of the building.

With the approval of Chief of Staff Meadows, Ornato also arranged for the Biden team to begin moving into the West Wing a couple hours before Biden officially became president. About a dozen senior Biden officials, including Dillon and incoming Chief of Staff Ron Klain, arrived at about ten a.m. and were welcomed by the few Trump officials still left, including outgoing National Security Advisor Robert O'Brien and outgoing White House Counsel Pat Cipollone. It was one small measure of civility after all that had happened, but it was appreciated by the Biden team.

The outgoing Trump staff did nothing to sabotage the offices that were now being turned over to the Biden team. There was nothing like the scene incoming aides for President George W. Bush found after the disputed 2000 presidential election, when the "w" keys were removed from some White House keyboards and some desk drawers were glued shut. But the Biden team did find that virtually every television set in the White House complex was tuned to Trump-friendly Fox News. Even in the offices with multiple televisions, every screen was tuned to Fox News.

About fifteen minutes before the official dawn of the Biden presidency, Chris Liddell took one last walk through the hallways of the West Wing. He stopped at the open door to the Oval Office. There were more than a dozen people quickly working to transform the place from Trump's office to Biden's. The carpet that had been used by Trump was already gone and new carpet was being brought in. The portrait of Andrew Jackson that had hung on the wall to Trump's left was gone. The White House construction team was hanging the artwork chosen by Biden. Trump was still technically the president, but he was already in Mar-a-Lago. The Oval Office was already Joe Biden's. Aside from the office up on the second floor where Liddell had been working, the White House was already in the hands of the soon-to-be Biden administration.

As Liddell walked back up to his office to retrieve his belongings, he looked back at the workers transforming the Oval Office and he smiled. After all that had gone down, the final minutes of the Trump presidency were quiet and uneventful. *Thank God,* he thought.

CHAPTER NINETEEN

EXILE IN MAR-A-LAGO

O utgoing presidents typically invite their successors to the White House prior to the inauguration. They give the new residents a tour of the place, introduce them to residential staff, most of whom serve presidents of both parties and spend decades working at the White House. Welcoming the new first family is the polite thing to do, but more important, it sends a message to the country that the incoming president will be the president for all Americans, regardless of how they voted. By tradition, the outgoing president meets the president-elect in the Oval Office while the outgoing first spouse hosts the incoming first spouse for tea in the residential area of the White House. The Obamas extended this courtesy to Donald and Melania Trump* even though Trump had waged a yearslong campaign to convince the country that Barack Obama wasn't a true American. The image of Trump and Obama together in

---

*The Obamas invited the Trumps to the White House twice before Donald Trump became president. The first time was on November 10, 2016—just two days after the election. The second time was on the morning of January 20, 2017—the morning of Trump's inauguration.

the Oval Office sent a powerful message to the country that even after a campaign as bitter as the one that elected Trump president, Americans could come together and wish the new president well. Trump would be everybody's president—even Obama's.

Donald Trump left the White House for the last time at eight a.m. on January 20, 2021, trashing one more American tradition on the way out the door, skipping town without welcoming the incoming first family to the White House.

It wasn't exactly surprising that Donald Trump failed to graciously welcome the Bidens to 1600 Pennsylvania Avenue. After all, he hadn't even called Joe Biden to acknowledge he won the election and he never conceded he lost. In a tense conversation five days after the Capitol riot, Kevin McCarthy told Trump it was time for him to finally call Biden. There are a total of at least five people who witnessed this call because Trump spoke to McCarthy over speakerphone.

"Are you going to call Joe Biden?" McCarthy asked.

"No, I cannot do that," Trump told him.

"Do you care what your grandchildren are going to think?" McCarthy asked him, and referring to the tradition of outgoing presidents leaving a letter in the Oval Office for an incoming president, McCarthy added, "You need to write a letter and put it in that desk for him."

After Trump said he hadn't decided whether to leave a letter, McCarthy appealed to Trump's own self-interest, warning him that if he didn't make some gesture of goodwill, he could lose everything.

"You are going to get impeached," McCarthy told him, "and there is a chance you will be convicted in the Senate."

Trump never made the call, but he did leave a letter for Biden on the desk in the Oval Office. A Biden administration official who has seen the letter told me it was handwritten, but the Biden White House has declined to make the letter public. Biden called it "a very generous letter" and his press secretary, Jen Psaki, said it "was both generous and gracious."

Trump had one final surprise before taking his last flight aboard Air Force One. It came right after a small farewell ceremony on the airport tarmac with family, a handful of his former advisors, and some other supporters, after Trump had walked along the red carpet and up the steps to Air Force One. Taking a seat in the presidential office at the front of the plane, he received a call from RNC Chairwoman Ronna McDaniel. She hadn't come to his send-off at the airport. She was back home in Michigan recovering from surgery to repair a broken ankle, but she called to wish him farewell. It was a very unpleasant conversation.

Donald Trump was in no mood for small talk or nostalgic goodbyes. He got right to the point. He told her he was leaving the Republican Party and would be creating his own political party. The president's son, Donald Trump Jr., was also on the phone. The younger Trump had been relentlessly denigrating the RNC for being insufficiently loyal to Trump. In fact, at the January 6 rally before the Capitol riot, the younger Trump all but declared that the old Republican Party didn't exist anymore.

"It should be a message to all the Republicans who have not been willing to actually fight, the people who did nothing to stop the steal," Donald Trump Jr. said on the morning of January 6. "This gathering should send a message to them: this isn't their Republican Party anymore. This is Donald Trump's Republican Party."

Now, with just three hours left of the Trump presidency, the elder Trump was telling the Republican Party chairwoman that he was leaving the party entirely. The description of this conversation and the discussions that followed come from two sources with direct knowledge of these events.

"I'm done," Trump told her. "I'm starting my own party."

"You cannot do that," McDaniel told Trump. "If you do, we will lose forever."

"Exactly. You lose forever without me," Trump responded. "I don't care."

Trump's attitude was that if he had lost, he wanted everybody around him to lose, too. According to a source who witnessed the conversation, Trump was talking as if he viewed the destruction of the Republican Party as a punishment to those party leaders who had betrayed him—including those few who voted to impeach him and the much larger group he believed didn't fight hard enough to over-turn the election.

"This is what Republicans deserve for not sticking up for me," Trump told McDaniel.

McDaniel told Trump that starting his own party wouldn't just destroy the Republican Party, it would also destroy him.

"This isn't what the people who depended on you deserve, the people who believed in you," McDaniel said. "You'll ruin your legacy. You'll be done."

Again, Trump said he didn't care. And he wasn't simply floating an idea. He was putting the party chairwoman on notice that he had decided to start his own party. It was a done deal. He had made up his mind. "He was very adamant that he was going to do it," a source who heard the president's comments later told me.

McDaniel immediately informed the RNC leadership about Trump's threat, and over the course of the next four days, there was a tense stand-off between Trump and the Republican National Com-mittee. Trump, morose in defeat and eager for revenge, plotted the destruction of the Republican Party. And the RNC played hardball, telling people close to Trump that leaving the party would cost him dearly.

"We told them there were a lot of things they still depended on the RNC for and that if this were to move forward, all of it would go away," an RNC official told me.

McDaniel and her leadership team made it clear that if Trump left, the party would immediately stop paying legal bills incurred during post-election challenges. But, more significant, the RNC threatened to render Trump's most valuable political asset worthless.

That asset was the campaign's list of the email addresses of forty million Trump supporters. In political terms, the list was pure gold—a way to reach out to the people most likely to donate money to Republicans. It's a list Trump had used to generate money by renting it to candidates at a steep cost. The list generated so much money that party officials estimated that it was worth about $100 million.

But the list was jointly owned by the RNC and the Trump campaign. And party officials threatened Trump that if he left the Republican Party, he would no longer be able to make money renting out the list. If he tried, they would give it away for free to any Republican who asked for it, effectively making it impossible for Trump to make money by renting it out.

Five days after that last flight aboard Air Force One, Trump backed down, saying he would remain a Republican after all. He later denounced news stories that he had considered starting his own party as "fake news." In my final interview with him for this book, Trump claimed to not recall his conversation with McDaniel on January 20. He told me "a lot of people suggested a third party, many people" but that he had never even thought about leaving the Republican Party.

"You mean I was going to form another party or something?" he asked me incredulously. "Oh, that is bullshit. It never happened."

But the truth is that Trump did more than consider leaving the Republican Party. He told the RNC chairwoman he had decided to do it and only backed down after he saw how much it would cost him.

Donald Trump's plan to start his own party quickly became a distant memory. He hadn't left the party. He had taken it over. When I visited him in March 2020 in his gilded exile at Mar-a-Lago, Trump was the undisputed leader of the Republican Party. Kevin McCarthy had visited him just eight days after the end of the Trump presidency, a mere three weeks after the Capitol riot. The two of them smiled as they posed for a picture in the glittery lobby of Mar-a-Lago. The photo sent the message that even after all that had gone down, Trump could still summon the most powerful Republican in the House to come see him. It was Trump's idea to take the photo and it was Trump who sent it out almost immediately after the meeting was over. He wanted the world to know he was still relevant—that the top Republicans were making the pilgrimage to Palm Beach. Over the next several weeks, a parade of other Republicans would make the trip, including several members of Congress and candidates who were hopeful to get Trump's endorsement for the next round of midterm elections. For these Republicans, Trump wasn't a pariah, he was the single most important endorsement for almost any Republican running for office. Trump loved it. He told me his resort was busier than Grand Central Terminal with all the Republicans coming down to get his blessing.

But as I sat down with Trump in the middle of the lobby at Mar-a-Lago, I found him to be consumed with bitterness and resentment aimed almost entirely at fellow Republicans, including the two top Republican leaders in Congress—Senator Mitch McConnell and Representative Kevin McCarthy. He blamed them directly for the fact he was no longer president of the United States.

"If McConnell and McCarthy fought harder, okay, you could have a Republican president right now," Trump told me. "They should have fought harder."

Trump absurdly claimed that the only reason McConnell had won reelection in solidly Republican Kentucky in 2020 was because he had endorsed him. "In retrospect," Trump told me about McConnell's reelection race, "I might have endorsed the Democrat."

During our conversation, Trump lashed out at the ten House Republicans who voted for impeachment and the seven Senate Republicans who voted to convict him in the Senate impeachment trial. He talked about several of them by name. He said he would oppose any of them who ran for reelection. He attacked the Republican governors in Georgia and Arizona for their roles in certifying the election results in their states. He ridiculed Senator Lindsey Graham, who had said he was done with Trump on the evening of January 6 but quickly came back into the Trump fold after he was harassed by Trump supporters the next day at the airport. "That's Lindsey," Trump told me, saying with a smile that Lindsey's separation from him lasted "maybe a few hours" until he was "attacked at the airport." Trump told me he didn't know if he could ever forgive Mike Pence for his role in presiding over the final certification of the election in Congress. He joyfully pointed out that several of those Republicans who had defied him, including Liz Cheney, were then quickly censured by the Republican Party organizations in their states. His list of Republican traitors was long. He offered biting insults aimed at all of them.

"I find this stuff so exhilarating and so interesting," he told me.

After his brutal loss, Donald Trump was aggrieved, blaming everybody but himself for what had happened. And he was loving every minute of it. There was one Republican whom he spoke fondly of during our conversation—Representative Marjorie Taylor Greene. Greene was the far-right congresswoman who had been a believer in the QAnon conspiracy theories and who later compared public health mandates requiring the wearing of masks to Nazi Germany. "As far as I am concerned, she is terrific," he told me, adding, "I don't think Kevin [McCarthy] has treated her properly."

The Senate impeachment trial didn't happen until after he left office. In the final vote—fifty-seven to forty-three—a solid majority voted him guilty, including seven Republicans, but the total fell far short of the two-thirds majority required for conviction. Mitch McConnell was not among the seven Republicans who voted to convict, but the speech he gave immediately after the trial ended was among the harshest condemnations of a president or former president ever given on the Senate floor. McConnell said he didn't vote to convict Trump because the trial had taken place after he left office.* But it's hard to square McConnell's words with his vote of not guilty. He said there was no question Trump was "practically and morally responsible" for provoking the events of January 6.

"This was an intensifying crescendo of conspiracy theories orchestrated by an outgoing president who seemed determined to either overturn the voters' decision or else torch our institutions on the way out," McConnell said.

He called the attack on the Capitol "a foreseeable consequence of the growing crescendo of false statements, conspiracy theories, and reckless hyperbole which the defeated president kept shouting into the largest megaphone on planet Earth."

In Mar-a-Lago after his acquittal, Trump was still shouting those false statements and conspiracy theories. He called Biden an

---

*McConnell was largely responsible for the timing of the Senate trial. He was the Senate majority leader until January 20 and rejected demands from Democrats to begin the trial before Trump left office, arguing there simply wasn't enough time.

"illegitimate president" and told me, "I have zero doubt I won the election." He went on and on repeating the same disproven claims of election fraud he talked about while he was still president. His megaphone may not be as large as it was when he was in the White House, but his influence over the party remained as large as ever. Precious few Republican leaders were using their megaphones to challenge Trump's hold on the party he had told the RNC chairwoman deserved to be destroyed. Among the megaphones that had fallen silent when it came to challenging Trump was Mitch McConnell's.

On May 28, the Senate voted to reject the formation of a bipartisan commission to investigate the January 6 riot. Only four Republicans voted in favor of the commission. Mitch McConnell opposed it and pushed others to do the same, perhaps because he believed the focus on the riot and Trump's behavior would hurt Republicans in upcoming midterm elections.

After the vote, Liz Cheney sent McConnell a text message expressing her belief that Senate Republicans had made a terrible mistake. By blocking the creation of a bipartisan commission, she believed Senate Republicans had become accomplices in the effort to whitewash or forget the actions of a president who inspired the effort to bring down American democracy. Her message to McConnell referred to a statue of a figure from Greek mythology that hangs above the corridor that connects the House and Senate chambers. It's one of the oldest pieces of artwork in the Capitol.

"Historian David McCullough has described the statue of Clio, the Muse of History, standing over the North door and Statuary Hall. She takes notes in her book, reminding all of us that our words will be measured by history," Cheney wrote in her text message to McConnell.

McConnell didn't respond to Cheney's message, but about a month later he called her. As she answered the call, she assumed he would be calling to explain why he had killed the January 6 commission and hoped he might even express a touch of regret for doing so. Instead, he was calling her to say she should stop criticizing Trump. McConnell agreed with almost everything Cheney had said about Trump. He had said much of it himself. But McConnell told her it was time to move on, that being so public about challenging Trump would hurt Republicans in the upcoming midterm elections—and make it more likely she would lose her own reelection campaign in Wyoming.

If the Muse of History was taking notes, she would have been unlikely to write much about McConnell's efforts to win a few more seats for Republicans in the midterm elections, but she would undoubtedly make note of Republican leaders who continued to allow Trump's lies to go unchallenged—even after the destruction of a presidency that almost brought down the republic with it. Clio, the Muse of History, had a bird's-eye view of the riot at the Capitol and the effort to undo the will of the people in the oldest democracy on the planet.

When I went down to see Trump in Mar-a-Lago I didn't expect him to show any remorse for what had happened or to express any regret for his actions. He is a man who believes an apology is a sign of weakness. But I was taken aback by how fondly he remembers a day I will always remember as one of the darkest I have ever witnessed. I asked him why on that night he had tweeted, "Remember this day forever."

It was, he told me, "a very beautiful time with extremely loving and friendly people—the largest crowd that I've ever spoken before—with tremendous spirit. And I'm referring to that."

He continued: "I'm referring to when I made a speech which was perfectly fine. Some people thought it was mild-mannered . . . it was a relatively mild-mannered speech."

As Trump continued to explain to me why he saw January 6 as a day to be remembered forever, he marveled at the size of the crowd that came out to see him.

"When I made that speech, it was a magnificently beautiful day," he told me. "They never gave the credit to the size of that crowd when the crowd went all the way back to the Washington Monument."

"And they were chanting 'Fight for Trump,'" I said.

"Then it was marred later on," he said, in the closest he has come to expressing any regret for what happened. "It was marred by what took place."

"But some people took what you said literally," I said. "You know—the election was being stolen, our country is being stolen, and they wanted to do anything possible to stop that."

"Well, I think it was a rigged election," he responded. "I never conceded the election. I think it was a rigged election, absolutely."

"Some people were saying it's 1776. If it's rigged, if it's being stolen, why not charge the Capitol?"

"I hadn't heard that, but the people were angry," he told me. "The press, the fake news, which is fake, never talked about the size of that crowd."

This was a remarkable conversation. I had pointed out that his rhetoric encouraged people to invade the Capitol and Donald Trump responded by complaining that the press had not given him enough credit for the size of the crowd that came out to hear him speak.

I asked him if he had been concerned about Vice President Pence's safety. After all, the Trump supporters who broke into the Capitol had been calling for Pence's execution. Even as Pence had been evacuated from the Senate chamber—even as he had spent more than five hours sequestered by a loading dock under the Capitol while the riot was going on—Trump had not even attempted to get ahold of his vice president to see if he was safe.

"Were you worried about him during the siege? Were you worried about his safety?" I asked Trump.

"No, I thought he was well protected, and I heard that he was in good shape," Trump answered.

"Because you heard those chants," I said. "That was terrible. I mean, you know, those—"

"Well, the people were very angry," he interrupted.

"They were chanting, 'Hang Mike Pence,'" I said.

And then, instead of expressing horror at the idea that his supporters would be calling for the death of his faithful vice president, Trump started to explain why they were doing it.

"Because it's common sense," he said. "How can you—if you know a vote is fraudulent, how can you pass a fraudulent vote to Congress? How can you do it?"

It boggled my mind that Trump was not only callously indifferent to the threats made against the vice president, but he also seemed to be justifying them. Trump had heard the chants from his supporters— the demands that Pence be *executed*—and here he was calmly and coolly explaining to me why the people chanting for Pence's death were so angry.

Republicans remained loyal to Trump even as he attempted to destroy the crown jewel of American democracy—the peaceful transition of power. His cruel mistreatment of Mike Pence was part of his assault on our democratic system. Americans were able to witness all that during the final days of the Trump presidency. Now the question is, will Republicans still remain loyal to Donald Trump when they read on these pages that even after January 6, he was attempting to justify the bloodlust of his supporters who thought Mike Pence deserved to die?

I've thought a lot about what John Kelly told me so long ago. That even if Trump chained himself to his desk in the Oval Office, the chains would be cut and he would be escorted out at noon on January 20. But Trump did something more brazen than refusing to walk out of the White House when his term was up, something more damaging than chaining himself to the Resolute desk. He convinced tens of millions of people to believe something that was not true—that a free and fair election was filled with fraud and that his successor had stolen it. He tried to stop the transfer of power by overturning the certified results of a presidential election. He didn't prevail. But there was no guarantee that he would fail. I didn't realize it at the time, but as I reported on this book, I became convinced that the peaceful transfer of power that happened, as scheduled, on January 20 was something of a miracle.

As he left the White House for the last time, Trump walked over to a group of White House reporters and said, "It was a great honor. The honor of a lifetime."

He's right. It was the honor of a lifetime. But unlike any of the forty-three presidents who served before him, he repaid that honor by betraying the very democratic system that made it possible for him to be president. We now live in a nation where a large part of the population does not trust our elections. There are many reasons for this, but none greater than Donald Trump and the lies he told about the 2020 election.

History will judge the Trump presidency harshly. His successes will rightfully be overshadowed by the lying, the incompetence, and, especially, the betrayal of democracy at the end. Future generations will wonder how Trump came to be president in the first place and how so many remained loyal to a man who offered loyalty to nothing but himself.

Our democracy—the one we have been taught is the greatest

system of government in the history of the world—survived his downfall. But his betrayal showed just how vulnerable our democratic system is. The continued survival of our republic may depend, in part, on the willingness of those who promoted Trump's lies and those who remained silent to acknowledge they were wrong, that it was a terrible mistake to put one man's ego above the truths we all should hold as self-evident.

ACKNOWLEDGMENTS

As just about anybody who has spoken with me over the past year or so knows, writing this book has been an obsession. Fortunately, I have been blessed with many friends and colleagues who have been willing to tolerate and feed this obsession—talking over themes and sharing insights as I struggled to make sense of the maddening events of 2020 and early 2021.

In many ways, Douglas Kennedy has been preparing me to write this book for nearly thirty years; it is an outgrowth of the conversations and debates we have been having about history and politics since we first met. Douglas was often the first person I called when I hit a roadblock or had a major breakthrough. He read every page of this book shortly after it was written and pushed me to write with moral clarity and to put the events described here in the proper historical context.

It's been said, in a quote almost certainly misattributed to Vladimir Lenin, that there are decades where nothing happens and there are weeks where decades happen. Recently we've lived through all too many of those weeks where decades seemed to happen. Katherine Faulders, Allison Pecorin, and Will Steakin helped me keep track of it all, helping me research this book and occasionally joining me on interviews. Allie played a big role in helping me with the research for

ACKNOWLEDGMENTS

Front Row at the Trump Show. This time around she brought her personal experience as a superb congressional reporter who was in the Capitol building during the January 6 insurrection. Will Steakin brought his experience and insights as an embedded reporter covering the Trump reelection campaign. Much of the groundbreaking reporting in the chapter "To Tulsa and Back" is Will's; he was there and kept reporting on this pivotal moment of the 2020 campaign long after the election was over. Katherine Faulders is a great colleague and one of the best investigative reporters in Washington; she helped me coax reluctant sources to tell their stories. All three of them made a mark on this book.

A group of good friends read the first draft of every chapter of this book as I wrote it and helped make the second and third drafts considerably better. My once and future podcast partner Rick Klein knows politics almost as well as he knows baseball and whiskey and was a valuable collaborator on this project, as he has been on so many others. Chris Donovan is one of the smartest and most well-read people I've ever met; he spotted my mistakes and omissions and suggested areas I needed to explore more thoroughly. Claire Brinberg cheered me on and offered her insights and suggestions along the way, as she did with about 95 percent of the scripts I wrote for ABC's *World News Tonight* during the Trump era.

My nephew Robert Karl Jr. is a software engineer and entrepreneur, but in writing this book, I also learned he is a really good editor. Nobody read my drafts more closely than Robert or did more to improve my writing.

I will be forever indebted to my ABC News colleagues with whom I worked side by side to cover the events of the past five years. From the 2016 election to the insurrection, I was especially fortunate to work with Cecilia Vega—as generous, hardworking, and wickedly funny a colleague as I have ever had. The ABC News Pennsylvania Avenue team helped navigate our way through those years and ultimately made it possible for me to write this book, including Justin

ACKNOWLEDGMENTS

Fishel, Jordyn Phelps, Karen Travers, Jon Garcia, Ben Gittleson, John Parkinson, Ben Siegel, Elizabeth Thomas, Trish Turner, and my fellow correspondents Rachel Scott and Mary Bruce. Rachel, Mary, and Cecilia are three of the very best correspondents who have ever worked at ABC News and, more important, they are good human beings and true friends.

My ABC News support network goes far beyond the Pennsylvania Avenue team. Kim Godwin came to ABC News as I was writing this book and immediately offered her enthusiastic support. Jonathan Greenberger supported and encouraged me and let me tap into his incredible memory of the events described in this book. Marc Burstein, Wendy Fisher, and Bob Murphy supported my work as a reporter and helped put me in a position to be able to write this book. I am also grateful for the support of Julie Townsend, Heather Riley, Kerry Smith, Caragh Fisher, Galen Gordon, and Peter Rice.

For me, the real first draft of this history was written in my scripts for *World News Tonight with David Muir*. Emily Cohen and Maggy Patrick produced most of the stories, and no matter how rough things got, I always loved working with them. David Muir and Almin Karamehmedovic have created the most-watched television news program in America; they also gave me the opportunity to do hard-hitting and in-depth reporting.

I am also deeply indebted to the team at *Good Morning America* for supporting crack-of-dawn reporting on the events of the Trump era—especially Shannon Crawford, Ellen Van de Mark, Chris Brouwer, Pete Austin, and Simone Swink.

I've had the opportunity to work with and learn from George Stephanopoulos for more than fifteen years; I've benefited from his counsel and am grateful for his support of this book and the reporting behind it. Martha Raddatz has been a friend and mentor for years. She shared her insights on the events at the Pentagon; no journalist has a deeper understanding of the US military than Martha. I've known Pierre Thomas since we were colleagues at CNN two decades ago. I benefited from his reporting on the Trump Justice Department and the struggle for racial justice. He's a first-rate reporter and a good friend.

I also benefited greatly from the work of ABC's investigative team, led by the legendary Chris Vlasto—including Aaron Katersky, Matt Mosk, Josh Margolin, Soorin Kim, and Ali Dukakis. John Santucci knows and understands the inner workings of Trump world as well as any reporter in the business. He is tireless, thoroughly sourced, and damn good at what he does.

I have been continually inspired by the professionalism and dedication of my ABC News family, including Dax Tejera, Devin Dwyer, Alex Mallin, Luis Martinez, George Sanchez, Matt Hosford, Mitch Alva, Dan Harris, Jenn Metz, Nancy Gabriner, Byron Pitts, Linsey Davis, Brad Mielke, Chris Dinan, Dee Cardin, Andrea Owen, Terry Moran, Alex Presha, Yoni Mintz, Treavor Hastings, Nate Luna, Pat O'Gara, Freda Kahen-Kashi, and the incredibly talented photographers, producers, desk assistants, editors, and technical and logistics staff that put me and fellow correspondents on the air every day. Sadly, we lost one of the best in 2021, the maestro Jim Sicile.

Diane Sawyer has been a constant inspiration since I first started at ABC News. She challenged me and encouraged me from the start. Ben Sherwood enthusiastically supported this book, just as he did *Front Row at the Trump Show* and he, too, read the early drafts. I am indebted to many colleagues no longer with ABC News but who helped and encouraged this project and so much more, including Barbara Fedida, Robin Sproul, Avery Miller, David Kerley, Tom Shine, Dennis Dunlavey, Robin Gradison, and James Goldston.

I am grateful for the way Bob Iger has supported my work and the work of my colleagues at ABC News. He has a passion for good journalism and an intense interest in politics.

Several political figures and public servants were immensely helpful in sharing their insights and recollections, including ABC contributors Chris Christie, Donna Brazile, Rahm Emanuel, Sarah

ACKNOWLEDGMENTS

Isgur, and Tom Bossert. Frank Luntz told me to set the bar high and make this the most important book about the Trump presidency. I may not have accomplished that, but I am grateful to have friends like Frank who have constantly pushed me to do better.

The Trump era has been a challenging one for journalists. Both Trump and his enemies have pushed reporters to act as an opposition party and harshly attacked good journalism. But there has been some monumentally important reporting on the Trump presidency by reporters who strived for truth and accuracy. It has been a privilege to work alongside some of the best and most fearless reporters to ever cover the White House, including Peter Baker, Maggie Haberman, Jonathan Swan, Josh Dawsey, Ashley Parker, Kristen Welker, Phil Rucker, Tamara Keith, Weijia Jiang, Doug Mills, Yamiche Alcindor, Olivia Nuzzi, Ryan Lizza, Michael Bender, Evan Vucci, Jabin Botsford, Paula Reid, Fin Gomez, Jeff Mason, Steve Holland, Kaitlan Collins, Kelly O'Donnell, Steve Portnoy, David Jackson, and Peter Alexander. Zeke Miller is a great reporter who worked closely with me during my time as president of the White House Correspondents' Association, a tenure that extended through many of the events recounted in this book. I am particularly indebted to Mike Allen, the hardest-working man in journalism and a true friend.

My literary agent, David Larabell, kicked this effort off by pushing me to write *Front Row at the Trump Show* (his title) and encouraging me to write the sequel. One of the best things about writing this book was having John Parsley, once again, as my editor. Thank you again to Cassidy Sachs for shepherding this book from start to finish and keeping me focused on meeting my deadlines.

Nobody read my drafts more quickly than Alan Berger—sometimes calling me with feedback less than an hour after having been emailed a draft chapter. As he did with my last book, he often called me, saying, "Where's the next chapter?" He's been a true believer in this project from the beginning and may have been the first person to tell me that I needed to write a sequel to *Front Row at the Trump Show*.

ACKNOWLEDGMENTS

Many of my closest friends offered encouragement and advice along the way, including Michael Feldman, Yousef al-Otaiba, Dave Almy (who survived four years as my college roommate), Franco Nuschese, Don Rockwell, Mary Ann Gonser, Wendell Allsbrook, Paul and Karen Freitas, Pete Madej, Brian Brown, Renae Schrier, Todd Surdez, Richard Dawson, and the legendary Scott Alexander.

This book was in many ways a family project. My daughters, Anna and Emily, are brilliant writers and editors and, whatever great things they accomplish in life, will always have the instincts and sensibility of great journalists. Sal and MaryAnn Catalano once again supported me in more ways than I could ever enumerate. Sal is an artist and a philosopher—his "Saints and Sinners" series of drawings serve as an inspiration. I am also grateful for the support and encouragement of Sal Catalano Jr.

My brother Allan Karl, a.k.a. Worldrider, inspired me to write both of my books on the Trump presidency by leading the way with his terrific—and decidedly apolitical—book, *Forks*, which details his global travels via motorcycle and his culinary discoveries.

This book is dedicated to my mom, Audrey Karl Shaff, because she is the one who taught me how to write and always encouraged me to do more of it. She read the first drafts of every chapter in this book. Her edits were light—but every single one of them made a difference.

Finally, the real driving force behind this book—and just about everything I have done during my career—is my wife, Maria. She was the very first reader of everything I wrote; only Maria knows how sloppy those initial drafts were. Fortunately, she is discreet enough to never tell. As always, Maria kept me grounded and sane. To an even greater degree than the last book, she loved me even when the stress of this project made me decidedly unlovable.

INDEX